The Paradoxical Balance of Rahu and Ketu: Desire to Detachment

The Paradoxical Balance of Rahu and Ketu: Desire to Detachment

Richa Shukla; MA, PhD
Jyotish Alankar, Jyotish Acharya
Faculty and Founding Director *Dev Jyotish*, Gurgaon, India

MOTILAL BANARSIDASS INTERNATIONAL
DELHI

First Edition : Delhi, 2026

© MOTILAL BANARSIDASS INTERNATIONAL
All Rights Reserved

ISBN : 978-93-47683-36-7

Also available at
MOTILAL BANARSIDASS INTERNATIONAL
H.O. : 41 U.A. Bungalow Road, (Back Lane) Jawahar Nagar, Delhi - 110 007
4261 (basement) Lane #3, Ansari Road, Darya Ganj, New Delhi - 110 002
203 Royapettah High Road, Mylapore, Chennai - 600 004
12/1A, 2nd Floor, Bankim Chatterjee Street, Kolkata - 700 073
Stockist : Motilal Books, Ashok Rajpath, Near Kali Mandir, Patna - 800 004

No part of this book may be reproduced in any form or by any electronic or mechanical means including information storage and retrieval systems without permission in writing from the publishers, excepts by a reviewer who may quote brief passages in a review.

Printed in India
MOTILAL BANARSIDASS INTERNATIONAL

Dedication

To my Ishtadev, my eternal light. To my father, Dr. J. P. Agnihotri—gentle, wise, and a spiritual guide whose love for Jyotish shaped my journey. To my mother, Nandini Agnihotri—practical, steadfast, and my greatest lesson in hard work, integrity, and resilience.

अतुलितबलधामं हेमशैलाभदेहं, अनुजवनकृशानुं ज्ञानिनामग्रगण्यम्।
सकलगुणनिधानं वानराणामधीशं, रघुपतिप्रियभक्तं वातजातं नमामि।

[I bow to Hanuman, the abode of incomparable strength, whose body shines like a golden mountain, who is swift as the wind and fire to his foes, foremost among the wise, treasure-house of all virtues, chief of the vanaras, and the beloved devotee of Lord Raghupati.]

Author's Note
Why This Book — From Sutra to Experience

When I look back upon the twenty-four years that I have walked hand in hand with astrology, what I see is so much more than just a catalogue of consultations or scattered research notes, I see a living treasury of human experiences that have repeatedly affirmed the laws of the cosmos as they operate through Rahu and Ketu. This book, therefore, is not the product of casual observation or abstract fascination, it has emerged from sustained practice, tested in the crucible of real lives, and verified through patterns that unfolded with unfailing regularity.

Astrology, for me, has never been about issuing proclamations or indulging in fleeting assertions suited for the stage or social media. An astrological law, if it is to deserve the name, must be demonstrable. It must withstand the rigour of replication, i.e., it must reveal its truth each time a planetary combination arises, and yield the same outcome across charts, across contexts. It is on this ground solely confidence in astrology can stand firm.

This is the ground I have cultivated across decades of practice. The knowledge in these pages is not speculative but distilled from patient observation, meticulous noting, and the living evidence of thousands of charts. When I shared fragments of these insights through a series on Rahu and Ketu on my YouTube channel, the resonance was overwhelming. More than ninety percent of the audience related closely to what I articulated. Through their feedback, I found a reassuring confirmation of the precision and truth contained within my work. That collective response gave me the conviction that the time had come to crystallise my experience into a book, for a book allows wisdom to endure beyond the transient medium of conversation or video, to take its place as a coherent body of knowledge.

For centuries, our guiding sutras on these shadow planets have come from the sages; they have been brief, powerful, and yet deliberately cryptic. Rahu, they told us, behaves like Saturn *(Shanivat)*; Ketu, like Mars *(Kujavat)*, but what does this resemblance truly mean? My years of research revealed a crucial nuance: when the sages compared Rahu to Saturn, it was not the Saturn of Capricorn they had in mind, but the Saturn of Aquarius. Likewise, when they declared Ketu to be like Mars, they implied the Mars of Scorpio, not of Aries. These distinctions, small at first glance, reshape the entire interpretive framework. The texts remained silent on such subtleties; only sustained practice could uncover them. It is this labour of decades that compels me to write now.

The Path from Desire to Detachment

Through observation, we see Rahu as bearing the qualities of air. Aquarius, being an airy sign, carries

Rahu's essence, while Capricorn, being an earth sign, does not. This is why Rahu co-owns Aquarius, though not as the sovereign lord. Its airy traits resonate most closely here. Similarly, Ketu finds its reflection in Scorpio, inheriting the depth, mysticism and secrecy of that sign.

This insight transformed my understanding of Mahadashas. When Rahu's Mahadasha begins, the house where Aquarius falls in a chart is inevitably stirred into life. In Ketu's Mahadasha, it is Scorpio that awakens. The dichotomy is clear: Rahu propels outward into uncharted realms of desire, while Ketu recalls inward, anchoring us to familiar roots from multiple past lives.

Rahu is the magnetic pull of untested possibilities; it's the restless urge to stretch towards experiences not yet tasted. While Ketu is the residue of memory, the weight of past life tendencies, the zone of comfort from which we hesitate to depart. Now we must bear in mind that roots nourish, but they also bind. The soul's growth requires the courage to step beyond Ketu's enclosure and into Rahu's unknown terrain. Rahu embodies risk; it demands courage. Ketu clings to memory, resisting change.

From this vantage, liberation itself acquires a new meaning. One does not escape desire by denial but by having lived it through. Only when the hunger is exhausted does freedom arrive. God has designed the universe in a particular way, a kind of harmony that is mirrored in astrological principles. The crux here is that we must understand how our roots must be watered, but not endlessly dug up. In Ketu's domain, the task is acceptance, to release the ego that insists on clinging, and to move forward into Rahu's domain, which is our present life's agenda too, while bearing in mind that both poles carry danger in some sense. How so? Over-identification with Ketu breeds stagnation, and intoxication with Rahu breeds insatiability. Rahu has no body, so it knows no measure; there's no natural limit. If left unchecked, the compulsions of desire can consume the very individual it sought to elevate. The purpose, then, is not to forsake one pole in favour of the other, but to sustain a harmony: roots are here to support us as desires extend us. Without this balance, life ends in regret and fulfilment continues to evade the most successful ones as well.

Balancing the Axis

The question becomes: how does one live this balance, or how to pursue desires without being consumed, and how to honour roots without being suffocated by them?

Through years of study, I found a consistent key, which is the strength of Rahu and Ketu's dispositor. When well-placed, whether in a central house *(kendra)*, trinal house *(trikona)*, or otherwise dignified, the native is naturally safeguarded against the distortions of both nodes. A strong dispositor of Rahu helps the individual channel ambition with awareness, ensuring that desires are pursued without crossing the bounds of wisdom or morality. Likewise, a strong dispositor of Ketu preserves the integrity of one's inner foundation, preventing detachment from turning into disconnection or apathy. Thus, when the dispositors of both Rahu and Ketu are fortified, the person moves through life with balance i.e., roots remain nourished, and aspirations remain achievable.

The truth of this balance is mirrored in the human body. Rahu and Ketu together represent the axis of the spine. Just as the Kundalini Shakti lies coiled within the spinal channel awaiting awakening, so too does the Rahu–Ketu axis carry the balance of the entire being. A misaligned spine throws the whole body into disorder; similarly, an imbalanced Rahu-Ketu axis unsettles the course of life. But when held steady, both body and destiny align. When desire is tempered by rootedness, and aspiration balanced by detachment, the soul discovers its equilibrium and moves onward with unshaken poise and enduring stability.

The Purpose and Progression of this Journey

Every book is born from a necessity to understand. *The Paradoxical Balance of Rahu and Ketu: Desire to Detachment* was conceived with the same impulse, to help readers comprehend the axis that binds longing and liberation. The purpose of this book is to guide the reader through the layered significance of Rahu and Ketu, from their mythological conception to astrological application, and ultimately toward spiritual discernment.

The sequence of chapters has been designed to reflect the same movement that Rahu and Ketu themselves represent: the journey from manifestation to release. The opening chapter explores their mythological origins, where the seed of duality first took birth. From there, Chapter Two elaborates on the cosmic paradox of desire and detachment, how fulfilment and peace are entwined in the eternal play of the lunar nodes.

Once this metaphysical groundwork is laid, Chapter Three undertakes a close examination of Rahu and Ketu as individual forces: their intrinsic nature, their signs of strength and weakness, their higher and lower expressions, and their subtle distinction from the planets they mirror. It is here that one begins to understand Rahu's intoxication and Ketu's mysticism, the two poles of the same invisible axis that governs the evolution of consciousness.

Chapter Four then brings this understanding into a structured astrological framework by examining the significance and interpretation of the Rahu–Ketu axis across the twelve houses. Building directly upon this, Chapter Five presents detailed case studies, translating theoretical principles into lived human experience. These narratives allow the reader to witness how the nodal axis operates dynamically within real horoscopes, revealing patterns of karma, conflict, growth, and release.

The preceding chapters exist to prepare the reader for this synthesis; without understanding Rahu and Ketu separately, and without observing their axis in motion through actual lives, one cannot fully comprehend their interdependent role in shaping destiny.

Author's Note (xiii)

From Chapter Six onward, the focus becomes progressively personal and applied. These chapters examine the distinct impact of Rahu and Ketu in each of the twelve houses and zodiac signs. They are intended as reference sections for readers who wish to study the nodal influence in their own horoscopes or apply the earlier philosophy to specific astrological contexts. This structure ensures that the book first builds a coherent foundation of understanding before turning toward individualized interpretation.

The concluding chapter offers resolution by addressing spiritual perspectives and remedial approaches that help harmonise the Rahu–Ketu paradox, allowing cosmic theory to be translated into conscious living.

In essence, every chapter of this book forms a step in the same pilgrimage, from intellectual curiosity toward spiritual awakening. Beyond being an astrological manual, this work serves as a contemplative journey through the anatomy of desire and the grace of detachment.

Each chapter has been placed with deliberation, for every preceding idea lays the groundwork for the next. The progression is both structural and spiritual, its continuity guiding the reader steadily forward until knowledge ripens into realization.

Preface

Ketu Mantra:

केतुः कालः कल्यित रुद्र देहः
हिरण्यवर्णः शशिवर्ण जातमः।
तमोमरेशं सुरपादपीठं
तं केतुमहं शरणं प्रपद्ये।

I take refuge in Ketu, the one with a body of dark-red hue, a form that radiates like molten gold, the one who brings challenges and obstacles but ultimately clears the path towards liberation.

Rahu and Ketu, known as the lunar nodes, have always held a unique place in the classical tradition. While every planet governs an aspect of life, these two reveal *how* an individual responds to the unfolding of circumstances; through fate yes, but also through inner orientation, instinct, and the residues of memory that rise unbidden. Their influence unfolds through choices, compulsions, recurring patterns, and the strange synchronicities that seem to pull a person toward certain experiences.

Much of the unease surrounding them stems from the fact that their workings are rarely spoken of with clarity. The ancient texts describe them in symbolic language, giving hints rather than elaborate explanations. Over time, this silence has led to speculation, exaggeration, and the kind of fear that emerges whenever understanding is absent.

This book seeks to bring lucidity where ambiguity has long prevailed. Instead of portraying Rahu and Ketu through the lens of fear or fatalism, it presents them as forces that shape *perspective* — the way one interprets events and the inner shifts that accompany life's turning points. Their presence marks the areas where one's perception is stretched, challenged or refined, often in ways unnoticed at first glance.

Drawing from years of observation and casework, the chapters ahead explore the nodes as markers of karma but also as indicators of how consciousness adapts and transforms through lived experience.

This book, "The Paradoxical Balance of Rahu and Ketu: Desire to Detachment" is born not merely from scholarly pursuit but from a heartfelt desire to dispel misconceptions and shed light on various aspects of Rahu and Ketu, ranging from their effects in different houses and signs to the influences they exert when in conjunction with various planets. It is a quest to replace fear-mongering mindsets with perception and understanding, channeling curiosity into astute insight.

Despite their far-reaching influence on individual destinies, a comprehensive and meticulously researched exploration dedicated solely to Rahu and Ketu has been conspicuously absent, further feeding fear among people. Driven by the earnest insistence of my students and clients, I am inspired to explore these celestial entities in depth.

Preface

At the heart of this book's exploration lies the recognition of Rahu and Ketu as the karmic fulcrum within the natal chart – a celestial axis that orchestrates the delicate balance of karma, the settling of debts, and the soul's journey towards higher realms. While other planets in the horoscope contribute their due role, it is Rahu and Ketu that primarily dictate the manner in which the overall life pattern evolves and the collective energies manifest their destined fruits.

This work draws upon long and steady practice in chart interpretation, presenting the Rahu–Ketu axis in a structured manner that is both accessible and rooted in classical principles, without dwelling on autobiographical detail.

Similarly, the invocation of Rahu embodies the quest for clarity and strength in overcoming material temptations:

Rahu Mantra:

ॐ अस्य श्री राहु मन्त्रस्य वामदेव ऋषि:।
अनुष्टुप् छन्द:।
राहु: देवता।
ॐ रां राहवे नम:।

This is the invocation for Rahu's mantra, paying homage to the shadow planet associated with desires, obsessions, and illusions, praying for clarity and strength to overcome material temptations.

Through rigorous research and a commitment to clarity, this book aims not only to educate but to empower. It invites readers to journey beyond the superficial, moving past what preys on collective insecurities. In offering this work, I extend a hand to all seekers of astrological truth, presenting a source of illumination amidst the complexities of the Rahu-Ketu axis. Readers can find assurance in the practical solutions and insightful material contained herein.

The intention is to assist those seeking astrological insight in honing their own judgment while making predictions, or to provide all the tools necessary for those eager to satiate their curiosity about the essence of the Rahu-Ketu axis and its cause-and-effect dynamics within a horoscope. May this book serve as a constant companion and guide, annihilating fear and illuminating the path towards light, self-discovery, and broader understanding.

Acknowledgements

To my father, Dr. J. P. Agnihotri, and my mother, Nandini Agnihotri, whom I thank from the deepest recesses of my heart's eye, for instilling in me a profound reverence for values and the power of words. I am endlessly indebted to both of you for your silently imparted wisdom and gentle guidance.

Father, this book is dedicated to you, the guiding force of my life, a man of wisdom, humility, and quiet strength. You have been my North Star, and your silent influence continues to inspire me every day. You have left an indelible mark on my life and spirit, and your gentle strength and countless acts of kindness will echo through time, carrying forward through generations.

Mother, your hard work, integrity, and practicality have taught me how to navigate this world with grace and discernment. You have shaped me into the person I am today, and for that, I am endlessly grateful. I dedicate this work to you, with heartfelt admiration for the strong and wise woman you are.

To my better half, Sharad Shukla, thank you for being my rock and my unwavering support. Your love has been my anchor, and your encouragement, the wind beneath my wings.

For Shivangi and Gaurav, my daughter and son-in-law, and for Sankalp, my son, who is both my greatest critic and my steadfast motivator, you all inspire me to continually strive for greater heights. Each of you brings immeasurable joy, purpose, and meaning to my life.

And to my precious granddaughter, Veda, the newest addition to our family, your presence fills every day with new brightness and meaning.

I also thank Luxmi, an astrology enthusiast, whom I met incidently, for constant support in the department of editing and proofreading.

I offer my deepest gratitude to my revered gurus at Bharatiya Vidya Bhavan, and to the eternal Guru Tattva, to whom I remain perpetually indebted for every lesson life has bestowed upon me. Beyond my teachers of Jyotish, I bow also to the many spiritual souls I have encountered along the way, each of whom has shaped the foundation of the knowledge that flows through me.

Contents

Dedication .... (v)

Author's Note .... (vii)

Preface .... (xv)

Acknowledgements .... (xix)

1. Rahu and Ketu: The Mythological Origins 1

2. Desire Fulfilled, Peace Found: Rahu and Ketu's Cosmic Paradox 5

3. Rahu and Ketu in Vedic Astrology 9

4. The Significance and Interpretation of Rahu-Ketu Axis Through 12 Houses 32

5. Rahu and Ketu Axis Through 12 Houses: Case Studies 75

6. The Impact of Rahu in Different Houses 148

7. The Impact of Ketu in Different Houses 174

8. The Impact of Rahu in Different Zodiac Signs 208

9. The Impact of Ketu in Different Zodiac Signs 231

10. Rahu and Ketu Conjunctions With
    Different Planets 264

11. Solutions for Rahu and Ketu 283

Chapter 1

Rahu and Ketu: The Mythological Origins

The Story of Samudra Manthan (Churning of the Ocean): The Origin of Rahu and Ketu

References: Brahma Purana, Bhagavata Purana, Mahabharata, Matsya Purana, Vishnu Purana, Rigveda

Samudra Manthan or the Churning of the Ocean of Milk (Kshirasagara) is a renowned episode from Hindu mythology, recounted in various Vedic scriptures. It begins with King Indra losing his kingdom to the Asuras due to a curse from Sage Durvasa. Seeking Lord Vishnu's counsel, the Devas forge an alliance with the Asuras to churn the ocean for the nectar of immortality (Amrit).

Mount Mandarachal serves as the churning rod, and Vasuki, the serpent king, as the churning rope. The churning releases treasures and perils, including the deadly poison Halahala, which was consumed by Lord Shiva to protect creation, thereby acquiring the name Neelakantha. The process also yields fourteen Ratnas (gems), symbolizing divine gifts. Amid many divine treasures was Goddess Lakshmi, who chose Lord Vishnu as her consort.

Dhanvantari emerges with the pot of Amrit, setting the stage for a fierce battle. Lord Vishnu transforms into Mohini, one of his Avataras in the form of a captivating enchantress, to deceive the Asuras. One of the Asuras, Svarbhanu, disguised as a Deva, manages to sneak a sip of Amrit but is exposed by Surya and Chandra. Bhagavan Vishnu's divine disc (Sudarshana Chakra) swiftly decapitates Svarbhanu—forming two parts: the upper half with just the head became known as Rahu, and the lower half, consisting of the body, became Ketu.

Despite this, the head (Rahu) and bodyless tail (Ketu) of Svarbhanu remained immortal, as the Amrit had seeped into his body before decapitation. In Vedic astrology, Rahu signifies insatiable desires and obsessions in the birth chart, highlighting areas of immaturity and unfulfilled yearnings. Ketu, on the other hand, signifies innate wisdom, past life gifts, and spiritual depth, revealing psychic insights and intuitive knowledge.

Blessed by Lord Brahma with a place among the Navagrahas, Rahu and Ketu continue to harbour animosity towards Surya and Chandra, cause solar and lunar eclipses in testament to their eternal grudge—for it was Surya and Chandra who caught Rahu during the consumption of nectar. As per mythological beliefs, Rahu and Ketu pursue the luminaries in vengeance, occasionally causing solar and lunar eclipses when they momentarily swallow the Sun and Moon. Although scientifically, eclipses occur due to the relative movements of the Sun, Moon, and Earth, this mythological narrative, recounted in ancient Puranic texts, underscores the enduring influence of Rahu and Ketu, who have a substantial say in determining an individual's course of destiny in unison with life's direction.

Symbolism and Representations

This Samudra Manthan episode symbolizes humanity's quest for spiritual immortality, with the ocean of milk representing human consciousness. The churning process signifies the integration of positive and negative energies within oneself, guided by concentration (Mandhara) and withdrawal of senses (Kurma). It illustrates the universal theme of inner transformation and divine intervention in orchestrating the cosmic balance.

Denoted as mathematical points in astrological calculations, Rahu and Ketu are referred to as 'Shadow Planets' (Chaaya Graha)—devoid of a physical existence. Irrespective of that, their influence is believed to impact human lives significantly. They are associated with eclipses and Rahu Kaal, an astrologically inauspicious period each day. Their mythological origin and astrological significance embody profound implications that steer the wheel of fortune and shape destinies, and celestial phenomena to this day.

To truly comprehend the nature of Rahu and Ketu, we must first contemplate the origin of their being. The mythic event of 'Samundra Manthan' that gave birth to these shadow planets is also connected to an unfulfilled promise, of yearning that turned into perpetual motion. Wherever Rahu is placed in the natal chart, the soul encounters a deep sense of deprivation at first, a certain denial of the very experiences or recognitions that the house signifies. The individual often strives in vain to secure validation within that sphere of life, feeling unseen, unacknowledged, or unappreciated. However, it is precisely through this vacuum that Rahu's hunger is born. The native becomes fiercely determined to master the lessons of that house, often willing to transcend norms and limitations to claim what was once withheld. Thus, Rahu's challenges become the fuel for its obsessive evolution.

Chapter 2

Desire Fulfilled, Peace Found: Rahu and Ketu's Cosmic Paradox

The shadowy planets Rahu and Ketu play a role that is more significant than just indicating karmic residues; they are agents of the soul's evolution. Their psychological and spiritual influence is profound, even though they are devoid of a physical form. Ancient sages, in their timeless wisdom, attributed co-rulerships over signs not traditionally associated with them to them—Rahu with Aquarius and Ketu with Scorpio.

[*Author's Note:* The connection between the fulfilment of desire and the emergence of detachment is a central theme developed through my own contemplative study of karmic astrology. While classical texts lay the foundation for Rahu and Ketu's symbolic roles, the insight is that *sukh* (4th house peace) can only arise after the soul has traversed its karma (10th house actions). In my personal interpretive synthesis, I have observed that it stems from observing how human experience itself matures from longing into release, from seeking into stillness.]

Rahu and the Co-Rulership of Aquarius: The Fire of Unfulfilled Desire

Aquarius, ruled by Saturn, is traditionally associated with collective progress, futuristic visions, and systemic change. But the deeper layers of this airy sign conceal a more electric and restless energy, which is a desire for innovation, rebellion, and transcendence. This is why our sages assign Rahu as a co-ruler of Aquarius, as Rahu is directly connected to the soul's desires.

Rahu, the head of the serpent, represents the insatiable hunger of the soul to experience, to possess, to become. Rahu governs what is foreign, futuristic, taboo-breaking, and intoxicating. When placed in Aquarius, Rahu manifests through an obsessive drive to change the system, push humanity forward, and redefine norms.

Shanivat Rahu—"Rahu is like Saturn"—because both deal with karmic challenges, long-term transformation, and breaking limitations. Yet unlike Saturn, Rahu does not proceed slowly or lawfully; he leaps, he manipulates, he distorts until the soul faces the mirror of illusion.

Why did the sages choose Aquarius? Because Aquarius is the zenith of desire for idealism, for utopia, for mental expansion, for impersonal revolution. It reflects Rahu's obsession not just with personal gain but with abstract, future-oriented desires, which are subtler and harder to satisfy.

Ketu and the Co-Rulership of Scorpio: The Mystic's Escape

Ketu, the tail of the serpent, is the force of detachment, renunciation, and *moksha*. It is headless because it sees with the inner eye, and it has no ambition because it remembers the truth.

While Mars traditionally rules Scorpio, sages have also attributed Ketu the co-rulership of Scorpio, for Scorpio is the sign of transformation, death, secrets, and occult penetration, which are all Ketu-like themes. Ketu is *Kujavat*—"like Mars"—because both are fiery and action-driven, but Ketu's fire is inward; it burns away attachments and destroys the ego.

Let's understand now why Scorpio only. Scorpio represents the underground transformation where the soul is stripped bare, where attachments rot away in the darkness, and where the ego dies. Ketu's presence here as co-ruler hints at the painful yet liberating process of letting go, an act not born of realization.

Karma, Desire and Happiness

The 4th house from Scorpio is Aquarius, showing that happiness (*sukh*) and emotional grounding (4th) for Scorpio, the seeker of truth through darkness, is discovered in Aquarius, the realm of collective and innovative vision. In this way, Rahu (desire) becomes essential for Scorpio's emotional fulfilment.

At the same time, the 10th house from Aquarius is Scorpio, pointing to the truth that the karma (action and responsibility) required to bring Aquarius's lofty visions into reality is rooted in Scorpio, where Ketu (detachment) holds sway. Only through deep inner work and transformation, the very energy of Ketu in Scorpio, can Rahu's futuristic goals be realized.

This reciprocal flow reveals a fundamental law that desire generates karma, karma ripens into detachment, and detachment, when genuine, becomes the doorway to peace. Thus, Rahu labors tirelessly, but its true reward is found in the satisfaction rooted in quietness of Ketu.

The Journey from Rahu to Ketu: When Desire Exhausts Itself

Let's go a layer deeper. Desire is not inherently evil; in fact, desire is the fuel of evolution. Rahu compels the soul to engage with the world, to chase dreams, to taste the bitter and sweet of maya. But true detachment arises when desire has been fulfilled, and cannot be born of forced renunciation.

This is why Ketu comes after Rahu in the zodiacal sequence; the south node cannot be understood or accessed until the north node's impulses are explored. One cannot truly renounce what has not been tasted. When the soul has chased Rahu's promises and still finds emptiness, Ketu emerges as the liberator. A Scorpio, transformed through inner churning, can experience the emotional peace (4th from Scorpio = Aquarius) only when Rahu's Aquarius-like ambitions have been exhausted.

Chapter 3
Rahu and Ketu in Vedic Astrology

Introduction to Rahu and Ketu in Vedic Astrology

The journey of life is often a swing between the axis of Rahu and Ketu. People chase after Rahu, only to realize in the end that they are running after an illusion, a mirage. Rahu represents our accomplishments, the fulfillment of desires, and the drive to achieve; however, when these desires spiral out of control, they lead us down a path of illusion and ultimately, self-destruction. If we harness our ambitions in a balanced manner and focus on a larger purpose—beyond personal gain, for the benefit of society—Rahu's influence can indeed be constructive, aligning with the higher values of the 11th house. Rahu also makes one believe that the grass is greener on the other side. Eventually, though, the true destination lies with Ketu, which symbolizes a return to our roots and a surrender to the divine.

Rahu's nature is to teach us that what we were pursuing was not reality but mere illusion. When we understand this, we return to Ketu, symbolizing spiritual truth and surrender to God and His will.

Rahu is not a malevolent planet; in fact, no planet is inherently bad. Each planet has its own assigned attributes and responsibilities, and they merely perform the duties entrusted to them.

The results influenced by Rahu and Ketu are significantly affected by their dispositors, making it crucial to thoroughly examine the dispositors on various parameters to accurately predict the outcomes associated with Rahu and Ketu.

Rahu and Ketu exhibit distinct characteristics and influence individuals in markedly different ways. Rahu is superficial, flamboyant, and operates on a more external level, often concerned with appearances and projections. It works primarily upon the mind, stirring restless thoughts and unfulfilled cravings. It represents role models and outward aspirations, influencing natives to be upfront, outspoken, and explicit about their desires and ambitions. Akin to the air element, Rahu's energy hovers above, absorbed in the external world, often creating an impression of intelligence and power but lacking depth in its approach. Ketu, by contrast, rules over the soul, drawing the native into an introverted, inward journey, turning attention away from surface realities toward inner truths and spiritual depth. Thus, while Rahu pushes outward, chasing illusions and worldly validation, Ketu pulls inward, guiding toward detachment, introspection, and liberation.

In contrast, Ketu presides over introspection, the 6th sense, and heightened intuition. Those predominantly influenced by Ketu delve deeply into the realms of self-awareness, engaging in thorough research and analysis. It embodies totality, thinking from the heart, and understanding things on a profound level. Ketu governs our inner desires and hidden emotions, guiding us through a path of introspection and spiritual growth. Natives influenced by Ketu tend to be secretive, introspective, and rarely express their ambitions or inspirations openly.

Ketu, like the roots of a tree, supports Rahu but reminds it to never forget its own origins. It is like the flag of a nation, representing the soul's identity and its karmic DNA. Ketu urges Rahu to pursue its desires but not at the cost of losing touch with its core values, its roots, and the truth of its existence. Ketu, the ruler of the 8th house, symbolizes the fundamental forces of life, much like the DNA of an individual, guiding us through the inner voice that calls us back to our true purpose. Ketu doesn't merely support Rahu's journey; it also ensures that the pursuit of external desires stays in alignment with inner values and spiritual truth.

The Ketu-Rahu axis functions as a powerful balancing act. Just as a tree cannot grow without nourishing its roots, our desires and spiritual pursuits must be anchored in our core beliefs and inner wisdom. When this balance is maintained, Ketu supports Rahu's quest for fulfillment, ensuring that desires are pursued in alignment with a higher purpose. If the balance is disturbed, however, it can lead to confusion, misplaced desires, and a loss of direction.

Sadhana (spiritual practice) plays a crucial role in maintaining this balance. When we focus on cultivating inner wisdom and self-awareness, Ketu empowers Rahu to fulfill its desires without losing touch with the soul's true purpose. Thus, it is not just about seeking material success or personal growth, but about understanding what to do and what to let go of in order to stay rooted in our higher calling.

Instead, they pursue their goals with a silent determination, focusing on inner development and spiritual practice. Ketu's energy is grounded and internal, revealing the deep-seated motivations and concealed feelings of individuals.

Let's understand the contrasts of Rahu and Ketu with another symbolism. When Lord Vishnu severed *Svarbhanu*, the head (Rahu) flew far away while the headless body (Ketu) fell at the feet of Lord Vishnu. This scene encapsulates and explains Rahu's association with the 'airy' element—representing mere thoughts or ideas—whereas Ketu is considered to be a *moksha-karaka* planet, signifying liberation or spirituality. This aligns perfectly with the notion that anyone who takes refuge at the feet of Lord Vishnu attains *moksha*, making Ketu the bestower of liberation or the highest order of spiritual pursuits.

Rahu is a futuristic planet, while Ketu signifies the past or even past life (lives), owing to its co-rulership of the 8th house. Between the past and future lies the realm of illusion (*Maya*), which Lord Vishnu presides over, being revered as the '*Mayapati*'. Following this analogy, Lord Vishnu is that deity in Hinduism who helps us transcend illusion and attain spiritual enlightenment. Among the Trimurti, Lord Vishnu governs the aspect of 'preservation'; his role as a preserver is described in various Vedic scriptures, viz. *Vishnu Purana* and *Bhagavad Gita*.

The *Vishnu Sahasranama Stotra*, Verse 1,

(शान्ताकारं भुजगशयनं पद्मनाभं सुरेशम्। विश्वाधारं गगनसदृशं मेघवर्णं शुभाङ्गम्।। लक्ष्मीकान्तं कमलनयनं योगिभिर्ध्यानगम्यम्। वन्दे विष्णुं भवभयहरं सर्वलोकैकनाथम्।।) — affirms Vishnu's role as the ultimate preserver. It depicts Lord Vishnu in serene repose on the serpent *Adishesha*, his navel adorned with a lotus, radiating supreme divinity over all gods and upholding the universe like the expansive sky and auspicious clouds. Vishnu, beloved of *Lakshmi* and the focus of yogic meditation, dispels the fears of worldly existence, asserting his sovereignty as the lord of all realms.

Understanding Rahu

Ardha kaayam maha veeryam chandraditya vimardhanam simhika garbha sambhutam tam rahum pranamamyaham

Rahu is the North Node of the Moon and is depicted as the head of the serpent, thus associated with cleverness, overthinking, and shrewdness. Rahu signifies excitement, desire, ambition, materialism, and worldly cravings. In astrology, Rahu is considered a malefic planet that can bring about sudden and unexpected changes, both positive and negative, depending upon its positioning in a horoscope—

planets it is conjunct with, houses it is affecting, and yogas/doshas it is forming. For Rahu is smoke, its influence can be blinding, obscuring clarity, and making the path forward unclear.

In an overarching sense, it is associated with innovation, obsessive tendencies, material desires, and transformation. People under the strong influence of Rahu may experience intense desires and ambitions and tend to pursue unconventional paths, as Rahu is the primary significator of "breaking the norm" or "breaking the boundaries," justifying its nature as that of a "foreign" or an "alien" planet.

As per the *Brihat Parashara Hora Shastra* (BPHS), Rahu is described as having a smoky appearance and a physique mixed with blue tones. He is said to reside in forests and is depicted as formidable and frightful. Rahu's temperament is likened to the wind, indicating swiftness and unpredictability, coupled with intelligence (*Ketu*, his counterpart, shares similarities with Rahu). The text paints a vivid picture of Rahu as possessing a hideous face, with four arms bearing a sword, shield, trident (*Shoola*), and a boon-bestowing gesture (*Vara*). His complexion is described as blue, and he is often depicted mounted on a lion, symbolizing power and dominance in Vedic astrology and mythology.

This is why Rahu rules the 11th house of desire, representing how our wants are insatiable, never truly dying. However, when unchecked, these endless desires can turn into greed, ultimately leading to grief. Rahu is willing to go to extreme lengths, even to the point of allowing its head to be severed, all in pursuit of its goals, reflecting its inherent extremism and refusal to tread the middle path. Only those who master control over their desires—true *sanyasis*—can transcend Rahu's influence and escape the cycle of earthly attachments, becoming unaffected by any planets, as they have "killed" desires altogether.

Rahu perpetually seeks a host, adapting and imitating the nature of the planet it disposes of. For instance, when placed in Virgo, Rahu harnesses Mercury's traits (as the ruler of Virgo) to achieve its objectives. It also imitates the characteristics of planets connected to it through aspects or conjunctions, using them as vehicles for its ambition.

To illustrate Rahu's nature, imagine having the freedom to consume whatever you desire, yet lacking the body to digest or extract value from the food. This analogy mirrors Rahu's essence: as the air element, Rahu represents thought without form, a craving without structure to fulfill it. Consequently, it assumes the characteristics of any planet it accompanies, using it as a vessel to realize its desires. Thus, understanding Rahu's behavior requires a careful analysis of the planets it interacts with, as Rahu manipulates these forces to fulfill its own objectives. Its adaptive yet deceptive nature epitomizes an insatiable desire that shapes—and sometimes distorts—the influences around it.

The Nature of Rahu's Intoxication

Rahu is known for its intoxicating and obsessive

influence in Vedic astrology, often leading the native to fixate intensely on areas of life represented by the planet it conjuncts. When Rahu merges with a planet, it amplifies the qualities of that planet, both positive and negative, gaining substantial strength that can profoundly shape or challenge the person's life path. Alone, Rahu's influence remains potent yet subtle, but in conjunction, it absorbs the essence of the other planet, mirroring its qualities and even "eclipsing" its innate nature. For instance, when Rahu aligns with Jupiter, it can obscure Jupiter's wisdom, leading to what is called *Guru Chandal Yog*. This configuration may prompt actions that, despite the awareness of ethical boundaries, veer towards self-serving or morally ambiguous choices, leaving others puzzled as to how a seemingly virtuous person could stray.

Rahu's influence demands careful interpretation of conjunctions, as it can obscure the core qualities of planets it joins, much like a shadow eclipsing light. Rahu's presence as the Varaha Avatar of Shri Hari Vishnu, who lifted the Earth from the depths of chaos and restored its form, symbolizes Rahu's potential to elevate or transform, albeit often through challenges that force one to confront illusions and gain a shape or form again.

Rahu represents the air element (*vayu tattva*), constantly in motion, restless, and without a fixed form. This quality reflects our own restless desires, which, without the guidance of spiritual wisdom, can lead us astray. As a rule of astrology, whenever two planets come into conjunction, they inevitably influence one another, sharing or exchanging their significations. Thus, if Rahu conjoins a planet that is naturally or functionally benefic in a horoscope, it can elevate Rahu to become one of the most beneficial forces in that chart. Conversely, when Rahu aligns with a malefic planet, it tends to magnify its harsher qualities, making Rahu one of the most challenging influences therein. This is because Rahu's very nature is to enhance, exaggerate, and amplify the attributes of whichever planet it associates with.

Yet, Rahu is not inherently negative. In Vedic astrology, no planet is purely good or bad; each has unique qualities (*karak tattvas*) and fulfills a distinct purpose. Rahu's purpose is to test us with desires and attachments, prodding us to recognize the impermanence of material achievements and redirect our focus toward deeper, enduring truths. It often compels us to confront our illusions and gradually, if conditions are right, leads us toward surrender, spiritual transformation, and ultimately inner peace.

In particular, Rahu's transformative potential is more evident in certain configurations, such as when Rahu is conjunct with the Sun or Moon, or when Saturn is conjunct with either luminary, as Rahu's energy resembles that of Saturn, a quality known as *Shanivat* (like Saturn). In such cases, Rahu may catalyze profound surrender and spiritual awakening, encouraging the native to detach from worldly pursuits and seek a higher purpose. However, Rahu's capacity to inspire transformation is conditional and may often first manifest as a period of stagnation or entanglement, pushing the native to ultimately realize that genuine fulfillment lies beyond worldly desires.

How to Differentiate a Positive Rahu From a Negative Rahu

A positive Rahu manifests in individuals who challenge established norms and contribute something new to society. These people are often tech-savvy, embodying the innovative spirit of a positive Rahu. When such natives are engrossed in activities like gaming, they are not merely participants but creators, constantly conceptualizing new ventures—for instance, they might come up with a whole new gaming concept of their own, demonstrating their inventive mindset. Such individuals do not easily subdue their desires, and their unyielding desires fuel restless nights spent envisioning ambitious dreams, driven by an insatiable thirst for achievement.

A positive Rahu encourages dreaming big and continuously aspiring for more. It inspires individuals to envision lofty goals and to take concrete steps toward turning those dreams into reality. Rahu's constructive influence is often visible in fields such as politics, media, and film, where its strength can propel one to remarkable achievements. Yet, its scope extends beyond worldly success. To one's surprise, when Rahu conjoins the 9th lord and is placed in a trine or kendra, it may open the doors to spirituality. Similarly, Rahu in conjunction with the lords of the 10th, 8th, or 12th houses can channel its expansive energy into spiritual pursuits, blending ambition with inner quest. Thus, Rahu, though typically seen as a force of material desire, can, under certain alignments, become a catalyst for profound spiritual awakening.

Another indication of a positive Rahu is the desire to carry forward the dreams and aspirations of your grandparents. This shows a connection to your heritage and a drive to fulfill the unaccomplished goals of previous generations—a beneficially functioning Rahu drives the native to leave behind a legacy.

Signs of a Weak or Negatively Functioning Rahu

Persistent difficulties in executing plans or a lack of clarity in pursuing aspirations often signify a weakened influence of Rahu. This may manifest as an inability to bring ideas to fruition or as uncertainty in the steps required to achieve success, reflecting a diminished sense of purpose and direction. Natives with a negative Rahu influence may find themselves abandoning dreams or deeming them unattainable, lacking the resilience and determination essential for persevering toward their goals. When thoughts and aspirations fail to take concrete form, despite continuous contemplation, or when individuals struggle to translate their ideas into action, it suggests that Rahu is functioning against their best interests. This obstruction of willpower, leaving plans unrealized and thoughts unmaterialized, reveals a Rahu influence that is clouded, hindering intuitive vision and execution.

Indecision and a flux of thoughts further underscore a weakened Rahu, where a tendency toward hesitancy and reluctance in making decisions—whether trivial or significant—prevails. Even in mundane tasks such as shopping, overthinking choices can betray a lack of confidence and assertiveness associated with a positive Rahu. Furthermore, health ailments such as migraines and other head issues can also be linked to a malefic Rahu in a horoscope, which prevents natives from maintaining a sense of balance and clarity in their lives.

Collectively, in a general sense, these symptoms point to the need for strengthening Rahu's positive attributes, fostering resilience, decisiveness, and a clear vision toward achieving personal and professional fulfillment.

Rahu as the Co-ruler of Aquarius/11th House (Shanivat Rahu)

In Vedic astrology, Rahu is regarded as a shadow planet, and it doesn't have traditional lordship over any house or sign. However, it is commonly associated with the 11th house and the sign of Aquarius. While Saturn holds primary rulership over Aquarius and the 11th house, Rahu is considered a co-lord due to its inherent qualities that overlap with the sign of Aquarius and the 11th house.

In the *Brihat Parashara Hora Shastra* (BPHS), it is stated that *"Shanivat Rahu"*—meaning Rahu behaves akin to Saturn. While a slow and cautious approach characterizes Saturn, Rahu contrasts sharply with its inherently reckless nature. Despite these apparent contradictions, the concept of *"Shanivat Rahu"* underscores their shared influence and role. Both planets contribute to shaping themes of gains, aspirations, and achievements/recognition in one's life, which we see from the 11th house of a horoscope or the sign of Aquarius. Rahu's association with Saturn in the most ancient text on astrology, *BPHS*, ascertains their combined impact on influencing ambition, discipline, and the pursuit of material and spiritual goals, albeit through different methods and perspectives.

The 11th house is considered the highest octave among the *trishadaya* houses, which include the 3rd, 6th, and 11th houses. Despite its reputation as the house of desire fulfillment, it is also acknowledged as potentially malefic due to its association with unbridled desires that can potentially lead to disruptions and challenges in life.

Rahu, as the co-lord of the 11th house, significantly influences its characteristics. Rahu intensifies desires associated with the 11th house, making them more pronounced and often more complex. This can lead individuals to pursue their aspirations with heightened intensity, sometimes at the cost of other aspects of life. Rahu's influence often directs desires toward material gains, status, and recognition in society. These desires, if unchecked, can become all-consuming, potentially overshadowing spiritual growth and personal well-being.

Rahu also brings a transformative quality to desires associated with the 11th house. It encourages individuals to explore unconventional paths and innovative approaches in their pursuit of goals, sometimes leading to unexpected outcomes. Despite the potential challenges posed by Rahu's influence on the 11th house, positive outcomes can be achieved under certain astrological conditions:

- The presence or aspect of benefic planets like Venus, Mercury, or Jupiter on the 11th house or its lord can mitigate Rahu's malefic effects. These planets promote desires that are harmonious and beneficial, fostering positive growth and fulfillment.

- When the lords of the trine houses (1st, 5th, and 9th houses) aspect or influence the 11th house or its lord, they bring supportive energies that enhance the likelihood of favorable outcomes. Their influence encourages desires aligned with higher principles and spiritual development.

Rahu's influence underscores the importance of conscious intentions behind desires. Desires aimed at selfless service, societal benefit, or spiritual evolution are more likely to yield constructive results, aligning with Rahu's potential for transformation and growth.

In essence, while Rahu's association with the 11th house can amplify desires and pose challenges, it also offers opportunities for personal evolution and achievement. By cultivating awareness and aligning desires with higher principles, individuals can harness Rahu's transformative energy to pursue goals that contribute positively to their lives and the world around them.

Understanding Ketu

Palasha pushpa sankaasham taraka graha mastakaam Roudram roudratmakam ghoram tam ketum pranamamyaham

Ketu is the South Node of the Moon and is depicted as the tail of the serpent—a headless planet symbolizing spirituality, detachment from worldly desires, and the essential spiritual lessons we need to learn in this life. Ketu is considered malefic in nature, yet its influence is primarily spiritual, revealing areas where one must exhaust past karma, as it represents the karmic DNA rooted in lineage, karmic lessons, and past-life influences.

Ketu embodies the characteristics of the 8th house, channeling both transformation and destruction, as well as an intense, research-oriented mind deeply invested in spiritual or metaphysical subjects. Unlike Rahu, who is showy and seeks prominence, Ketu operates in the background, working intensely and silently, suggesting that true success and depth make noise only through substance, not surface.

While Rahu can lead to illusions and superficial recognition, Ketu's "silent-destruction" manifests as addictions, mental aberrations, and overthinking, making it more malefic than Rahu in certain respects; Ketu's influence can even lead to self-destruction, extreme isolation, sleep disorders, or identity issues, at times severe enough to result in experiences such as seeing spirits or other entities.

People under Ketu's influence often feel a profound sense of introspection, exhibiting a strong spiritual inclination and preferring solitude or research-focused pursuits. These individuals may be introverted, driven by a desire to disconnect from material attachments and dedicate themselves to their craft or spiritual calling.

Ketu's presence is known as a 'flagbearer' that sets one apart for skills honed over lifetimes, producing an individual who often excels in particular areas. However, the mysticism surrounding Ketu is sometimes overstated, as the initial seed of spirituality originates from Rahu, and only matures under Ketu's transformative energies, provided it is connected to the Moon, Sun, or Lagna Lord.

The Nature of Ketu's Mysticism

Ketu, symbolized as the 'body' without a head, signifies the karmic obligations that must be fulfilled and the lessons each soul must learn. Its position in the horoscope highlights the past karmas that require addressing, emphasizing the physical acts and sacrifices necessary to exhaust these debts. Here lies the subtle catch with Ketu: the karmas associated with the house it occupies must be exhausted, and the duties connected to that sphere of life must be fulfilled. Yet, one must take care not to remain bound too tightly by its strings. For instance, when Ketu is placed in the 4th house, it creates strong ties to the mother, the home, and the comforts of domestic life. While it is essential to honor and fulfill these responsibilities, excessive attachment to them can hinder personal growth and spiritual evolution. Ketu, by its very nature, functions like invisible threads, binding and pulling the native toward past-life obligations. The path forward is to discharge those karmas with sincerity while learning to gradually loosen the attachment, so that growth and liberation become possible.

Due to Ketu's lack of identity, it continuously prompts introspection, driving individuals to ask questions such as "Who am I?" and "What realms has my soul traversed?" This quest epitomizes Ketu's core aim—to uncover the origins of one's soul's journey and realize one's ultimate purpose. If Ketu is not positively placed, this relentless questioning can lead individuals into states of depression, addictions, or other mental health challenges.

When Ketu is well-positioned, it can propel individuals to extraordinary heights, such as those who have overcome countless challenges by persistently refining their inner selves. A powerful Ketu, especially when associated with the Ascendant or Lagna Lord in a Kendra (angular) position, can mark individuals who achieve remarkable success in their fields. Notable figures, such as Amitabh Bachchan, embody this never-give-up attitude, using introspection as a tool for constant self-improvement. Conversely, a poorly aligned Ketu may lead to a complete loss of self, plunging an individual into extremes—where Ketu's energies provide no middle ground but instead alternate between the highest peaks and lowest lows.

Ketu signifies the completion of unfinished karmic business from previous lifetimes, guiding individuals toward ultimate spiritual evolution. Its presence in a horoscope highlights areas marked by detachment and karmic completion, steering individuals toward isolation, inner peace, and the transcendence of worldly bonds.

How to Differentiate a Positive Ketu From a Negatively Ketu

A positive, well-aligned Ketu endows individuals with profound introspection and a quest to understand their spiritual lineage, prompting deep inquiry into the journey of their soul through various planes of existence. Those with a positive Ketu have a natural affinity for mystical practices, whether through meditation, *sadhana*, or mantra chanting, as well as an inherent aptitude for fields such as astrology, healing, or occult knowledge.

Furthermore, a strong Ketu manifests in individuals drawn to hidden realms of knowledge, such as astrology, history, and archaeology, or those pursuing metaphysical studies. These individuals master the nooks and corners of such ethereal subjects in a considerably short span of time. Their affinity for understanding the essence or roots of phenomena signifies a strong connection to Ketu's spiritual dimensions. Individuals engaged in *tantra sadhana*, secluded sanctuaries, or secretive agencies often exhibit prominent Ketu influences.

However, when Ketu's influence is positive, it can drive individuals toward finding their higher purpose. They may immerse themselves in spiritual practices, *sadhana*, and deep research, seeking enlightenment and profound personal transformation.

Signs of a Weak or Negatively Functioning Ketu

A weak or negative Ketu manifests through traits such as fearful or misguided intuition, fostering apprehension or a sense of imminent danger. Misusing spiritual practices or hidden knowledge for harmful purposes reflects a negative Ketu, as does indulging in selfish behaviors under the guise of spiritual pursuits. For instance, running an ashram for personal gain.

When Ketu is functioning negatively in a horoscope, it can lead to severe forms of addiction and mental health challenges. This includes complete annihilation through addictions such as drugs and the onset of serious psychological disorders like bipolar disorder and schizophrenia. As Ketu is symbolically represented as a body without a head, it causes a lack of understanding and awareness, often leading individuals to seek escape from reality. They may find themselves trying to forget their own identity in an attempt to avoid facing their inner turmoil.

By dedicatedly engaging in meditative practices and following a spiritual routine, one can harness the positivity of Ketu, which it inadvertently embodies; through introspection aimed at connecting with the inner self or the higher power, one channelizes the positive potential of Ketu to work in their favor.

Ketu as the Co-ruler of Scorpio/8th House (Kujavat Ketu)

In Vedic astrology, Ketu, like Rahu, is considered a shadow planet without traditional lordship over any house or sign. However, it is commonly associated with the 8th house and the sign Scorpio. While Mars holds primary rulership over Scorpio and the 8th house, Ketu is regarded as a co-lord due to its inherent qualities that resonate with the transformative, mystical, and introspective nature of Scorpio and the 8th house.

In the *Brihat Parashara Hora Shastra* (BPHS), Ketu is described as "Kujavat Ketu," meaning Ketu behaves similarly to Mars. This description is especially apt when examining Scorpio's dual rulership by both Mars and Ketu. While Mars in Aries expresses itself with directness and outward aggression, Mars in Scorpio—aligned with Ketu's subtle and introspective nature—exudes a secretive, strategic, and controlled energy, marked by a quiet but intense poise.

Scorpio, symbolized by Mars' covert side, shares with Ketu an unbreakable connection to the past. Ketu, like the 8th house, often holds onto past experiences and is wary of hidden threats or "enemies." With placements such as Ketu in the 8th or 4th house or a connection to the 8th Lord, individuals can be highly vigilant, recognizing threats that may lurk in secrecy and capable of launching silent, calculated responses. Scorpio Mars avoids public confrontations, preferring internalized challenges where it is in constant personal transformation, embodying a warrior who battles within.

Ketu embodies a more subtle and spiritual approach to the same themes of transformation and intensity. The concept of 'Kujavat Ketu' underscores their shared influence and role, with both planets contributing to themes of transformation, hidden knowledge, celibacy and deep psychological insight that are prevalent in the 8th house and Scorpio. Ketu's association with Mars in BPHS affirms their combined impact on shaping one's journey through transformation, mysticism, and the exploration of the unknown. Ketu's influence in the 8th house and Scorpio guides individuals toward spiritual growth, encouraging them to delve into the mysteries of life, confront their fears, and seek deeper truths beyond the material realm. This alignment highlights Ketu's role in facilitating profound personal and spiritual evolution, albeit through a more introspective and detached lens compared to Mars.

The 8th house is one of the most enigmatic and transformative houses in Vedic astrology, associated with secrets, mysteries, celibacy, *sadhana* and sudden changes. It represents death and rebirth, both in a literal and metaphorical sense, dealing with deep psychological transformation, hidden knowledge, and the occult. This house also governs matters related to inheritance, taxes, insurance, and other people's money or unearned wealth. Ketu, as a co-lord of the 8th house, significantly influences its characteristics, intensifying the themes associated with the 8th house, making them more intense and often more complex. This can lead individuals to delve deeply into the mysteries of life, confront their deepest fears, and seek spiritual enlightenment.

As discussed above, Ketu's influence often directs attention away from material pursuits toward spiritual growth and inner transformation. These pursuits, if not balanced, can lead to detachment from worldly responsibilities and personal relationships. Ketu also brings a transformative quality to the areas governed by the 8th house. It encourages individuals to explore unconventional paths and embrace the unknown, sometimes leading to heightened spiritual awakening.

Despite the potential challenges posed by Ketu's influence on the 8th house, positive outcomes can still be realized under certain astrological conditions, such as the presence or aspect of benefic planets like Venus, Mercury, or Jupiter on the 8th house or its lord, mitigating Ketu's malefic effects. These planets promote healing, wisdom, and positive transformation, fostering growth and spiritual enlightenment. Likewise, when the lords of the trine houses (1st, 5th, and 9th houses) aspect or influence the 8th house or its lord (Ketu, here), they bring supportive energies that enhance the likelihood of favorable outcomes. Their influence encourages a balanced approach to transformation and spiritual development, aligning with higher principles and greater understanding.

Ketu's influence underscores the importance of conscious introspection and spiritual intentions. Activities aimed at self-discovery, healing, and spiritual practices are more likely to yield constructive results, aligning with Ketu's potential for deep transformation and growth. In a nutshell, while Ketu's association with the 8th house can amplify challenges and intensify inner struggles, it also offers opportunities for remarkable personal evolution and spiritual awakening. This duality is critical to understand: if the influence of Ketu is negative, it can lead to complete destruction, annihilation, or an absolute loss of identity, resulting in a state of total dissolution. However, if the influence is positive, it can foster significant evolution and growth. By constantly cultivating awareness and aligning pursuits with higher spiritual principles, individuals can harness Ketu's transformative energy to navigate the complexities of the 8th house. This navigation can lead them to emerge with greater wisdom and enlightenment on the other, often untapped or unexplored, side of life.

Chapter 4

The Significance and Interpretation of Rahu-Ketu Axis Through 12 Houses

Note: The benefic or malefic influences (aspects or conjunctions) on Rahu and Ketu and their dispositor will significantly alter the overall effects, polarity and magnitude of the results produced by them, along with the overall strength of the dispositor.

Significance of Rahu Ketu Axis

The Rahu-Ketu axis in Vedic astrology is known as a karmic axis, I call it 'the power axis' or 'the mysterious axis', because its placement reveals the karmic baggage native is supposed to settle in this lifetime. It wields considerable influence over an individual's life. This axis could be symbolically compared to the spinal cord, which forms the central structure around which an individual's existence revolves. When we dissect the Rahu and Ketu axis in a natal chart, we are met with deep insights into the native's karmic patterns, desires, and life purpose. Rahu represents our current life's desires and the karma we accumulate, while Ketu signifies our past life's karmic legacy, lineage, and karmic exhaustion. Rahu and Ketu are inherently incomplete on their own, creating a sense of unfulfillment that drives an individual's actions and experiences.

Rahu and Ketu are two shadow planets that affect human destiny in the most karmic manner and are positioned in a horoscope representing the two areas of life where most of the karma has to be exhausted in the present birth; everything else, orchestrated by other planets, that happens with a native eventually is serving the purpose as signified by this Rahu-Ketu axis in their horoscope.

Rahu is one of the malefic planets that brings obsession, confusion, and materialism. It is said to have the power to magnify and intensify the areas of life it touches, leading to insatiable desires and relentless pursuit of worldly achievements. Ketu, on the other hand, is a spiritual planet that brings detachment, liberation, and enlightenment. It is associated with past life karmas and is believed to guide individuals toward spiritual growth by making them confront their karmic residues. Both Rahu and Ketu are seen as karmic nodes that create a balance between material and spiritual pursuits, pushing individuals toward their ultimate life purpose.

The Rahu-Ketu axis in astrology is crucial in determining where your energy will be focused and which areas of life will present challenges or breakthroughs. Rahu and Ketu symbolize the karmic nodes of the moon, revealing your past life's mastery and current life's desires. Understanding their significance can help navigate life's journey more effectively.

Ketu represents what we have already mastered in our past lives. It carries the legacy of our skills, knowledge, and experiences accumulated through multiple births. This shadow planet shows the areas where we have deep-seated talents and where our subconscious expertise lies. Recognising and embracing these talents can provide a solid foundation for personal growth in this lifetime.

Rahu, on the other hand, symbolizes our current life's desires and ambitions. It represents the uncharted territories we seek to explore and conquer. These are the areas where we feel an intense, almost obsessive drive to achieve and succeed. However, without understanding and integrating the lessons of Ketu, our efforts towards Rahu's desires may feel incomplete or frustrating.

The relationship between Rahu and Ketu's dispositors (the planets ruling the signs they occupy) is significant. If these dispositors have a harmonious relationship, such as being in quadrants or angles from each other, it enhances the native's chances of success. This harmony suggests that the individual is well-positioned to learn their karmic lessons and fulfill their soul's mission. Benefic influences on these dispositors further amplify this potential, offering support and ease in achieving life's purpose.

Understanding the mutual relationship between Rahu and Ketu's dispositors is crucial – a positive connection between them indicates that the native will likely assimilate their karmic lessons effectively, fulfilling their life's purpose and contributing something valuable to society as indicated by the Rahu-Ketu axis.

To truly harness the power of the Rahu-Ketu axis, one must integrate the lessons of Ketu. By leveraging the skills and knowledge from past lives, individuals can pave the way for fulfilling Rahu's desires. This integration process involves recognising and accepting the areas of past life's mastery and using them as a stepping stone for current life's aspirations.

Achieving balance between the energies of Rahu and Ketu is essential. This balance allows individuals to progress smoothly towards their goals, overcoming obstacles, and breaking free from limitations. Success becomes more attainable when past lessons are acknowledged, and present desires are pursued with a holistic understanding.

The Rahu-Ketu axis reveals where an individual will invest their energy, where challenges will arise, and where breakthroughs will occur. By understanding and embracing the legacy of Ketu, native can effectively work towards fulfilling the desires presented by Rahu for the current birth. A consonance between their dispositors can significantly amplify one's chances of success, guiding them towards achieving their life's purpose and delivering meaningful contributions to society. Remember, the journey of life is about learning all the lessons indicated by this karmic axis, and only then can you truly progress and find fulfillment.

Interpretation: Rahu and Ketu Axis Through 12 Houses

1. 1/7 Rahu-Ketu Axis (1st and 7th House) — The Axis of Selfhood and Union

When the Rahu-Ketu axis forms in the 1st and 7th house of a horoscope, we uncover a karmic interplay between the native's identity/sense of self and relationships/partnerships/marriage.

Rahu in the 1st House, Ketu in the 7th House

The 1st house, or ascendant, represents our personality and being as a whole – it's associated with our head and also referred to as 'Tanu Bhava' in Vedic astrology. Rahu, an amplifier and magnifier of desires, when positioned in the 1st house, makes the native exceedingly ambitious and, at times, arrogant. Such individuals are driven by a constant need for more, as Rahu itself is incomplete, symbolized only by a head without a body.

These natives are aware of their potential for greatness and have a profound sense of identity, feeling destined to achieve something significant. However, this relentless ambition often leads to dissatisfaction with their achievements, prestige, and social image. They remain constantly hungry for more, their desires insatiable. This intense self-focus can make them forget the importance of the counterpart, Ketu, which signifies the body and resides in the 7th house. While they strive to build a substantial identity, they inherently recognise their incompleteness, creating an underlying desire for relationships to achieve a sense of wholeness.

While, the 7th house represents the counterparts—one's spouse, marriage, partnerships and business partners. With Ketu in this house, the native desires a perfect relationship to feel complete within himself. However, these natives often make extravagant or unrealistic promises in relationships, failing to give their partners the respect and importance they deserve. This behaviour stems from past life tendencies where the native might have manipulated relationships for personal gain, as indicated by Ketu's karmic legacy.

In this life, the native continues to exhibit selfish tendencies, prioritising their ambition over their partner's needs. They may use their spouse for comfort and support but struggle to give back equally. Despite putting effort into relationships, they often harbour a deep desire for independence and a strong personal identity. Persistently giving into these deep-seated behavioural patterns leads to a cycle of failed relationships, where the native's dissatisfaction and relentless pursuit of personal goals overshadow and often damage their partnerships or relationships.

In order to efficaciously resolve this karmic pattern, the native must show humility and respect towards the spouse. These individuals must help their partner build an identity, fulfilling the promises they made to them and supporting their spouse's growth alongside their own. By doing so, they can achieve a harmonious balance, exhausting their karmic baggage and finding true fulfilment in life. The native must avoid being self-centred, recognising that true satisfaction comes from nurturing their relationships and respecting their partner's identity.

Ketu in the 1st House, Rahu in the 7th House

When Ketu is positioned in the 1st house, the native often battles with an identity crisis. Ketu, being a headless planet, while symbolizing past life's karmic residues, indicates that the native might have suppressed someone's identity in a previous life. Consequently, in this life, the native's identity is intrinsically linked to the 7th house, where Rahu resides. These individuals often seek identity through relationships, marrying into prestigious families or partners with strong social standings, thus gaining recognition through their spouse.

Ketu in the 1st house demands that the native works diligently to build their identity, the native tends to rely on their spouse for the same. This position suggests that the native's past life actions necessitate a balanced approach in this life, ensuring they do not repeat the mistakes of the past by overshadowing or demeaning their partner.

With Rahu in the 7th house, the native becomes an explorer in relationships, seeking fulfilment through partnerships. When under benefic influences, it can lead to loyalty and strong, fulfilling relationships. However, a malefic influence or a weak dispositor can result in multiple relationships, dissatisfaction, and a constant desire for more, sometimes leading to inter-religious or foreign partnerships.

The native must exercise caution, ensuring they do not exploit their spouse for personal gain or identity formation, only to betray them later as there's a tendency to indulge in that with this placement of Rahu. Loyalty and respect towards the spouse are crucial for mitigating karmic debts. Failure to honour these principles can lead to severe consequences, including identity crises, defamation or bodily troubles, as the native repeats past life mistakes.

The example of Amitabh Bachchan illustrates this dynamic. When he married Jaya Bachchan, her identity was more prominent than his. This demonstrates how the native's identity can be remarkably shaped by their spouse, emphasising the importance of mutual respect and support in relationships.

In summary, the Rahu-Ketu axis in the 1st house and 7th house creates a karmic interplay between self-identity and relationships. For natives with Rahu in the 1st house and Ketu in the 7th, the journey involves balancing ambition with humility in partnerships. Conversely, for those with Ketu in the 1st house and Rahu in the 7th, the challenge lies in building a strong personal identity while respecting and supporting their spouse's identity. Embracing these lessons helps natives mitigate karmic debts and achieve true fulfilment in both personal and relational spheres.

Balancing the Axis of Identity and Relationship: Lessons and Remedies

For those with Rahu in the 1st house and Ketu in the 7th, the journey involves balancing ambition with humility in partnerships. Conversely, for those with Ketu in the 1st house and Rahu in the 7th, the challenge lies in building a strong personal identity while respecting and supporting their spouse's identity.

To navigate this axis successfully, the native must:

- **Humility and Respect in Relationships:** Natives must learn to respect their partners' identities and support their growth, fulfilling promises and being genuinely supportive.
- **Balancing Personal Ambitions and Partnerships:** Ambition should not overshadow the importance of relationships. Natives must recognize that true fulfilment comes from a balanced approach that values both personal success and partnership.
- **Loyalty and Integrity:** Maintaining loyalty and integrity in relationships is crucial. Natives should avoid using their partners for personal gain and ensure that they honour their commitments.

By embracing these lessons, natives can resolve their karmic patterns, achieve a harmonious balance in their lives, and find true fulfilment in both personal and relational spheres.

2. 2/8 Rahu-Ketu Axis (2nd and 8th House)— The Axis of Family Roots and Mystical Pursuits

This axis suggests that the native's financial and family dynamics are deeply intertwined with their karmic lessons and spiritual evolution. The individuals may find themselves constantly oscillating between the pursuit of material wealth and the need for deeper, spiritual fulfilment. The key to balancing the 2/8, 8/2 Rahu-Ketu axis lies in understanding that true success and satisfaction come from integrating both the material and spiritual aspects of life. Once the native achieves a harmonious balance between family, finances, and spiritual growth, it will lead to the exhaustion of his karmic debts, settling the energetic dues and thereby the attainment of true fulfilment in life.

Rahu in the 2nd House, Ketu in the 8th House

The 2nd house in Vedic Astrology encompasses family, early learnings in terms of values, speech, and finances, and it also gives insight into an individual's mental aptitude. It is the first *upachaya* house from the ascendant, indicating the growth and expansion of the Ascendant (native) in life.

When Rahu, the foreign and unconventional planet, is positioned in the 2nd house, being an outcast and representative of different cultures, it suggests that the native's family is either liberal or unconventional. Regardless of the country, the family environment will be markedly different from typical families. Rahu as the significator of wealth indicates a strong desire in the native to become rich and successful, a drive often inspired by the family.

This position of Rahu makes the native's speech potentially enigmatic and enchanting, yet it can also be harsh or deluding depending on Rahu's strength and its dispositor. When in strength, Rahu can bestow a magical voice, making the native a renowned orator, philosopher, banker, gambler, or a successful share market trader. The native may also excel in financial institutions, driven by the desire to amass wealth.

Rahu's influence makes the native feel that their strength lies in their family's unconventionality and unique ways. This can lead to a sense of being ungrounded. During the early years, Rahu may make the native flamboyant with an intense desire for wealth, but they may struggle to understand how to achieve it.

The 8th house in astrology is associated with transformation, secrets, inheritance, the occult and the unknown. It is a house of deep, often hidden changes and experiences that shape our lives. When Ketu, the spiritual planet symbolizing detachment and past life karmas, is positioned in the 8th house, it brings an emphasis on spiritual growth and confronting karmic residues. This placement indicates that the native may have experienced significant upheavals or transformations in past lives, leading to a deep understanding of life's mysteries.

With Ketu in the 8th house, the native is likely to have a natural inclination towards spiritual practices and may possess an innate ability to delve into occult or esoteric knowledge. The 8th house in astrology is a mystical realm that encompasses themes such as death, longevity, secret services, research, occult science, insurance, in-laws, tantra, mantra, sudden gains, and meditative practices. This house represents the hidden aspects of life and the transformations that arise from deep, often mysterious experiences. As Ketu is an inherently spiritual and detached planet, it's well placed in the 8th house. Besides, the 8th house corresponds to Scorpio in the fixed zodiac *(Kaalpurush Kundali)*, a sign where Ketu is exalted. This exaltation signifies that the native could have been an expert in the occult or spiritual realms in past lives, potentially reaching high levels of mastery in meditative practices or conducting significant research.

Natives with Ketu in the 8th house possess a naturally curious mind, well-suited for research and exploration of hidden knowledge. This placement indicates that the native's true strength lies in their ability to delve deep into complex subjects, particularly those related to the occult and spiritual practices. The native might feel an inherent pull towards these areas, driven by past life expertise in occult sciences, meditation, and high-level research. It also bestows the native with an intricate understanding of spiritual and occult practices. This placement suggests that the native has spent multiple lifetimes honing these skills, making them an adept occultist or spiritual guide in the present life. The native's expertise in these areas is not just an interest but a deeply ingrained part of their soul's journey, reflecting lives of accumulated knowledge and practice.

With Ketu in the 8th house, the native is likely to excel in roles that require a deep understanding of spiritual and occult knowledge. They could become influential spiritual guides, orators, or astrology-related speakers. The native's ability to articulate complex spiritual concepts and occult knowledge with clarity and authority makes them stand out in these fields. When the native speaks on these subjects, their profound expertise shines through, captivating and enlightening their audience.

To fully harness the power of Ketu in the 8th house, the native should embrace their innate talents in research, spiritual practices, and occult sciences. By acknowledging and utilising the skills acquired in past lives, the native can achieve mastery and recognition in these fields. Whether through teaching, writing, or public speaking, the native's contributions to spiritual and occult knowledge can leave a lasting impact. When the native speaks on these subjects, their depth of understanding and eloquence will make it evident that they are a true expert. Their audience will recognise the native's unique ability to convey intricate spiritual and occult concepts, often feeling that no one could explain these topics better.

Ketu in the 2nd House, Rahu in the 8th House

The 2nd house in astrology governs family,

speech, values, early learning, and finances. Ketu, known for its detachment and spiritual nature, in this house directs the native's initial life focus towards family matters. The native often finds themselves heavily invested in family responsibilities, expending considerable wealth and mental energy in tending to their family's needs. Individuals with Ketu in the 2nd house feel a strong sense of duty towards their family. Their primary concern revolves around supporting and guiding their family members, often feeling an incessant need to contribute more and more.

Speech becomes a critical area of focus. Despite their intentions to support and nurture their family, their words can sometimes cause misunderstandings or bitterness, leading to separation or discord. Thus, these individuals must be mindful of their speech, thinking carefully before speaking to avoid conflicts. Furthermore, finances are another significant concern, the native's wealth is often directed towards family obligations, making it essential for them to balance financial strategies to maintain harmony between personal ambitions and familial responsibilities.

The 8th house is associated with death, longevity, occult sciences, in-laws, shared resources, and transformative experiences. Rahu, representing obsession and insatiable desires, when placed in the 8th house, drives the native towards the mystical and hidden aspects of life. Individuals with Rahu in the 8th house possess an innate curiosity for the occult, spiritual practices, and the hidden truths of life. They seek to uncover deep, mystical knowledge and often become experts in fields that require intense research and understanding of secrets. There is a strong desire to achieve something monumental, a magnum opus that would make the native's name immortal. They aim to leave a lasting legacy, driven by the urge to transcend ordinary reality and achieve extraordinary success.

The 8th house also represents darker aspects such as money laundering, betting, and deceit. If Jupiter, and the dispositor of Rahu, is not well-placed, the native may be tempted into activities that bring infamy or disrespect to their family. The manifestation of positive or negative aspects depends significantly on the strength and placement of the dispositor.

The dynamic between Ketu in the 2nd house and Rahu in the 8th house often indicates a strong familial legacy. The native might carry forward the expertise and knowledge inherited from their ancestors. For example, if the native's grandfather was an astrologer, and the native learns astrology from him, they can achieve extraordinary success in this field by positively utilising Ketu's influence in harmony with Rahu's desires. This alignment allows the native to build on their family's legacy and achieve great heights. Conversely, if the dispositor of Rahu is afflicted or weak, the native might tarnish the family's reputation or fail to uphold the legacy, leading to adverse outcomes.

Balancing the Axis of Familial Roots and Mystical Pursuits: Lessons and Remedies

For those with Rahu in the 2nd house and Ketu in the 8th, the journey involves balancing the pursuit of material wealth with spiritual growth and understanding deep, transformative experiences. Conversely, for those with Ketu in the 2nd house and Rahu in the 8th, the challenge lies in fulfilling family responsibilities while exploring and mastering mystical and occult knowledge.

To navigate this axis successfully, the native must:

- **Balance Family and Finances:** It is crucial to maintain a harmonious balance between family obligations and financial strategies. The native should ensure they are not overly consumed by family responsibilities to the detriment of their personal growth.

- **Mindful Communication:** Given the potential for speech-related conflicts, the native should practice mindfulness in their communication, carefully considering their words to avoid misunderstandings and maintain familial harmony.

- **Strategic Detachment:** When family dynamics start hindering personal progress, the native should mentally detach slightly to prevent discordant behaviour and ensure their own success. This detachment should be strategic, allowing them to fulfil familial responsibilities while pursuing their personal goals.

- **Embrace Spiritual and Mystical Pursuits:** Leveraging their inherent curiosity and past life expertise in occult and mystical practices, the native should embrace these pursuits, striving to achieve mastery and recognition in their chosen field.

3. 3/9 Rahu-Ketu Axis (3rd and 9th House)— The Axis of Worldly Achievements and Spiritual Gains

The axis of Rahu in the 3rd house and Ketu in the 9th house presents a tug-of-war between worldly achievements and higher learning. This placement brings forth a journey where mastering communication skills and courage complements the pursuit of spiritual wisdom and advanced knowledge. The main lesson for natives with the 3/9, 9/3 Rahu-Ketu axis is to transcend petty issues and focus on higher learning and spiritual growth.

Rahu in the 3rd House, Ketu in the 9th House

The 3rd house in Vedic Astrology governs communication skills, media, siblings, travelling, society, neighbourhood, marketing, willpower, finances (as it is the 2nd from the 2nd house), and health (as it is the 8th from the 8th house). It also signifies gains due to past life good deeds (being the 11th from the 5th house) and encompasses performing arts and sports.

Rahu thrives in the 3rd house, where its unconventional and ambitious nature aligns well with the natural significations of the house. This placement bestows the native with exceptional communication and networking skills, which can manifest in various forms. If the dispositor is favourably placed, Rahu can make the native an eloquent and effective communicator. Conversely, if the dispositor is afflicted or Rahu is under malefic influences, the native might incline towards foul language or deceptive speech. A beneficial aspect from Jupiter can refine this communication, making it elegant and measured – native will weigh his words before speaking.

The 3rd house also represents courage and bravery. Rahu's presence here imbues the native with immense courage and an indomitable spirit. This courage can manifest in positive ways, such as standing up against societal evils, or in negative ways, depending on the overall influences on the dispositor.

Rahu in the 3rd house imparts a go-getter attitude, with a relentless "I can do it" and "I will do it" mindset. Natives with this placement tend to tackle challenges head-on, often without a pre-planned strategy, and figure out solutions as they go. This boldness makes them excel in areas requiring perseverance and courage, such as performing arts, sports, media, and marketing.

An illustrative example from the teachings of Shri KN Rao highlights a woman with Rahu in the 3rd house who became a renowned dancer during a time when societal norms restricted women's public roles. This placement gave her the courage to break societal boundaries and pursue her passion, gaining significant popularity.

The 9th house, diametrically opposite the 3rd house, signifies long-form communication, publishing, books, philosophy, gurus, father, righteousness, religion, wisdom, foreign travel, and foreign jobs as well for it's 10th from the 12th house. Ketu, representing past life expertise and skills, brings a depth of knowledge and a strong inclination towards spirituality and philosophy. Ketu in the 9th house suggests that the native carries significant spiritual and philosophical wisdom from past lives. This placement emphasises the importance of higher learning and continuous education. The native is drawn to understanding and knowledge that expand his horizons of mind, often seeking lifelong learning, advanced degrees, or deep spiritual practices.

For success, natives with Ketu in the 9th house must focus on higher learning rather than trivial matters represented by the 3rd house, such as social media, gossip, and fleeting trends. To excel in their chosen field, whether in media, sports, or performing arts, they must acquire technical expertise and in-depth knowledge, underscoring the necessity of continuous learning and skill development. The native's ultimate success lies in harmonising the practical, hands-on approach of the 3rd house with the philosophical and educational pursuits of the 9th house. By utilising the higher knowledge and skills acquired in past lives, the native can achieve significant accomplishments in the present incarnation.

By understanding and integrating the lessons of both houses, the native can navigate their karmic path with greater clarity and purpose, achieving a harmonious balance between material success and spiritual fulfilment.

Ketu in the 3rd House and Rahu in the 9th House

The placement of Ketu in the 3rd house and Rahu in the 9th house creates a tension between short-form communication and the pursuit of higher knowledge. This axis highlights the journey from engaging in trivial matters to embracing significant, meaningful learning and spiritual growth.

The 3rd house in Vedic Astrology is associated with communication skills, media, siblings, travelling, society, neighbourhood, marketing, and willpower. It also relates to finances, health, and gains due to past life good deeds. When Ketu, the planet of past life expertise and skills, is placed in the 3rd house, it signifies that the native carries an inherent proficiency in short-form communication and small-scale problem-solving.

If Ketu is well-aspected and its dispositor is strong, the native may excel in writing, mediating conflicts, and counselling. They possess an intuitive ability to navigate social media, data analytics, and other communication-related fields. This placement makes the native a natural peacemaker, adept at resolving minor disputes and issues. However, if Ketu is ill-placed or the dispositor is weak and afflicted by malefic influences, the native may exhibit rigidity, harshness, and cruelty in communication. They might possess a dictatorial attitude, believing they inherently know how to rule over others due to past life memories of authority.

The 9th house represents long-form communication, publishing, philosophy, gurus, father, righteousness, religion, wisdom, foreign travel, and foreign jobs. Rahu, the planet of unconventional and ambitious pursuits, in the 9th house, encourages the native to seek higher learning and spiritual wisdom.

Rahu in the 9th house signifies a break from traditional faith and religious structures. The native may develop an unconventional attitude towards religion and spirituality, influenced by a liberal or non-traditional father. This placement fosters an open-minded approach to learning, where the native is inclined to explore various religious texts and philosophies, integrating valuable insights from different sources into their life.

Rahu in the 9th house drives the native to seek higher truth and advanced knowledge. They are unlikely to follow religious practices blindly but will instead use their discernment to filter and adopt beliefs that resonate with them. This placement encourages breaking societal boundaries and embracing a broader, more inclusive perspective on spirituality and learning.

The primary challenge for natives with Ketu in the 3rd house and Rahu in the 9th house is to rise above trivial matters and focus on higher learning and spiritual growth. Ketu in the 3rd house suggests a preoccupation with minor issues in past lives, while Rahu in the 9th house urges the native to pursue something more meaningful and significant in the present life.

Balancing the Axis of Worldly Achievements and Spiritual Gains: Lessons and Remedies

For those with Rahu in the 3rd house and Ketu in the 9th, the journey involves harmonising the practical, hands-on approach of the 3rd house with the philosophical and educational pursuits of the 9th house. Conversely, for those with Ketu in the 3rd house and Rahu in the 9th, the challenge lies in balancing the preoccupation with trivial issues and the urge to pursue something more meaningful and significant in the present life.

The main lesson for natives with this placement is to transcend petty issues and focus on higher learning and spiritual growth. By rising above trivial matters and embracing continuous education and philosophical exploration, the native can harmonise the energies of Ketu in the 3rd house and Rahu in the 9th house.

To navigate this axis successfully, the native must:

- **Rise Above Trivial Matters:** Overcome the tendency to focus on minor issues, such as disputes with siblings or neighbours, and instead channel energy towards more significant pursuits.

- **Pursue Higher Learning:** Embrace continuous education and spiritual growth. The native must leverage their innate communication skills to delve into advanced knowledge and philosophical studies.
- **Integrate Past Life Expertise:** Utilise the practical skills and expertise from past lives, as indicated by Ketu in the 3rd house, to support the pursuit of higher goals and spiritual wisdom represented by Rahu in the 9th house.
- **Adopt an Open-minded Approach:** Be flexible and open to learning from various sources and philosophies. This will allow the native to expand their understanding and integrate diverse perspectives into their spiritual journey.

By understanding and integrating the lessons of both houses, the native can achieve a harmonious balance between his worldly desires, communication skills, trivial aspects of life and the pursuit of higher learning, spirituality, and philosophical gains leading to a more fulfilling and enlightened life.

4. **4/10 Rahu-Ketu Axis (4th and 10th House)—The Axis of Domestic Comfort and Professional Aspirations**

Rahu and Ketu's 4th house and 10th house axis suggests a karmic correlation between an individual's domestic comfort and professional ambition. This placement presents a journey where the experience of homely peace and comfort from past lives contrasts with the relentless pursuit of career success and public recognition in the present life. The key to balancing the 4/10, 10/4 Rahu-Ketu axis lies in mastering the balance between personal tranquillity and professional achievement.

Rahu in the 4th House, Ketu in the 10th House

The axis of Ketu in the 4th house and Rahu in the 10th house creates a karmic tug-of-war between domestic comfort and professional ambition. This placement presents a journey where the experience of homely peace and comfort from past lives contrasts with the relentless pursuit of career success and public recognition in the present life. The main lesson for natives with the Rahu-Ketu axis being formed between the 4th and 10th house is to master the balance between personal life and professional achievements.

In Vedic Astrology, the 4th house represents our home, mother, comfort, luxury, vehicles, emotions, harmony, peace, happiness, and satisfaction. When Rahu is placed in the 4th house, it brings an unconventional atmosphere to the home. For instance, a person living in India might have Italian marble, imported chandeliers, and other foreign elements in their house, making it stand out as unique. These individuals are often driven to constantly improve the look and feel of their home, frequently renovating and adding new elements.

When Rahu occupies the 10th house, the individual is driven by an intense desire to achieve success and make a significant name for themselves. Rahu owing to its nature, bestows an innate feeling of being different and destined for greatness. These individuals often feel initially out of sync with their environment but possess an unwavering belief that they will eventually create something of immense value. Rahu instils a relentless pursuit of immortality through one's profession, pushing the native to achieve fame and build a lasting legacy.

To fully understand Rahu's impact, it's essential to analyse the strength and condition of the 10th house lord along with Saturn, the natural *'karmakaraka'* and one of the significators of the 10th house. This analysis helps determine whether Rahu will bring fame or defamation. Individuals with Rahu in the 10th house, work tirelessly towards their goals, never satisfied with their achievements and always setting new milestones.

This placement also suggests that the native may be heavily influenced by their father or aspire to be like him. The father might have had an unconventional career or risen from humble beginnings to great success. If the dispositor of Rahu is ill-placed or malefically aspected, the native's relationship with their father could be strained. Nonetheless, these individuals are born with a drive to pour their energy into their work, aiming to create something monumental and achieve immortality through their professional endeavours.

Rahu in the 10th house often leads to unconventional professions. Fields related to artificial intelligence, game development, digital marketing, and social media fall under Rahu's domain. In the current age, dominated by technology and innovation, Rahu's influence is particularly strong.

Ketu's placement in the 4th house indicates that the native has experienced homely peace, comfort, luxury, and harmony in past lives. In the present life, however, Rahu in the 10th house drives the native to work hard and achieve these comforts through professional success. Despite attaining material comforts, the native might not find deep satisfaction in them, as Ketu's energy pushes them to continually seek more achievements. Their focus remains outward, towards professional milestones, rather than inward, towards domestic tranquillity.

With Ketu in the 4th house, the native's mother might be involved in an unconventional profession or possess a unique approach to spirituality and wisdom. The relationship with the mother carries a karmic connection from past lives, which could be positive or negative, depending on the aspects and influences on Ketu in unison with the strength of its dispositor. The native may have a deep love for their mother and be willing to make significant sacrifices for her, striving to settle past karmic debts.

However, excessive attachment to the mother can hinder professional success. The native must balance their karmic obligations towards their mother with their professional aspirations. Once the karmic debts related to the mother are resolved, the native can truly rise in their career.

Ketu in the 4th House and Rahu in the 10th House

Rahu in the 10th house signifies a deep, insatiable desire to achieve professional success and gain public recognition. Natives with this placement often feel a unique sense of destiny, believing they are meant to accomplish something remarkable. They are driven by the ambition to make a significant name for themselves, create a lasting legacy, and be remembered for their work. This placement fuels a tireless work ethic, with individuals constantly striving to reach new heights in their careers.

However, Rahu's influence also suggests that the native's professional journey may be unconventional. They may be drawn to innovative fields such as artificial intelligence, digital marketing, or any profession that breaks traditional boundaries. The desire to stand out and do something extraordinary is a hallmark of Rahu in the 10th house.

The native's relationship with their father can also be significant, either as a source of inspiration or challenge. The father might have had an unusual career path or achieved notable success, influencing the native's own professional aspirations.

Ketu in the 4th house indicates that the native has experienced comfort, luxury, and domestic harmony in past lives. In the present life, these individuals might find it challenging to derive satisfaction from their home environment, as their focus is drawn outward towards achieving professional milestones. Despite acquiring material comforts, there is often a sense of dissatisfaction and a continual pursuit for more. If the 4th lord is poorly placed or under malefic influences, Ketu's placement in the 4th house could lead to accidents involving vehicles or the need to sell assets.

This placement also highlights a karmic connection with the mother, who may be involved in an unconventional profession or possess unique spiritual wisdom. The native may have a deep bond with their mother, feeling a strong sense of duty and willingness to make sacrifices for her. However, excessive attachment to domestic life can impede professional growth.

Balancing the Axis of Worldly Achievements and Spiritual Gains: Lessons and Remedies

The primary challenge of this axis lies in balancing personal and professional life. The native must learn to prioritise appropriately between these two spheres. In essence, the native's journey involves mastering the art of work-life balance. They must understand when to prioritise personal life over professional ambitions and vice versa. Achieving this balance is crucial for fulfilling their desires and life purpose as indicated by the Rahu-Ketu axis in the 4th and 10th houses. By effectively navigating this balance, the native can harmonise domestic affairs and work life, leading to a more integrated and fulfilling existence.

By understanding and integrating the lessons of both houses, the native can navigate their karmic path with greater clarity and purpose, achieving a harmonious balance between material success and spiritual fulfilment.

To navigate this axis successfully, the native must:

- **Achieve Work-Life Balance:** Maintaining a harmonious balance between domestic responsibilities and professional ambitions is crucial. The native should ensure they are not overly consumed by work to the detriment of their home life, and vice versa. Finding this balance is key to fulfilling both personal and career aspirations.

- **Cultivate Emotional Detachment at Home:** With Ketu in the 4th house, the native may have a deep attachment to their home and mother. However, it is essential to practice emotional detachment to some extent, allowing for professional growth without being hindered by domestic issues. This detachment should be balanced and strategic, enabling the native to support their family while pursuing career goals.

- **Embrace Unconventional Professional Paths:** Rahu in the 10th house drives the native towards unconventional and innovative career paths. The native should leverage this placement by exploring non-traditional professions, such as those related to technology, digital marketing, or any other fields that break societal norms.

Embracing these unconventional paths can lead to significant professional success and public recognition.

- **Utilise Past Life Wisdom in Career:** With Ketu's influence, the native brings past life wisdom and experience into their current life. This inherent knowledge can be a valuable asset in their professional journey. The native should tap into this wisdom, using it to guide their career decisions and strategies, ultimately leading to greater achievements and satisfaction.

By understanding and integrating the lessons of both houses, the native can achieve a harmonious balance between his inner peace and professional aspirations leading to a more fulfilling and enlightened life.

5. 5/11 Rahu-Ketu Axis (5th and 11th House)— The Axis of Learning and Gains

The Rahu-Ketu axis in the 5th and 11th houses represents an interplay between personal creativity, intellectual pursuits, and social gains. This axis is essential for understanding how individuals balance their unique talents and desires with their ability to connect, network, and achieve social success.

Rahu in the 5th House, Ketu in the 11th House

The 5th house in Vedic astrology is a realm of knowledge, intellect, creativity, self-expression, romance, past life merits, sudden gains like lotteries, and progeny. When Rahu, the planet of unconventionality and expansion, occupies the 5th house, it brings a unique flavour to these areas of life. Individuals with Rahu in the 5th house often exhibit an unconventional approach to romance, preferring modern arrangements like live-in relationships over traditional marriage. Progeny can also come about through non-traditional means, such as IVF or surrogacy. These natives might even have children without the institution of marriage, reflecting Rahu's boundary-breaking nature.

Creativity and intellectual pursuits take on an extraordinary quality with Rahu in the 5th house. Creativity is marked by a desire to explore taboo or avant-garde topics. For example, a filmmaker with this placement might create content that challenges societal norms. Their children are likely to have unique interests, possibly aspiring to careers in fields like space exploration, video game development, or other unconventional professions. Rahu's influence leads to deep imagination and a continuous quest for unique knowledge, driven by the dispositor's placement, which narrows down the exact interests.

In terms of courage in creativity, these individuals are willing to push boundaries. Whether in arts or entertainment, they transform dramatically for their roles, taking on controversial or groundbreaking projects with ease. Rahu's presence endows them with the courage to undertake what others might consider daunting or extreme.

The 11th house signifies gains, income, networking, friends, elder siblings, and the fulfilment of desires. It represents the rewards of our karma and the growth of our social image. When Ketu, the planet of detachment and past-life mastery, resides in the 11th house, it highlights a different aspect of these significations. Natives with Ketu in the 11th house have an inherent knack for networking, and projecting themselves with poise and ease, particularly on social media. This skill is a carryover from past lives where they honed these abilities. They are adept at manoeuvring through social settings and can achieve significant social status and rewards due to their inherent expertise.

Professional achievements and recognition come naturally to these individuals. As Ketu is in the 2nd house from the 10th, they often find themselves in high-ranking positions. They have a natural talent for climbing the professional ladder, having already achieved significant success in past lives. They can win international awards and recognition, embodying the skills and savvy needed to navigate complex social and professional landscapes. For example, a prominent figure like Narendra Modi, with Ketu in the 11th house, exemplifies this success.

Despite their accomplishments, Ketu's nature brings a sense of dissatisfaction. These natives are perpetual seekers, always on a quest for something more, never fully content with their social or professional achievements. This constant search drives them to keep honing their craft and striving for greater heights, yet they might never feel completely fulfilled in the areas governed by the 11th house.

To successfully navigate the 5th/11th Rahu-Ketu axis, the native must strive to harmonise personal creative pursuits with the need for social recognition and networking. Embracing the unique talents and interests bestowed by Rahu in the 5th house, they can leverage Ketu's networking prowess in the 11th house. Using Rahu's influence, these individuals explore and excel in unconventional and innovative fields, such as technology, digital marketing, or any non-traditional profession that breaks societal norms.

Tapping into the inherent skills and wisdom brought by Ketu, past-life mastery can guide their professional decisions and social interactions, leading to significant achievements. These individuals must seek inner peace and contentment, understanding that true fulfilment comes from within. While Rahu drives the pursuit of external success, Ketu's placement reminds them to look inward for lasting satisfaction.

Maintaining a balanced social presence is essential, leveraging inherent networking skills to build and maintain a strong social image. However, they must remain mindful of Ketu's detachment, ensuring that social interactions are genuine and fulfilling rather than purely strategic. By addressing these key aspects, the native can effectively balance the demands of their personal creativity and social ambitions, ultimately achieving harmony and satisfaction in both areas.

Ketu in 5th House, Rahu in 11th House

The Rahu-Ketu axis in the 11th and 5th houses represents a correlation between personal wisdom, creativity, and the fulfilment of desires and social gains. This axis is essential for understanding how individuals balance their inherent knowledge and past-life merits with their aspirations for social recognition and material success.

The 5th house in Vedic astrology, as we discussed, governs knowledge, intellect, creativity, self-expression, past life merits, mantra sadhana, and progeny. When Ketu, the planet of detachment and spiritual wisdom, occupies the 5th house, it indicates that the native has extensively exhausted their karma related to learning, education, and progeny in past lives. This placement bestows the native with a vast reservoir of knowledge and wisdom accumulated over multiple lifetimes.

A well-placed Ketu in the 5th house enhances the native's intellect, endowing them with a sharp mind and high IQ. These individuals possess a charismatic personality, often becoming eloquent speakers or orators whose words can influence and captivate others. If Ketu is weak, under malefic influence, or if its dispositor is weak, the native may have knowledge but not perfect or complete understanding. However, with a strong Ketu, their success becomes inevitable once they identify their true passion or calling.

This placement also indicates that the native's children may be high achievers or instrumental in helping the native polish their skills and knowledge from past lives. For instance, a native with Ketu in the 5th house and the Sun in the 8th house might possess in-depth knowledge of astrology or the occult, perhaps inherited from ancestral lineage. Such individuals need only to awaken this latent knowledge, and it will flow naturally into their conscious mind.

The 11th house is associated with gains, income, networking, friends, elder siblings, and the fulfilment of desires. It represents the rewards of our karma and the growth of our social image. When Rahu, the planet of desires and materialism, is placed in the 11th house, it aligns perfectly with the house's significations, creating a formidable combination for success.

Rahu in the 11th house is considered one of the best placements for Rahu, as it amplifies the native's ambitions and aspirations. This placement brings about new sources of wealth and continuous growth, especially after the age of 42 or 48. If Rahu is aspected by the 11th lord or one of the significators of the 11th house, or if the 11th lord is strongly placed in a trinal or quadrant house, the native experiences the fulfilment of their deepest desires.

Individuals with Rahu in the 11th house have a profound hunger for appreciation, awards, and recognition, often more so than for material wealth alone. They aspire to be part of prestigious groups and network circles, seeking validation and acknowledgement from influential and renowned personalities. This desire for social elevation and importance usually manifests fully after the age of 48, making them late bloomers. However, once they bloom, they achieve remarkable success in alignment with the efforts they have invested and there's no looking back for such individuals.

Balancing the Axis of Learning and Gains: Lessons and Remedies

To effectually navigate this axis, natives must harmonise their inherent wisdom and creativity with their social aspirations and material desires. Embracing the deep knowledge and sharp intellect provided by Ketu in the 5th house, they can leverage Rahu's ambition in the 11th house to achieve significant social and material success.

To navigate this axis successfully, the native must:

- **Harmonise Wisdom and Ambition:** Natives must harmonize their inherent wisdom and creativity with their social aspirations and material desires. Embracing the deep knowledge and sharp intellect provided by Ketu in the 5th house, they can leverage Rahu's ambition in the 11th house to achieve significant social and material success.
- **Pursue True Passions:** Focus on identifying and pursuing true passions, utilizing the profound understanding and past-life merits to excel in chosen fields. By tapping into Ketu's spiritual wisdom, natives can maintain

a sense of inner fulfilment even as they chase external recognition and rewards.

- **Balance Intellectual and Social Goals:** Balance personal intellectual pursuits with social and material goals. While Rahu drives natives towards external achievements and recognition, Ketu's placement reminds them to seek inner peace and satisfaction from their inherent wisdom and spiritual growth.
- **Avoid Overemphasis on Children**: Ensure they do not get caught up with just children throughout their whole lives. It is important to balance familial responsibilities with personal and professional aspirations to achieve overall fulfilment.

By understanding and integrating the lessons of both houses, the native can achieve a harmonious balance between their inherent wisdom, creativity, social aspirations, and material desires, leading to significant social success and inner fulfilment. By leveraging past-life merits and pursuing true passions, while balancing intellectual pursuits with external achievements, they can navigate the challenges of the 5th/11th Rahu-Ketu axis and achieve a more fulfilling and enriched life.

6. 6/12 Rahu-Ketu Axis (6th and 12th House) – The Axis of Materialism and Spirituality

The 6th/12th Rahu-Ketu axis signifies a karmic interplay between materialism and spirituality in a native's life. This axis brings a balance between the pursuit of material wealth and the quest for spiritual liberation, shaping the individual's journey through karmic challenges and opportunities.

Rahu in the 6th House, Ketu in the 12th House

Let's understand the 6th house first, the 6th house represents karmic debts, fears, litigation, diseases, routine, jobs, enemies, and service. It also encompasses the growth of children, father's fortune, medicine, and healing. The presence of Rahu, an amplifier and a malefic planet, in this house is paradoxically beneficial. As the 6th house is a *trik* and an *upachaya* house, malefic planets like Rahu perform well here. Classics illustrate that malefic planets destroy the significations of the houses they occupy. Thus, Rahu in the 6th house tends to destroy enemies, debt, and disease, bestowing the native with tremendous courage and a fighting spirit. Competitors and adversaries rise, only to be overcome by the native's indomitable will.

This placement of Rahu indicates a deep desire for material prosperity. Individuals with this placement often start working at a young age, driven by a strong urge to accumulate wealth and material comforts. They may feel envious of others' success and might go to great lengths to achieve material abundance. The extent of these tendencies depends on Rahu's dispositor and aspects. Rahu in the 6th house can also lead to addictions, such as liquor, smoking, or physical pleasures, depending on the zodiac sign in the 6th house. While this placement provides significant advantages in fields like law, medicine, the corporate sector, and technical fields, it can also pose challenges, such as issues with medicine consumption or exacerbating existing medical conditions. The native may excel as a consultant or even a judge if Rahu is aspected by Jupiter, and a high-ranking government position is possible if Rahu is associated with the Sun.

On the other end of the axis, the 12th house signifies liberation, expenditure, sleep, charity, renunciation, bed pleasure, isolated places, and foreign lands. Ketu's placement here suggests that the native was highly spiritual in their past life, reaching close to spiritual enlightenment and mastering meditative practices. These individuals were benevolent, charitable souls who now, in this life, seek to hoard material success. Despite their achievements, they find peace and satisfaction in solitude and spirituality. They prefer aloofness and often seek peacefulness in isolation. At some point, they may feel compelled to renounce all material success, embracing a simpler, more spiritual life. This can manifest as quitting the rat race and living in an *ashram*, joining a spiritual community, or dedicating themselves to meditative practices.

Rahu in the 12th House, Ketu in the 6th House

The placement of Rahu in the 12th house and Ketu in the 6th house embodies the tension between material desires and spiritual aspirations in a reverse manner to the aforementioned.

The 12th house, as we discussed, represents spirituality, renunciation, imagination, dreams, foreign lands, and expenditure. When Rahu, a planet associated with foreign elements and exploration, occupies the 12th house, it amplifies the native's urge for freedom and boundless experiences. Such individuals are often itinerant, feeling stifled by confinement or routine. This placement can be worrisome, as Rahu's disregard for morality may lead the native to explore harmful or immoral activities. However, Rahu in the 12th house also sparks interest in subjects like astronomy and space, and natives may have a profound sense of detachment from worldly life, sometimes resulting in an early or sudden departure from this world.

Rahu in the 12th house can manifest as a propensity for multiple romantic affairs, particularly with foreigners, due to the house's association with bed pleasures and foreign lands. The native may be a spendthrift, indulging in luxury items such as watches, cars, and fine dining. This Rahu placement can also drive the native towards renunciation, depending on the aspects and condition of the 12th lord. Innovation is another hallmark of Rahu, making these individuals potential inventors. They often harbour a desire to explore and settle in foreign countries, seeking new experiences and cultures. Their approach to religion is flexible, preferring to explore various beliefs before choosing one to practice. Ultimately, Rahu in the 12th house pushes the native to understand spiritual matters, urging him not to be entirely consumed by material pleasures.

On the other end, Ketu in the 6th house brings significant lessons through diseases, enemies, or debt, the primary significations of this house. Natives might also learn from legal battles or litigations. Ketu's influence emphasises the importance of organisation and discipline, symbolized by the watch. Until the native aligns their life with disciplined routines, they may struggle to grow or enjoy material prosperity. Overcoming the challenges represented by the 6th house is crucial for these individuals. They must confront their greatest fears, whether related to health, enemies, or financial issues, to progress towards the luxury and freedom indicated by Rahu in the 12th house.

Balancing the Axis of Materialism and Spirituality: Lessons and Remedies

The primary lesson of this axis is to transcend material enjoyment and sensory pleasures to achieve spiritual fulfilment. Natives must balance their actions and desires, forming a bridge between their external pursuits and inner growth. By mastering the lessons of the 6th house, they can relish the luxuries associated with the 12th house, like staying in luxurious hotels. This balance is essential for leading a life of completion and overall abundance.

To navigate this axis successfully, the native must:

- **Harmonise Wisdom and Creativity with Aspirations:** Balance inherent wisdom and creativity with social aspirations and material desires. Utilise your deep knowledge and sharp intellect to inform your ambitions and goals.

- **Embrace Discipline and Organisation:** Cultivate discipline and organisation in your life, as emphasised by Ketu in the 6th house. Aligning your daily routines and responsibilities with a disciplined approach helps overcome challenges related to health, enemies, and financial debts, ensuring overall growth and stability.

- **Balance Material and Spiritual Goals:** Balance the deep desire for material comforts and luxury brought by Rahu in the 12th house with spiritual growth. Engaging in meditative practices, exploring various religious philosophies, and seeking inner peace helps harmonise material and spiritual aspirations. Tap into Ketu's spiritual wisdom to maintain inner fulfilment while seeking external recognition and rewards. This ensures you are not solely driven by material success but also find peace and satisfaction from within.

- **Tap into Spiritual Wisdom to Seek Inner Fulfillment:** Prioritise inner fulfilment despite material success. Spending time in solitude, engaging in charitable activities, and practising renunciation brings a sense of peace and satisfaction that transcends material wealth.

The Rahu-Ketu axis between the 12th and 6th houses compels the native to navigate a path that balances their material desires with spiritual growth. By integrating the lessons of both houses, they can achieve a harmonious existence, where external success is matched by inner peace and fulfilment.

Chapter 5

Rahu and Ketu Axis Through 12 Houses: Case Studies

Case Study 1
Rahu in the 1st House, Ketu in the 7th House

Example Chart 1 - Raj Kapoor (Actor, Director and Producer)

With Rahu placed in the ascendant in Cancer, conjunct the Moon, Raj Kapoor's life exemplifies the creation of a larger-than-life persona. Here, Rahu magnifies the qualities of the ascendant lord, and since the Moon rules Cancer and sits alongside Rahu in its own sign, his emotional depth and imaginative nature were greatly enhanced. This made him someone who felt and expressed life on a grand scale. His cinematic vision was unconventional and ahead of its time, as seen in films like "Mera Naam Joker", which initially failed at the box office but later came to be appreciated for its brilliance. Rahu in the first house made him restless and ambitious, driven to explore new artistic frontiers, while the Moon's strong placement infused his work with creativity, emotion, and universal appeal. This combination allowed him

Example Chart 1: Raj Kapoor (Actor)

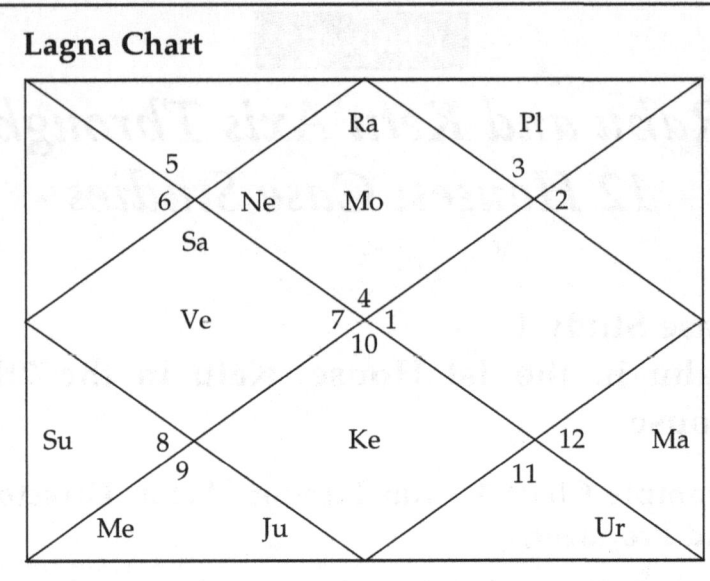

to merge his personal identity with his artistic legacy, becoming a visionary who reshaped Indian cinema.

Ketu in the 7th house in the sign of Capricorn reveals a past-life mastery over relationships and audience connection. The seventh house represents both the masses and partnerships, and Kapoor naturally understood how to captivate people, whether through his performances, his on-screen storytelling, or his real-life relationships. This innate skill allowed him to draw audiences effortlessly and build lasting associations with collaborators like Nargis and Mukesh. However, Ketu's detachment also created turbulence in his personal life. Though deeply connected to many, including his wife, Krishna Kapoor, he could never fully anchor himself in a single relationship. The strength of Saturn, the dispositor of Ketu, exalted in the fourth house alongside Venus, kept him firmly tied to his family and sense of duty, preventing him from abandoning those bonds despite challenges. Both dispositors in strong Kendra houses, Moon in its own sign and exalted Saturn, gave him the ability to balance his inner ambitions with his outer responsibilities. This alignment helped him nurture his relationships while still pursuing his Rahu-driven vision, ultimately allowing him to honour his past mastery even as he forged a powerful, individual legacy in the world of cinema.

Example Chart 2 - Jaya Kishori (Spiritual Orator and Devotional Singer)

Jaya Kishori has Rahu in the 1st house in Libra, positioned in Swati nakshatra, Rahu's own nakshatra,

Example Chart 2: Jaya Kishori (Spiritual Orator and Devotional Singer)

Lagna Chart

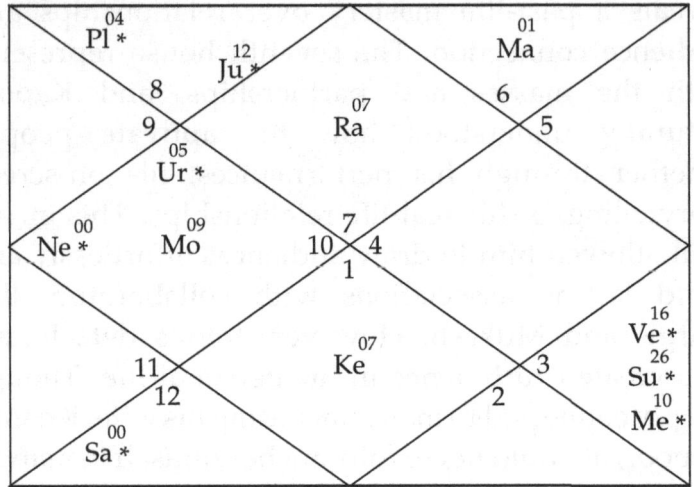

Lagna Chart

			Me¹⁰ Ve¹⁶
Sa⁰⁰*	Ke		Su²⁶
		Birth Details **Jaya Kishori** Jul 13, 1995 Time 14: 0: 0 Time Zone 5.5 Latitude 27: 41: N Longitude 74: 28: E	
Ur⁰⁵* Ne⁰⁰* Mo⁰⁹			
	Pl⁰⁴* Ju¹²*	Ra⁰⁷ Asc¹³	Ma⁰¹

making this a highly potent placement. Libra is a sign of balance, beauty, and the masses, and Rahu here amplifies her ability to connect with people on a grand scale. From the age of just seven, she began delivering Kathas, an unconventional and rare phenomenon, especially for a young girl, thus breaking societal norms. Swati's nature is to rise independently and reach great heights, and Rahu here gave her complete focus on her own identity and mission. This explains why she could stand apart so early in life and create a unique space for herself as a spiritual voice for the modern generation. The dispositor of Rahu, Venus, is strongly placed in the 9th house along with Sun and Mercury, which channelled Rahu's ambitious energy into a path aligned with dharma. Because the 9th house is a trikona house of faith and guidance, this placement gave her access to the right mentors, environment, and opportunities, ensuring her rise was both divinely protected and spiritually oriented. Thus, even though Rahu is naturally materialistic and restless, its strength was harmonized and directed toward spreading spiritual teachings with a modern outlook.

On the other side of the axis, Ketu is in the 7th house in Aries, indicating past-life mastery in relationships and partnerships. This made it natural for her to connect with audiences and form bonds with people, which is evident from the massive following she has today. However, the dispositor of Ketu, Mars, is placed in the 12th house, a position that pulls the soul away from worldly connections toward seclusion, detachment, and spiritual transcendence. This suggests that while she excels at captivating the masses, there is a lack of personal focus on nurturing one-to-one relationships, such as marriage or deep companionship. As a result, the 7th house may remain undernourished. If she continues to focus solely on Rahu, building her personal brand and public mission without periodically "watering" her Ketu, she may later experience feelings of isolation or imbalance. This could manifest either as complete renunciation or a sense of longing for companionship later in life.

Her chart demonstrates how a strong Rahu, supported by a powerful dispositor, can lead to extraordinary success and influence, especially when aligned with dharma. At the same time, it highlights the importance of balance. While Rahu has been beautifully channelled through Venus in the 9th house, Ketu's domain requires conscious attention. If nurtured, it can bring inner fulfilment alongside outer success; if neglected, it may create a void that even fame and spiritual achievement cannot fill.

Case Study 2
Ketu in the 1st House, Rahu in the 7th House

Example Chart 1 - Amitabh Bachchan (Cinema Icon)

Amitabh Bachchan has Ketu in the 1st house in Aquarius and Rahu in the 7th house in Leo. Ketu in the ascendant often makes the native unsure of personal direction, which is why people with this placement

Example Chart 1: Amitabh Bachchan (Cinema Icon)

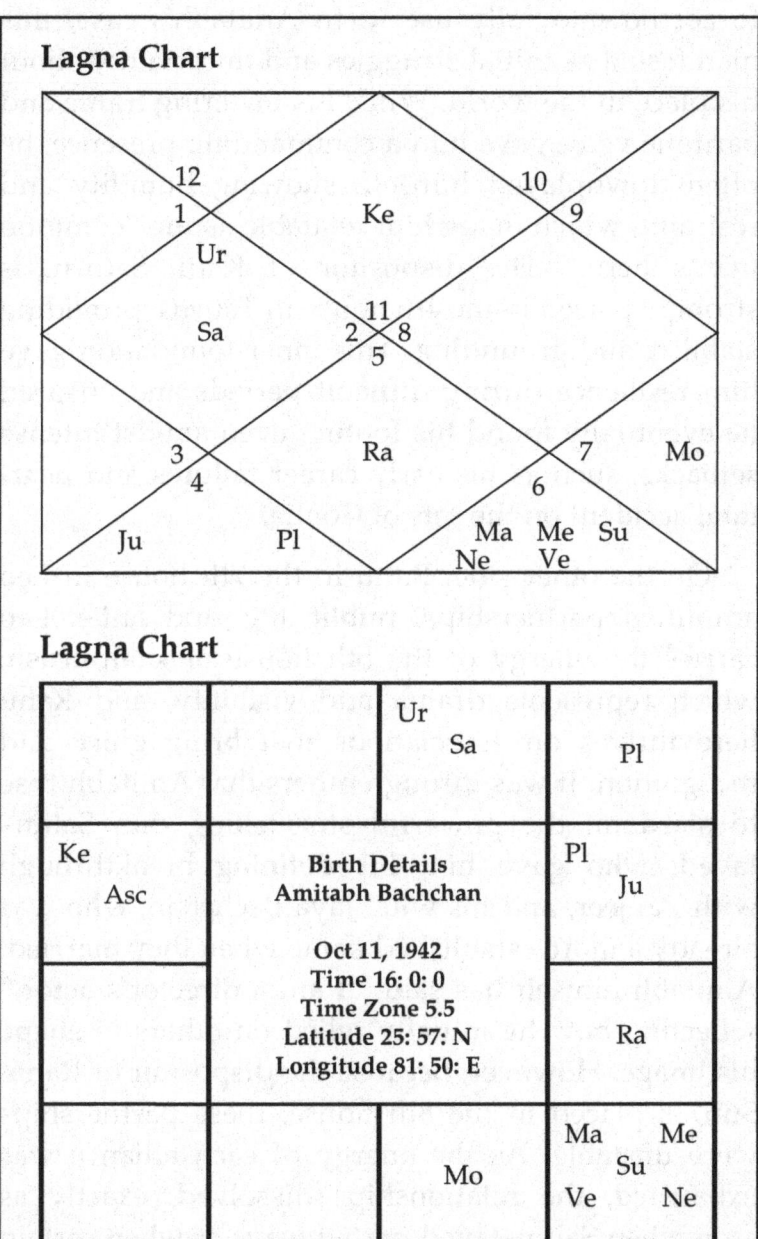

often carry past-life self-mastery but, in this lifetime, forget how to fully use it. In Amitabh's case, this manifested as initial struggles and uncertainty about his place in the world. While his towering frame and baritone voice gave him a commanding presence, he often downplayed himself, showing humility and restraint, which made him relatable as the "common man's hero." The dispositor of Ketu, Saturn, is strongly placed in the 4th house in Taurus, providing stability and grounding. This inner foundation gave him resilience during difficult periods and ensured he eventually found his footing even amidst intense setbacks, such as his early career failures and near-fatal accident on the sets of Coolie.

On the other side, Rahu in the 7th house in Leo amplified partnerships, public life, and fame. Leo carries the energy of the 5th house of kaalpurush, which represents drama and visibility, and Rahu here thrives on associations that bring glory and recognition. It was through others that Amitabh rose to stardom: the powerful storytelling duo Salim–Javed, who gave him his defining breakthrough with Zanjeer, and his wife, Jaya Bachchan, who was already a more established name when they married. Amitabh himself has said, "I am a director's actor," reflecting how he initially relied on others to shape his image. However, because the dispositor of Rahu, Sun, is placed in the 8th house, these partnerships were unstable. As the energy of each alliance was exhausted, the relationships dissolved, exactly as seen when Salim–Javed parted ways or when certain directors stopped collaborating with him. This instability reflects Rahu's transient nature when its dispositor is challenged.

Over time, the setbacks brought by Ketu realigned him with his inner self. While Rahu initially propelled him to fame through others, life's trials, such as bankruptcy, betrayals, and near-death experiences, forced him to reclaim his own mastery. In later years, he evolved into "Big B," a self-sustained icon whose presence no longer depended on collaborators. This journey shows how the soul first runs toward Rahu's hunger for external validation, only to be reminded by Ketu to return inward. By integrating both energies by projecting humility while commanding the public stage, Amitabh created a lasting legacy and a persona revered for both his extraordinary talent and his grounded simplicity.

Example Chart 2 - Sheikh Hasina (Prime Minister of Bangladesh)

Sheikh Hasina has Ketu in the 1st house in Scorpio and Rahu in the 7th house in Taurus, both exalted, creating a potent axis of self-mastery versus public alliances. Scorpio in the ascendant enhances her resilience, strategic acumen, and depth, while Ketu here reflects past-life self-mastery. Yet in this life, she faced a profound identity question, "Who am I?", as she needed external cues to define herself. The dispositor of Ketu, Mars, is placed in the 12th house, signifying exile, foreign connections, and hidden struggles. This placement manifested as Hasina's

Example Chart 2: Sheikh Hasina (Ex-PM of Bangladesh)

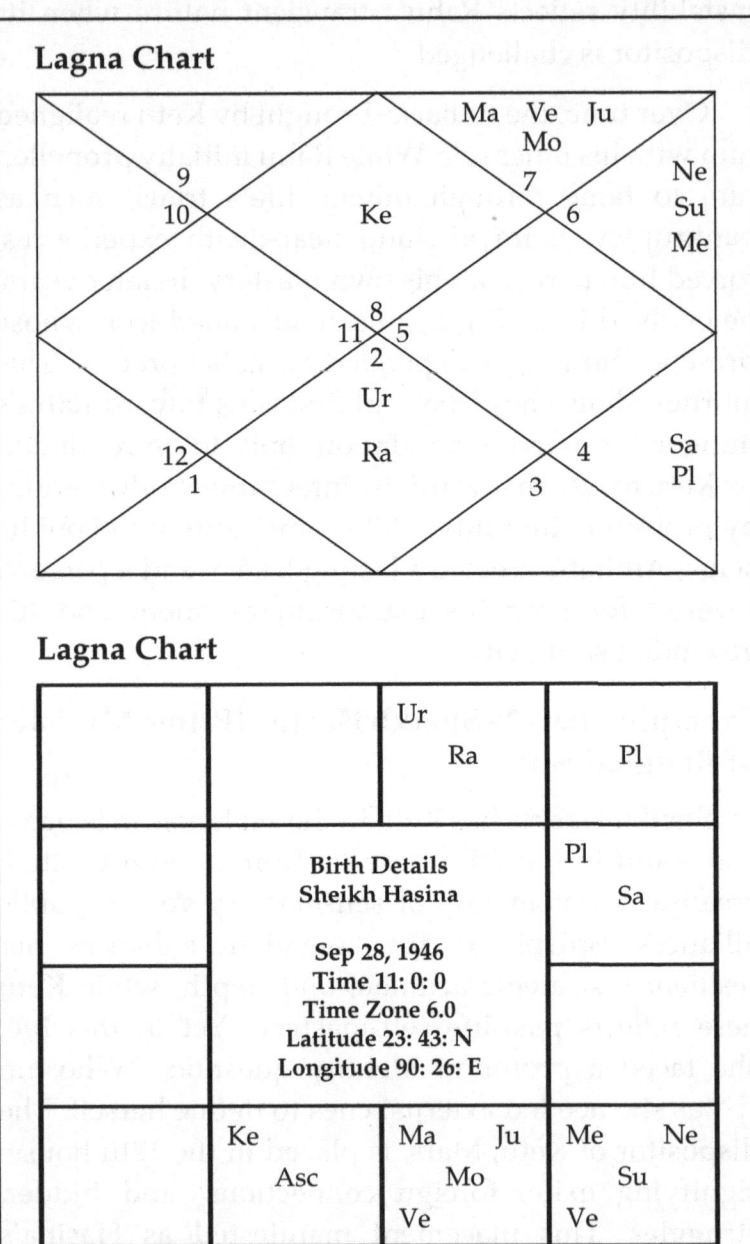

years in Germany, a period of political exile where she had to confront her own sense of self while being away from her homeland. Ketu in the ascendant gave her inner strength and detachment, but without the support of a well-placed dispositor, the early years were marked by uncertainty, introspection, and reliance on external guidance.

Meanwhile, Rahu in the 7th house in Taurus brought immense recognition through partnerships, alliances, and public life. Taurus gives Rahu a steady and material-oriented energy, magnifying her capacity to engage with others effectively. Its dispositor, Venus, is also in the 12th house in Libra, further connecting her success to foreign support, international alliances, and public perception. This explains how both her personal partner, Dr. M. A. Wazed Miah, and foreign nations became pivotal in shaping her authority and influence. Rahu's exalted energy fueled her rise to prominence, yet the axis was imbalanced: too much focus on Rahu and self-promotion created challenges, such as political rivalries and exile. By navigating these trials, she learned to integrate Ketu's wisdom, rooted in humility, resilience, and inner composure, with Rahu's outward hunger for recognition. This balance allowed her to consolidate power, command respect both domestically and internationally, and emerge as one of South Asia's longest-serving and most influential leaders.

Her chart exemplifies the essence of the Rahu–Ketu axis as to how the soul begins by chasing validation through Rahu, relying on partners and alliances, but true mastery and lasting success arrive only when one reconnects with Ketu, grounding oneself while harmonizing public ambition with inner wisdom. Hasina's journey illustrates both the blessings and the challenges of exalted Ketu and Rahu, showing how the axis can produce extraordinary resilience, leadership, and legacy when navigated consciously.

Case Study 3
Rahu in the 2nd House, Ketu in the 8th House

Example Chart 1 - A. R. Rahman (Composer, Singer, Oscar Winner, Global Musical Icon)

A.R. Rahman has Rahu in the 2nd house in Taurus and Ketu in the 8th house in Scorpio, creating a powerful axis that combines creativity, transformation, and challenges in personal relationships. Taurus, ruled by Venus, enhances Rahman's artistic inclination, giving him a unique, unconventional voice and a deep connection to music. The 2nd house governs speech, expression, and family lineage, and Rahman's life reflects a soul-driven desire to create something extraordinary in the creative field, breaking conventional family patterns and redefining his lineage through music. Rahu's dispositor, Venus, is placed in the 8th house along with Ketu, indicating early life challenges related to family finances, transformations, and a need to navigate intense personal or material crises. These difficulties shaped his determination to succeed and achieve recognition through his talent, while also catalyzing a change in family or personal dharma.

Example Chart 1: A.R. Rahman (Composer, Singer, Oscar Winner, Global Musical Icon)

Lagna Chart

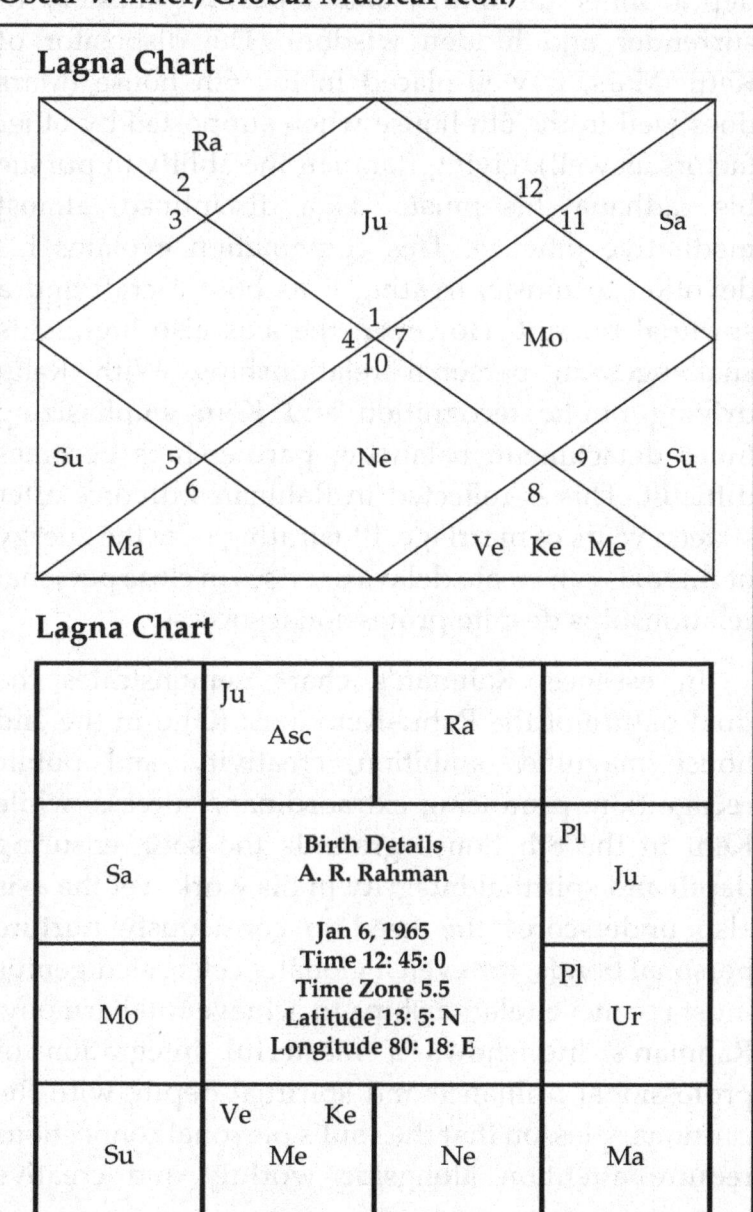

Lagna Chart

	Ju Asc	Ra	
Sa	**Birth Details** **A. R. Rahman** Jan 6, 1965 Time 12: 45: 0 Time Zone 5.5 Latitude 13: 5: N Longitude 80: 18: E		Pl Ju
Mo			Pl Ur
Su	Ve Ke Me	Ne	Ma

Ketu in the 8th house in Scorpio brings spiritual depth, inner discipline, and a past-life mastery of surrender and hidden wisdom. The dispositor of Ketu, Mars, is well-placed in the 6th house (Mars does well in the 6th house when supported by other factors as well), giving Rahman the ability to pursue his sadhana, his music, as a disciplined, almost meditative practice. This combination explains his devotion to music, treating it as both a craft and a spiritual pursuit. However, the axis also highlights challenges in personal relationships. With Rahu driving public recognition and Ketu emphasizing inner detachment, balancing partnerships becomes difficult. This is reflected in Rahman's divorce after sixteen years of marriage, illustrating how the energy of this axis can create delays or crises in close personal relationships despite professional success.

In essence, Rahman's chart demonstrates the dual nature of the Rahu–Ketu axis: Rahu in the 2nd house magnifies ambition, creativity, and public recognition, producing extraordinary success, while Ketu in the 8th house grounds the soul, ensuring depth and spiritual integrity in his work. Yet the axis also underscores the need to consciously nurture personal bonds, for even a globally celebrated genius must reconcile relationships to achieve full harmony. Rahman's life shows a masterful integration of professional brilliance and spiritual depth, with the cautionary lesson that the soul's personal connections require attention alongside worldly and creative pursuits.

Example Chart 2 - Dharmendra (Bollywood Icon)

Dharmendra's Rahu in the sign of Sagittarius is placed in the 2nd house of speech, family, and accumulated wealth, which endowed him with a natural drive for recognition, material prosperity, and charismatic self-expression. True to this placement, his dialogue delivery became iconic, creating a distinctive style that left a lasting mark on Bollywood. Rahu here also inspired ambition to rise above modest beginnings, ensuring that he achieved financial success and fame while projecting his voice and personality in compelling ways.

Balancing this outward hunger is Ketu in Gemini, in the 8th house, which carried past-life mastery over transformation, crisis management, and spiritual depth. Ketu here provided Dharmendra with resilience, humility, and the ability to navigate upheavals, both personal and professional, with composure. This energy is reflected in his enduring adaptability, from his early roles as a romantic hero to becoming a respected veteran actor. The placement of Ketu's dispositor, Mercury, in the ascendant strengthened his connection to family and roots, enabling him to maintain bonds across complex relationships. Even with two marriages, he managed to honor both families, keeping ties intact and demonstrating Ketu's stabilizing, grounding influence.

Rahu's dispositor, well placed in the ascendant, reinforced his determination to safeguard family

Example Chart 2: Dharmendra (Bollywood Icon)

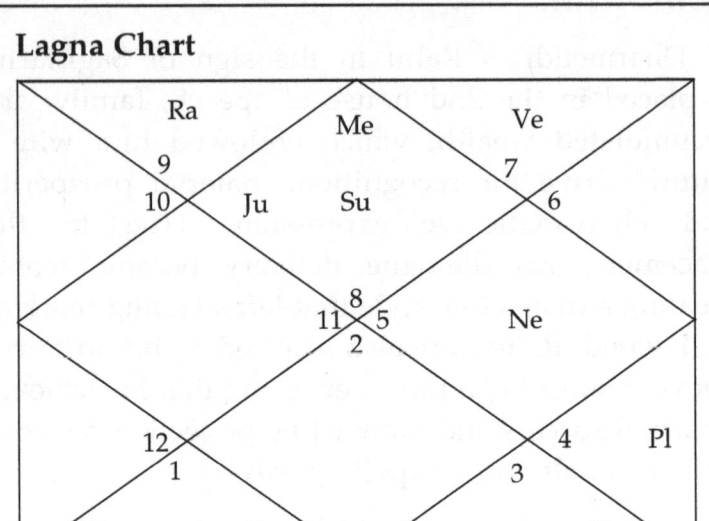

Lagna Chart

	Ur Mo		Ke
Sa	**Birth Details** **Dharmendra** **Dec 8, 1935** **Time 6: 0: 0** **Time Zone 5.5** **Latitude 30: 56: N** **Longitude 75: 52: E**		Pl
Ma			Ne
Ra	Su Me Asc Ju	Ve	

welfare, ensuring that material success was not pursued at the expense of loved ones. Together, these dispositors created a balanced axis, while Rahu demanded projection, wealth, and public acclaim, while Ketu anchored him internally, offering insight, spiritual resilience, and mastery over personal transformations.

In Dharmendra's life, this Rahu–Ketu axis expresses the journey from inner wisdom to outer achievement. Ketu in the 8th house provided the inner fortitude to endure societal judgment and personal upheavals, while Rahu in the 2nd house translated this depth into public recognition, iconic dialogue delivery, and enduring fame. His ability to balance familial responsibilities, personal choices, and professional ambitions exemplifies how the soul uses past-life mastery (Ketu) to fulfill present-life desires (Rahu), leaving behind a legacy of charisma, talent, and relational integrity.

Case Study 4
Ketu in the 2nd House, Rahu in the 8th House

Example Chart 1 - Rajinikanth (Actor, Cultural Icon)

Ketu in the 2nd house in Virgo endowed Rajinikanth with detachment from material security and early-life stability, reflecting past-life mastery over speech, values, and family-related dynamics. The 2nd house governs speech, accumulated skills, and family lineage, while Virgo lends precision, analytical

Example Chart 1: Rajinikanth (Actor, Cultural Icon)

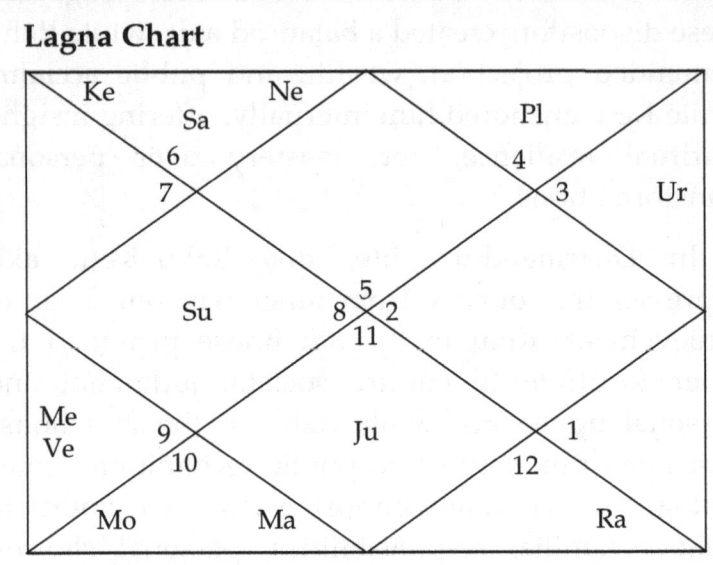

depth, and subtlety to expression. Born into modest circumstances, he faced childhood hardships and worked various jobs, including as a bus conductor, before entering the cinema. Ketu's influence cultivated humility and simplicity in his speech and demeanor, qualities that remained central to his persona even as he rose to superstardom. The dispositor of Ketu, Mercury, is placed in the 5th house, strengthening his creative expression, command over dialogue, and mastery in performance, as the 5th house governs skill, intelligence, and artistic flair. This combination facilitated his iconic style, from dialogue delivery to charismatic hand movements, leaving a lasting impression on audiences.

Balancing this inner mastery, Rahu in the 8th house in Pisces propelled Rajinikanth toward transformation, sudden upheavals, and encounters with unseen dimensions of life. The 8th house governs rebirth, regeneration, and intense life experiences, while Pisces adds visionary imagination, empathy, and a connection to the collective unconscious. Rahu here amplified his magnetic screen presence and capacity to captivate audiences with an almost hypnotic allure. The dispositor of Rahu, Venus, is exalted in the 1st house, ensuring that his worldly recognition, fame, and artistic collaborations were firmly anchored in charm, grace, and personal magnetism. Rahu's influence also manifested in his spiritual inclinations, meditation practices, and philosophical approach, infusing his public persona with an aura of mystery and reverence.

The Rahu–Ketu axis in Rajinikanth's chart exemplifies a harmonious balance between inherited mastery and worldly manifestation. Ketu in the 2nd house provided him with humility, detachment, and a natural command over speech and personal values, while Rahu in the 8th house demanded transformation, visibility, and public recognition. By channeling Ketu's depth through Rahu's drive for extraordinary impact, he turned early hardships into a narrative of personal and cultural rebirth. His rise from obscurity to superstardom illustrates how past-life mastery (Ketu) can be actualized through Rahu's worldly purpose, creating a legacy that resonates both spiritually and across mass audiences.

Example Chart 2 - Ravi Shankar (Sitar Virtuoso, Composer, Global Cultural Ambassador)

Ravi Shankar has Ketu in the 2nd house in Aries and Rahu in the 8th house in Libra, forming an axis that beautifully balances inherited mastery with transformative worldly expression. The 2nd house governs speech, family heritage, accumulated skills, and creative expression, and Ketu here reflects past-life mastery over these domains. Aries adds pioneering energy and initiative, giving his musical expression originality, courage, and dynamism. Ketu's placement endowed him with effortless mastery over classical music, an intrinsic spiritual connection to sound, and the ability to channel centuries of Indian musical tradition through the sitar. This placement also instilled detachment from material concerns,

Example Chart 2: Ravi Shankar (Sitar Virtuoso, Composer, Global Cultural Ambassador)

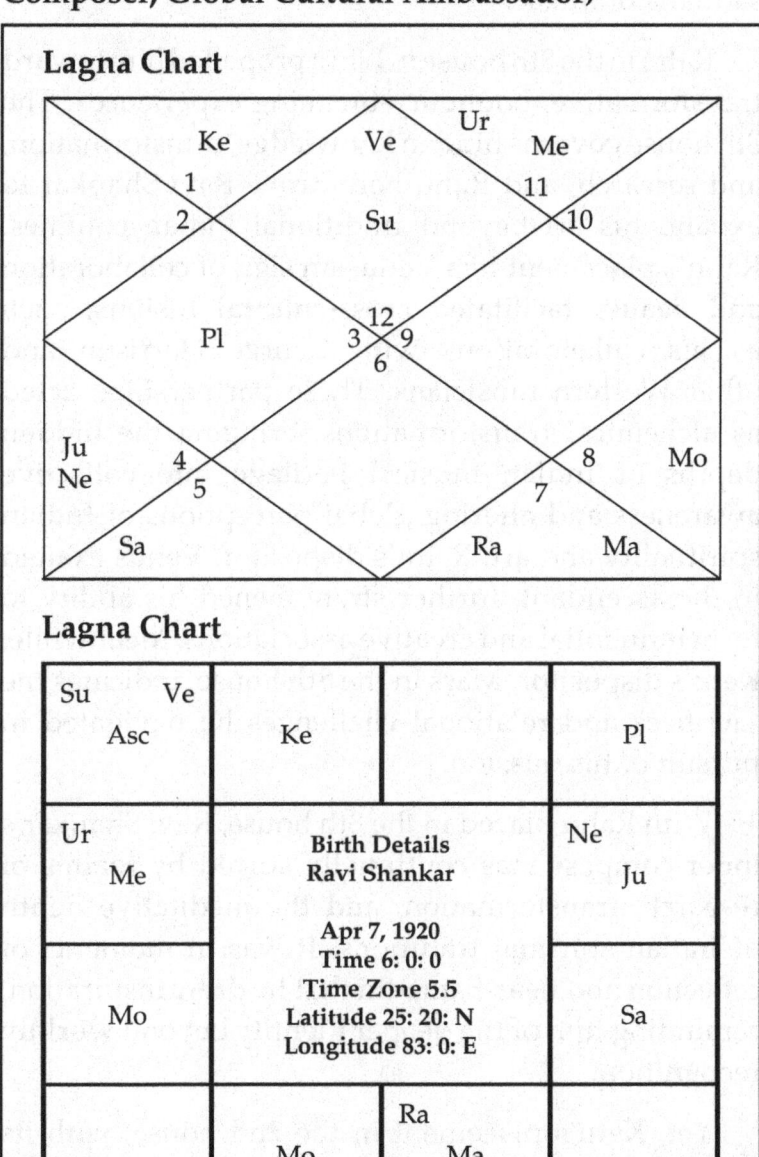

allowing him to focus on the purity of his art and the sadhana of music.

Rahu in the 8th house in Libra propelled him toward transformative, boundary-breaking experiences. The 8th house governs hidden knowledge, transformation, and research, and Rahu here drove Ravi Shankar to expand his art beyond traditional Indian confines. Rahu's placement in a Venusian sign of collaboration and beauty facilitated cross-cultural fusions, such as his collaborations with George Harrison and other Western musicians. These partnerships acted as alchemical transformations, bringing the hidden depths of Indian musical heritage into collective awareness and altering global perceptions of Indian spirituality and art. Rahu's dispositor, Venus exalted in the ascendant, further strengthened his ability to form influential and creative associations. Meanwhile, Ketu's dispositor, Mars in the 8th house, indicates the sacrifices and relational challenges he navigated in pursuit of his mission.

With Rahu placed in the 8th house, Ravi Shankar's inner compass was continually stirred by realms of research, transformation, and the meditative depth of Indian spiritual traditions. It was in moments of reflection and near-Samadhi that he drew inspiration, reminding him of the deeper identity beyond worldly recognition.

Yet, Ketu's placement in the 2nd house, with its dispositor Mars in the 8th, made family harmony fragile. He struggled to protect bonds, and relationships often fractured, as seen in his turbulent personal life, where his marriage to Annapurna Devi eventually broke down, and even ties with children bore strain. The karmic weight of this placement could be seen in repeated ruptures within his intimate circle.

This axis illustrates the integration of past-life mastery and worldly innovation. Ketu in the 2nd house endowed Ravi Shankar with innate genius, spiritual depth, and discipline, while Rahu in the 8th house prompted him to transform that mastery into a global impact and collaborative breakthroughs. The axis allowed him to become a bridge between cultures, elevating Indian classical music to international prominence.

Case Study 5
Rahu in the 3rd House, Ketu in the 9th House

Example Chart 1- S.D. Burman (Music Composer, Singer, Icon of Indian Cinema)

S. D. Burman's chart presents Rahu in the 3rd house in Leo and Ketu in the 9th house in Aquarius, forming the axis of self-effort and destiny. The 3rd house governs initiative, communication, and creativity, while Leo infuses this placement with a desire to leave a personal mark, achieve recognition, and assert individuality. Rahu here magnifies ambition, courage, and entrepreneurial spirit, driving the native to create something unique that stands out in the public eye. The dispositor of Rahu, the Sun, is placed in the 5th

Example Chart 1: S.D. Burman (Music Composer, Singer, Icon of Indian Cinema)

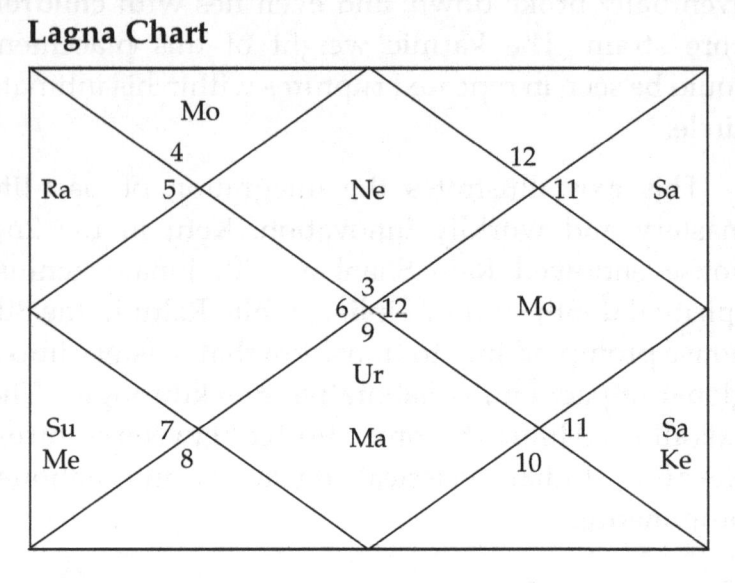

house in Libra, linking Rahu's ambitions to creativity, artistic talent, and entertainment. This alignment naturally drew Burman toward music, allowing him to craft a distinctive identity while leaving a lasting impression in the realm of Indian cinema. Burman fused classical training with folk traditions from Bengal, Assam, and Tripura, producing music that was rooted in heritage yet daringly modern. His distinctive, raw singing voice reflects Rahu's drive to make the unconventional compelling, enabling him to reach audiences far and wide. Rahu pushed him to step confidently into the world, leaving an enduring imprint through creativity, performance, and innovation.

Ketu in the 9th house in Aquarius, conjunct Saturn, imbues the native with a disciplined approach toward higher learning, spirituality, and dharmic pursuits. The 9th house governs wisdom, higher education, and connection with mentors or gurus. Ketu here suggests past-life mastery over philosophical or spiritual domains, while Saturn brings patience, structure, and a deep respect for tradition. This placement ensured that Burman's pursuit of creative innovation was always tempered with integrity, reverence for classical forms, and sustained effort, creating a harmonious balance between self-effort (Rahu in the 3rd) and the guidance of destiny (Ketu in the 9th).

The Rahu–Ketu axis in Burman's life reflects the integration of personal drive with dharmic discipline. Rahu in Leo gave him the courage and ambition to innovate in music, experimenting with fusion, folk, and contemporary sounds. Meanwhile, Ketu in the 9th anchored him in tradition, guiding him to honor the wisdom of his mentors and incorporate classical elements into his compositions. This balance allowed him to leave a unique mark on Indian music, blending originality with timeless artistry. His legacy, both in innovation and in respect for tradition, exemplifies how a well-maintained 3rd–9th house axis enables the harmonious realization of talent through both self-effort and dharmic alignment.

Example Chart 2 - B. R. Ambedkar (Social Reformer, Architect of the Indian Constitution)

B.R. Ambedkar's horoscope presents a balanced Rahu–Ketu axis that perfectly illustrates the integration of self-effort and destiny in the service of social transformation. Rahu in the 3rd house empowered him with extraordinary courage, revolutionary initiative, and the ability to confront entrenched societal norms. The 3rd house governs communication, personal effort, and daring action, and Rahu's placement here instilled in him an insatiable drive to create something new and enterprising for the people of India. His mastery over language, eloquence in speeches, and prolific writings exemplify Rahu's energy, allowing him to mobilise masses, challenge orthodox structures, and enact reforms that reshaped the nation.

Rahu's dispositor, Venus, in the 12th house in Aquarius and conjunct Jupiter, the ascendant lord, highlights his dedication to public service and the

Example Chart 2: B. R. Ambedkar (Reformer, Architect of the Indian Constitution)

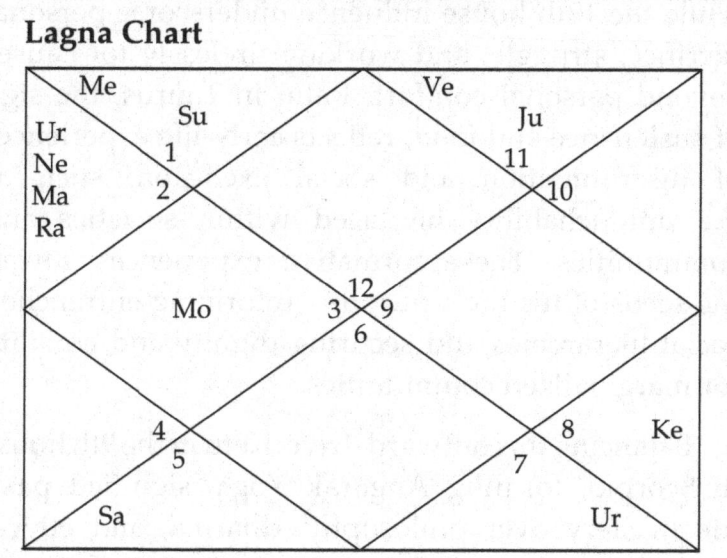

masses. Aquarius, a sign of reforms, shows that his efforts were aligned with collective upliftment, while the 12th house influence underscores personal sacrifice, struggle, and working tirelessly for causes beyond personal comfort. Rahu in Taurus, the sign of sustenance and food, reflects early-life experiences of discrimination and social exclusion, such as the untouchability he faced within societies and communities. These formative experiences sowed the seeds of his life's purpose: reforming entrenched social hierarchies and securing dignity and equality for marginalized communities.

Balancing this outward drive, Ketu in the 9th house in Scorpio, forming Angarak Yoga, signified past-life mastery over philosophy, dharma, and ethical discernment. It also reflected the need to transform old structures, question outdated traditions, and redefine societal norms. The 9th house placement, combined with Mars as Ketu's dispositor, reinforced the courage and strategic vision to challenge entrenched systems. With the 9th lord in the 3rd house, Ambedkar's philosophical inquiry became inseparable from his active social engagement, allowing him to merge inner wisdom with practical reformist action.

Together, this Rahu–Ketu axis illustrates the seamless integration of personal mastery and worldly purpose. Rahu in the 3rd catalyzed bold communication, social action, and revolutionary ideas, while Ketu in the 9th provided philosophical depth, detachment from convention, and ethical clarity. Ambedkar's life exemplified selfless effort for the greater good, combining strategic intellect, moral courage, and transformative vision. His journey from personal marginalization to becoming the principal architect of India's legal and social reforms demonstrates how past-life mastery (Ketu) and present-life ambition (Rahu) can harmoniously coalesce to fulfil a soul's mission on both personal and collective levels.

Case Study 6
Ketu in the 3rd House, Rahu in the 9th House

Example Chart 1 - Paramhansa Yogananda (Spiritual Teacher, Author of Autobiography of a Yogi)

Paramahamsa Yogananda had Ketu in the 3rd house in Libra, Rahu in the 9th house in Aries. Dispositor of Ketu, Venus, is placed in the 4th house in Scorpio; dispositor of Rahu, Mars, is placed in the 8th house. This axis reflects the integration of past-life mastery in communication, courage, and inner discipline with a present-life mission of spiritual expansion and dissemination.

Ketu in the 3rd house endowed Yogananda with innate proficiency in communication, fearlessness, and discernment, gifts refined across past lifetimes. The well-placed dispositor Venus in Scorpio, positioned in a Kendra, amplified his mastery over sadhana, occult knowledge, meditation, and spiritual discipline. From an early age, he exhibited vivid visions, extraordinary perception, and an inner focus on liberation

Example Chart 1: Paramhansa Yogananda (Spiritual Teacher, Author of Autobiography of a Yogi)

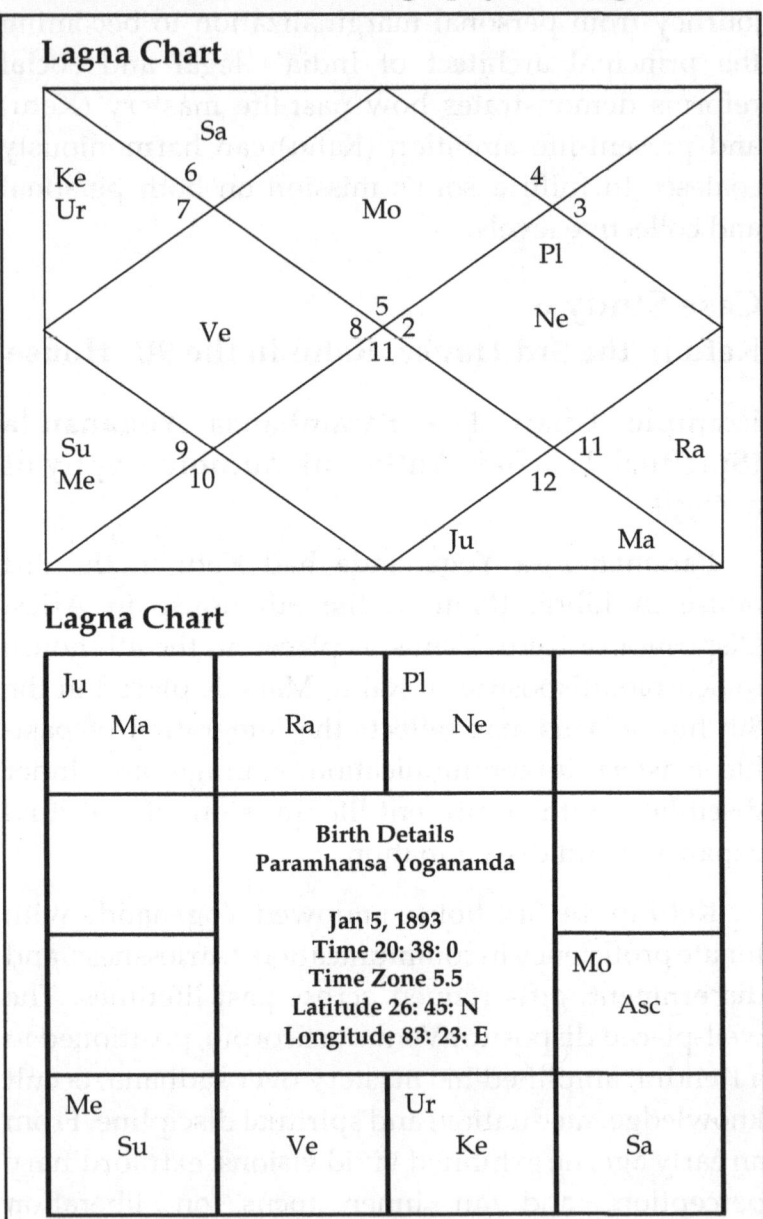

rather than worldly success. His detachment from conventional sibling and familial dynamics allowed him to channel his energies entirely toward higher realms, manifesting in an effortless ability to convey profound spiritual truths with clarity, humility, and grace. This Ketu-driven mastery made him uniquely capable of teaching complex concepts in ways that were accessible, authentic, and transformative.

Rahu in the 9th house propelled him outward, instilling an insatiable drive to cross cultural and geographical boundaries in pursuit of dharma. The 9th house governs higher learning, philosophy, teachers, and the broader currents of destiny. Its dispositor, Mars, placed in the sign of Pisces in the 8th house, reinforced the need for long-distance efforts, international engagement, and service beyond personal or familial confines. Rahu's influence manifested in his journey to the United States in 1920, where he founded the Self-Realization Fellowship, introducing yoga, meditation, and India's spiritual heritage to a global audience. His seminal work, Autobiography of a Yogi, became a spiritual classic, inspiring countless seekers, including figures like George Harrison and Steve Jobs.

The interplay of Ketu and Rahu in Yogananda's chart reflects a harmonious alignment of inner mastery and outward purpose. Ketu in the 3rd house provided the depth, detachment, and communicative skill necessary to articulate spiritual truths, while Rahu in the 9th guided him to expand these gifts internationally, fostering cross-cultural spiritual exchange. The alignment of both dispositors with Scorpion (longevity) energies further ensured that his work would endure, leaving a lasting legacy. Institutions founded in his name, the continued influence of his teachings, and the global resonance of his philosophy testify to the longevity of his mission, which is a direct expression of Rahu's expansive drive supported by Ketu's mastery.

Even his final act of entering mahasamadhi after delivering a speech emphasizing spiritual unity between India and the West epitomizes this axis: past-life mastery of communication (3rd house Ketu) employed in the service of universal spiritual vision (9th house Rahu). Yogananda's life demonstrates how the soul integrates inherited skills with present-life purpose, channeling detachment and discipline into a transformative, globally impactful mission.

Example Chart 2 - Suraiya (Actress and Singer)

Suraiya's chart exemplifies the Rahu–Ketu axis of communication, courage, and destiny. Ketu in the 3rd house endowed her with innate mastery over speech, artistic expression, and performance. This placement reflects past-life refinement, allowing her to command the stage and screen with effortless poise and emotive depth. Her voice, acting, and subtle gestures conveyed emotions with a natural elegance that felt both timeless and instinctive. The dispositor of Ketu, Venus, placed in the 9th house, further reinforced her connection to higher arts and creative pursuits, imbuing her talents with grace, aesthetic sensibility, and a subtle spiritual depth.

Example Chart 2: Suraiya (Actress and Singer)

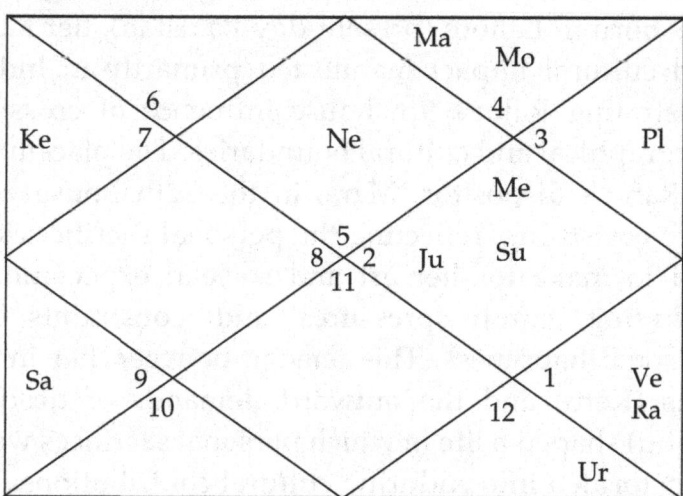

Rahu in the 9th house drove her toward broader horizons, compelling her to achieve recognition beyond her immediate surroundings. Although she was born in Lahore (present-day Pakistan), her fame and cultural impact manifested primarily in India, illustrating Rahu's 9th house influence of crossing geographical and cultural boundaries. The placement of Rahu's dispositor, Mars, in the 12th house was not very strong, reflecting the personal sacrifices she had to make for her art and societal expectations, including family pressures and constraints on personal happiness. This tension between her inner gifts (Ketu) and the outward demands of destiny (Rahu) shaped a life in which personal sacrifices were transformed into enduring cultural contributions.

Suraiya's Rahu in the 9th house reflects a karmic call to uphold righteousness and parental authority, even at the cost of her own joy. Despite her deep love for Dev Anand, she bowed to her grandmother's stern command and sacrificed personal happiness. The path of dharma, as defined by family and tradition, outweighed her own heart's longing, a choice that left her unmarried for life, but consistent with the 9th house theme of surrendering the self to uphold inherited values.

The interplay of Ketu and Rahu in Suraiya's life illustrates the journey from mastery of inner gifts to realization of public purpose. Ketu in the 3rd supplied natural courage, artistry, and detachment, allowing her to focus entirely on her craft, while Rahu in the 9th propelled her toward recognition, broader impact, and cultural legacy. The dispositor placements ensured that her creativity aligned with spiritual and higher principles, giving her performances a timeless resonance. Yet, in keeping with Rahu's 9th house demand, she sacrificed her personal happiness to honor familial righteousness, embodying the archetypal conflict between love and duty.

Case Study 7
Rahu in the 4th House, Ketu in the 10th House

Example Chart 1 - M. S. Subbulakshmi (Indian Carnatic Singer)

In M. S. Subbulakshmi's chart, Rahu is placed in the 4th house in Capricorn with its dispositor Saturn in the 10th house, while Ketu is positioned in the 10th house in Cancer with its dispositor Moon in the 7th house which displays a highly powerful and harmonious Rahu–Ketu axis, with both dispositors strongly placed in houses directly connected to karma, public recognition, and relationships with society. This is a classical configuration for someone who becomes a monumental figure, leaving behind a lasting cultural and spiritual legacy.

Ketu's placement in the 10th house indicates past-life mastery of career, social standing, and worldly achievements. In this lifetime, it manifested as a natural detachment from fame and public recognition. Subbulakshmi did not seek the limelight or work with ambition; rather, she approached her art as a form of devotion. Her performances were not displays

Example Chart 1: M. S. Subbulakshmi (Indian Carnatic Singer)

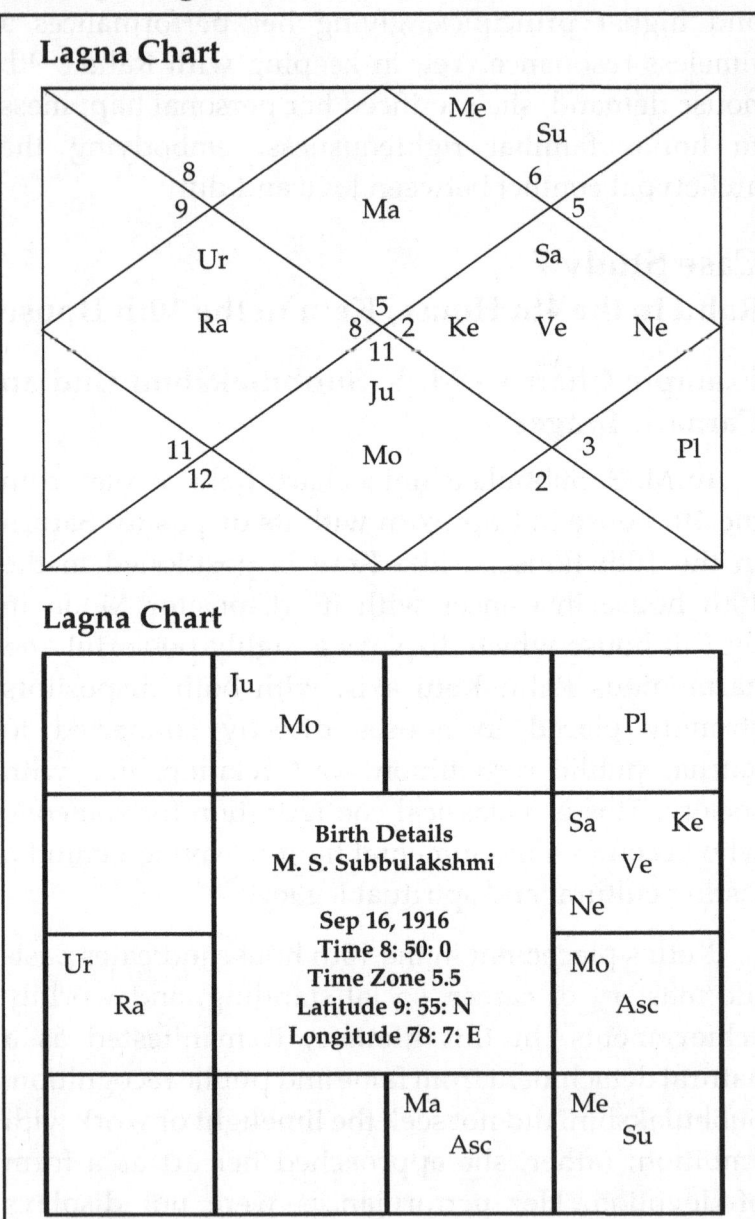

of personal glory but sacred offerings, embodying purity and surrender. This timelessness and depth in her singing reflected Ketu's influence, allowing her to move beyond the ego-driven dimensions of a career and into the realm of spiritual service.

What makes this combination especially powerful is the position of Ketu's dispositor, the Moon, in the 7th house. The 7th house is 10th from the 10th, representing the highest octave of karma and public recognition. This placement amplified her ability to connect with audiences and communities through her work, showing that her devotion and mastery were meant to reach the collective in profound ways. It also represents harmony and balance, which she maintained beautifully, navigating career, relationships, and cultural responsibilities with grace.

Rahu in the 4th house propelled her toward serving her homeland and connecting deeply with her roots. The 4th house represents motherland, emotional foundations, and cultural heritage. Its connection with Rahu shows that her destiny was tied to bringing glory to her country through her music. The fact that the dispositor of Rahu, Saturn, is strongly placed in the 10th house of karma and achievements indicates a life dedicated to creating an enduring mark on the nation. This is why she was honoured with Bharat Ratna, India's highest civilian award. The blending of the 4th house (motherland) and 10th house (recognition and awards) through Rahu and its dispositor directly reflects her journey, i.e., her devotion to her homeland was acknowledged at the highest level.

Ketu in the 10th gave her past-life mastery and detachment, allowing her to sing with purity and grace without personal ambition. Rahu in the 4th, supported by a strong dispositor, pushed her to channel this devotion outward, honouring her homeland and elevating its cultural heritage. She turned the stage into a temple, her voice into a prayer, and her life into a service to art and nation. This placement also shows how she seamlessly integrated the private emotional world of the 4th house with the public professional stage of the 10th house. Her music, though deeply personal and devotional, resonated with millions, creating a bridge between the sacred inner space of bhakti and the collective consciousness of society, transcending the boundaries of a normal career, becoming a part of India's spiritual and cultural identity.

Example Chart 2 - Serena Williams (Tennis Champion, Global Icon)

Serena Williams' chart beautifully illustrates the interplay between detachment from worldly recognition and the pursuit of deep emotional roots. Rahu in the 4th house in Cancer shows a powerful drive to establish an inner sanctuary and a profound connection to her family and homeland, while Ketu is positioned in the 10th house in Capricorn. The dispositor of Rahu, the Moon, is placed in the 5th house in Leo, a house associated with creativity,

Example Chart 2: Serena Williams (Tennis Champion, Global Icon)

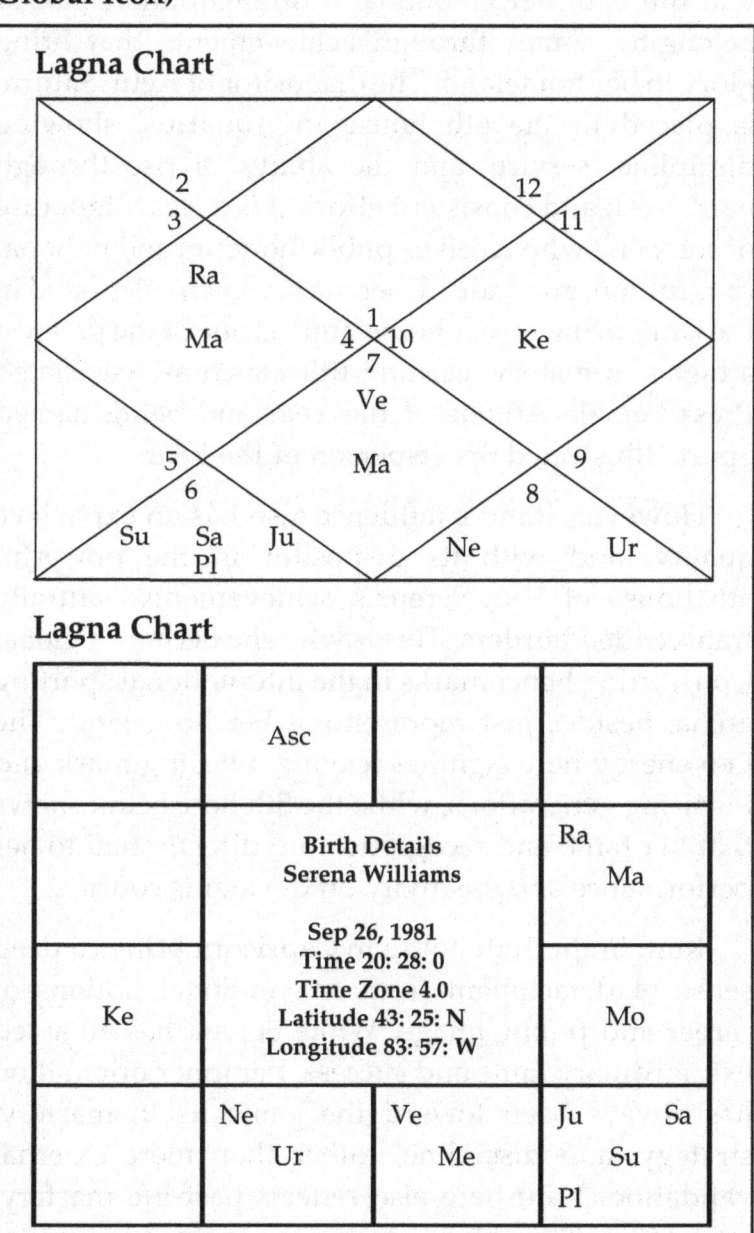

recognition, and awards. This placement indicates that much of her emotional fulfillment and sense of belonging comes through achievements that bring glory to her homeland. The dispositor of Ketu, Saturn, is placed in the 6th house in Aquarius, showing discipline, service, and the ability to rise through hard work and consistent effort. It is a clear signature of someone who receives public honours and national recognition, and indeed, Serena has been celebrated in the United States (her homeland) as one of the greatest athletes in history, earning titles such as Associated Press Female Athlete of the Year and being named Sports Illustrated Sportsperson of the Year.

However, Rahu's influence also has an expansive quality, and with its dispositor in the powerful 5th house of Leo, Serena's achievements naturally transcended borders. This is why she became a global icon, setting benchmarks in the international sporting arena, besides just representing her homeland. The Leo energy here signifies leaving a lasting mark and inspiring generations, while the 5th house link shows that her fame and recognition are directly tied to her performance and creativity on the tennis court.

Ketu in the 10th house in Capricorn brings a deep sense of detachment from conventional notions of career and public image. While Serena has amassed extraordinary fame and success, her inner orientation has always been toward the game itself, mastery, strategy, and discipline, rather than mere external validation. Ketu here also reflects past-life mastery, explaining her natural instincts, composure under pressure, and ability to perform at peak levels consistently.

The dispositor of Ketu, Saturn, is placed in the 6th house, a house of competition, struggle, and opponents. Though 6th house placements are generally considered challenging, in Serena's case, this became her greatest strength because she chose a career in sports, which is an inherently competitive field. Instead of being overwhelmed by obstacles or rivals, she channelled the 6th house energy into excellence, using competition as a vehicle for growth and dominance. This placement also highlights her resilience in facing injuries, setbacks, and even life-threatening health challenges, such as complications during childbirth, and returning stronger each time.

The synergy between these placements is remarkable. Rahu's dispositor in the 5th house of awards and fame ensured that Serena would bring honour to her homeland and be celebrated nationally and internationally. Ketu's detachment in the 10th, supported by Saturn in the 6th, allowed her to focus on the game rather than the noise surrounding it, turning obstacles into stepping stones.

Her journey reflects this axis perfectly: a woman who rose to the pinnacle of tennis, took breaks to focus on family and motherhood (Rahu in the 4th), and then returned to reclaim her place at the top, demonstrating unparalleled resilience and emotional strength.

Case Study 8
Ketu in the 4th House, Rahu in the 10th House

Example Chart 1 - Mahatma Gandhi (Freedom Leader, Spiritual Reformer)

Mahatma Gandhi's chart has Ketu in the 4th house in Capricorn, showing detachment from homeland, family comforts, and the conventional idea of "home," while Rahu is placed in the 10th house in Cancer. The dispositor of Rahu, the Moon, is joined with Rahu in the 10th house, intensifying his public life and amplifying his role as a national figure. The dispositor of Ketu, Saturn, is placed in the 2nd house, reflecting austerity, simplicity in speech and sustenance, and the karmic weight of values that shaped his mission. In Gandhi's life, this manifested as a disconnection from personal comforts and domestic bonds. Born into a respected Gujarati family, he had access to stability and privilege, yet his soul was restless. This restlessness drove him beyond familiar surroundings, first to England for studies, then to South Africa, and later across India.

For individuals with Ketu in the 4th, true purpose is only discovered by stepping away from the known and venturing into foreign lands. Gandhi's pivotal moment came in South Africa, where he encountered racial discrimination firsthand. This experience ignited the emotional trigger that set his life's mission into motion. Once Rahu's path was activated through this event, Gandhi returned to India to fight untouchability and lead the freedom struggle,

Example Chart 1: Mahatma Gandhi (Freedom Leader, Spiritual Reformer)

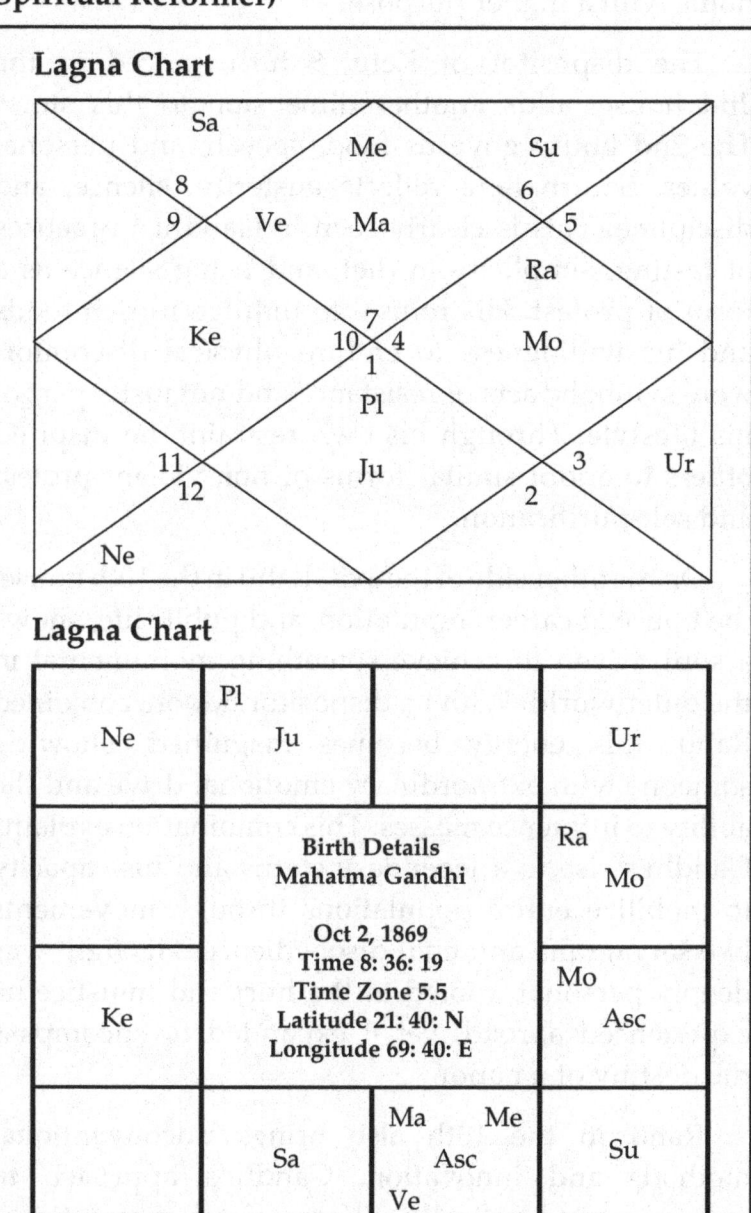

showing how the journey outward helped him return home with a higher purpose.

The dispositor of Ketu, Saturn, placed in the 2nd house, adds another dimension to this story. The 2nd house governs food, speech, and personal values. Saturn here reflects austerity, silence, and discipline. This is clearly seen in Gandhi's practices of fasting, simplicity in diet, and using silence as a form of protest. His refusal to indulge in rich foods and his willingness to endure physical discomfort were symbolic acts of resistance and not just a part of his lifestyle. Through his own restraint, he inspired others to adopt similar forms of non-violent protest and self-purification.

On the other side of the axis, Rahu in the 10th house, the house of career, reputation, and public life, shows a soul driven to achieve something monumental in the outer world. With its dispositor, Moon, conjoined Rahu, this energy becomes magnified, showing someone with extraordinary emotional drive and the ability to influence masses. This combination explains Gandhi's rise to a legendary status and his capacity to mobilize entire populations through movements like satyagraha and civil disobedience. His fight was deeply personal, rooted in the hurt and injustice he experienced abroad, yet it expanded to encompass the destiny of a nation.

Rahu in the 10th also brings unconventional methods and innovation. Gandhi's approach to resistance was radically different from conventional politics as he used moral and spiritual principles as tools for collective liberation. This is Rahu's boundary-breaking influence working through the highest house of action.

When we view this axis together, it becomes clear: Ketu in the 4th gave Gandhi mastery over detachment, freeing him from the distractions of personal life and comforts, while Rahu in the 10th directed that mastery into massive public impact. His repeated acts of renunciation, from leaving his homeland to adopting a minimalist lifestyle, built the moral foundation necessary for him to lead millions.

Example Chart 2 - Rabindranath Tagore (Poet, Visionary Educator)

In Rabindranath Tagore's chart, Ketu is in the 4th house in Gemini and Rahu is in the 10th house in Sagittarius, illustrating the tension between detachment from domestic anchors and the call toward global recognition. The dispositor of Rahu, Jupiter, is exalted in the 5th house, blessing him with creative brilliance, philosophical depth, and the power to inspire through education and literature. The dispositor of Ketu, Mercury, is placed in the 2nd house along with the exalted Sun, endowing him with eloquence, a radiant voice, and the ability to express cultural and spiritual truths with authority. Ketu in the 4th denotes a profound detachment from conventional comforts of home, familial security, and cultural norms. Although born into the illustrious Tagore family, surrounded by wealth, tradition,

Example Chart 2: Rabindranath Tagore (Poet, Visionary Educator)

Lagna Chart

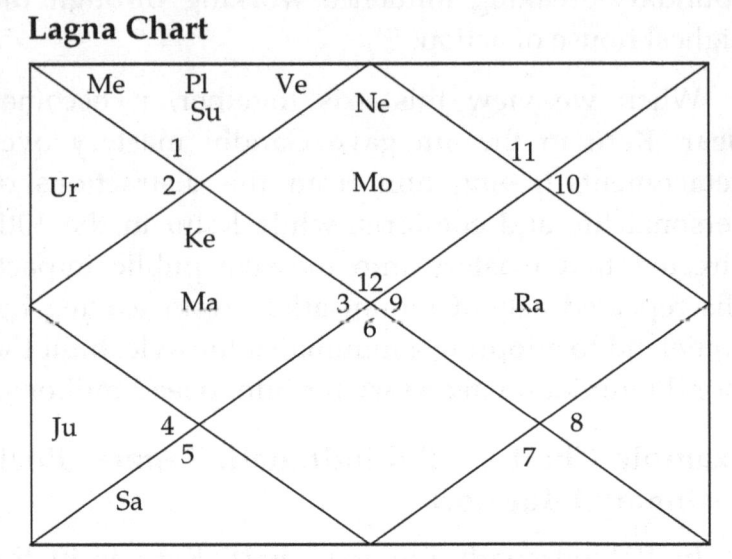

Lagna Chart

Mo Ne Asc	Me Ve Su Pl	Ur	Ke Ma
	\multicolumn{2}{c}{}	Ju
	Birth Details Rabindranath Tagore May 7, 1861 Time 2: 27: 41 Time Zone 5.5 Latitude 22: 30: N Longitude 88: 25: E	Sa
Ra			

and artistic heritage, Ketu instilled a restlessness that prevented him from feeling fully anchored in these privileges. This placement, in a mercurial sign, carried innate literary and communicative skills, though initial confidence was low; early praise and recognition were necessary for him to fully realize his potential. The Gemini influence emphasized travel and intellectual exploration, which became crucial for aligning with his soul's purpose. Tagore's formative travels to England at the age of 17, where he studied and immersed himself in Western literature and culture, illustrate this trajectory. These experiences expanded his horizons, introduced him to global ideas, and helped him shape a literary and philosophical vision that transcended his local environment.

Opposite Ketu, Rahu in the 10th house in Sagittarius magnified his public aspirations. Its exalted dispositor, Jupiter in the 5th house, endowed him with exceptional creativity. Rahu here propelled Tagore to channel his inner detachment and literary mastery into tangible societal contributions: founding Shantiniketan, revolutionizing Indian education, composing timeless works of poetry, music, and literature, and promoting cultural and philosophical discourse worldwide. His international travels, including lectures in Europe, the United States, and Japan, reflect Rahu's boundary-crossing energy, expanding his influence far beyond India. The 10th house Rahu also underscores his pursuit of recognition in spheres where actions impact society, explaining accolades like the Nobel Prize in Literature in 1913 and enduring international renown.

The Ketu–Rahu axis in Tagore's chart exemplifies the dynamic interplay between inner mastery and outer achievement. Ketu in the 4th provided emotional depth, detachment from familial anchors, and a foundation of intellectual and spiritual insight carried from past lives while Rahu in the 10th translated these gifts into transformative societal impact. His early travels, literary experiments, and cross-cultural engagements were all expressions of this axis, demonstrating how restlessness and detachment from the familiar catalyzed outward expansion and public legacy.

Case Study 9
Rahu in the 5th House, Ketu in the 11th House

Example Chart 1 - Rukmini Devi Arundale (theosophist, dancer and choreographer)

In Rukmini Devi Arundale's chart, Rahu is in the 5th house in Virgo and Ketu is in the 11th house in Pisces, which reflects a karmic pull toward creative innovation and cultural transformation. The dispositor of Rahu, Mercury, is placed in the 9th house, linking her artistic quest with higher learning, philosophy, and the transmission of tradition across borders. The dispositor of Ketu, Jupiter, sits with Ketu itself in the 11th house, emphasizing detachment from conventional social circles and directing her energy instead toward spiritual associations and visionary networks. Rahu in the 5th infused her with an insatiable drive for learning, experimentation, and creative expansion. This placement demanded

Example Chart 2: Rabindranath Tagore (Poet, Visionary Educator)

Lagna Chart

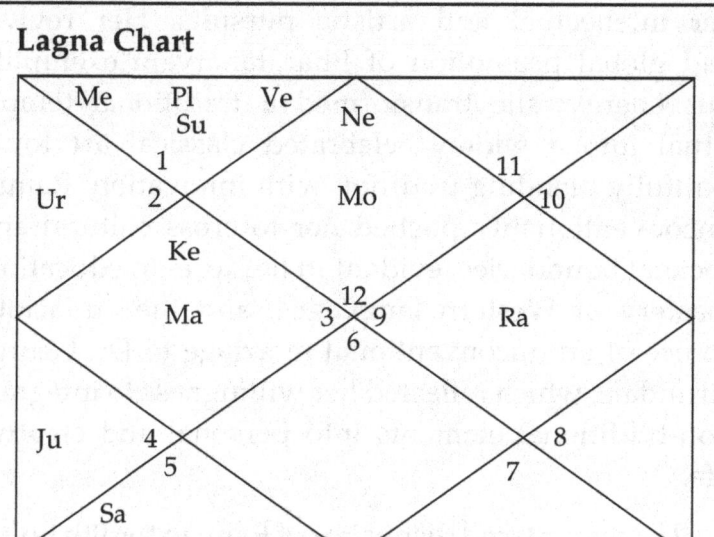

Lagna Chart

Mo Ne Asc	Me Ve Su Pl		Ke Ma
		Ur	
	Birth Details Rabindranath Tagore		Ju
	May 7, 1861 Time 2: 27: 41 Time Zone 5.5 Latitude 22: 30: N Longitude 88: 25: E		Sa
Ra			

continuous growth, ensuring that she never rested on past achievements but constantly evolved in her intellectual and artistic pursuits. Her revival and global promotion of Bharatanatyam exemplify this energy: she transformed a traditional temple ritual into a widely celebrated classical art form, skillfully blending tradition with innovation. Rahu's unconventionality pushed her to cross cultural and societal boundaries, evident in her foreign education, mastery of Western languages, and the audacious choice of an unconventional marriage to Dr. George Arundale, which reflected her willingness to integrate non-traditional elements into personal and creative life.

The well-placed dispositor of Rahu in the 9th house amplified her ability to harmonize global learning with cultural roots, allowing her to institutionalize her vision. The founding of Kalakshetra in 1936 stands as a tangible manifestation of this alignment: an educational and artistic institution that preserved Indian classical arts while introducing innovative pedagogical methods. Rahu here drove her to leave a lasting, transformative impact on dance, music, and cultural education, ensuring that her creative ambitions were realized on both national and international scales.

Ketu in the 11th house endowed Rukmini Devi with natural detachment from material success, social accolades, and superficial networking. This placement, coupled with its Jupiterian sign, reflects past-life mastery over collective endeavors, allowing her to navigate societal structures with clarity, purpose, and emotional equanimity. Her selective relationships and purposeful engagement with cultural and Theosophical circles enabled her to maintain focus on her mission, deriving fulfillment from spiritual and societal contribution rather than personal gain.

The interplay of Rahu in the 5th and Ketu in the 11th created a powerful synergy, allowing Rukmini Devi to innovate, educate, and lead without being swayed by conventional expectations or the pursuit of recognition.

Example Chart 2 - Maharishi Mahesh Yogi (Spiritual Teacher, Founder of Transcendental Meditation)

In Maharishi Mahesh Yogi's chart, Rahu is in the 5th house in Aries and Ketu is in the 11th house in Libra, reflecting a karmic focus on self-expression, innovation, and transcending traditional boundaries. The dispositor of Rahu, Mars, is placed in the 6th house, highlighting disciplined effort, service, and the transformative application of knowledge in daily life. The dispositor of Ketu, Venus, is situated in the 9th house, emphasizing detachment from ordinary social networks and a deep orientation toward spiritual wisdom and higher learning. Rahu in the 5th energized him with an insatiable drive to innovate, teach, and expand the boundaries of knowledge. This placement governs self-expression, teaching, and the ability to inspire through novel methods,

Example Chart 2: Maharishi Mahesh Yogi (Spiritual Teacher, Founder of Transcendental Meditation)

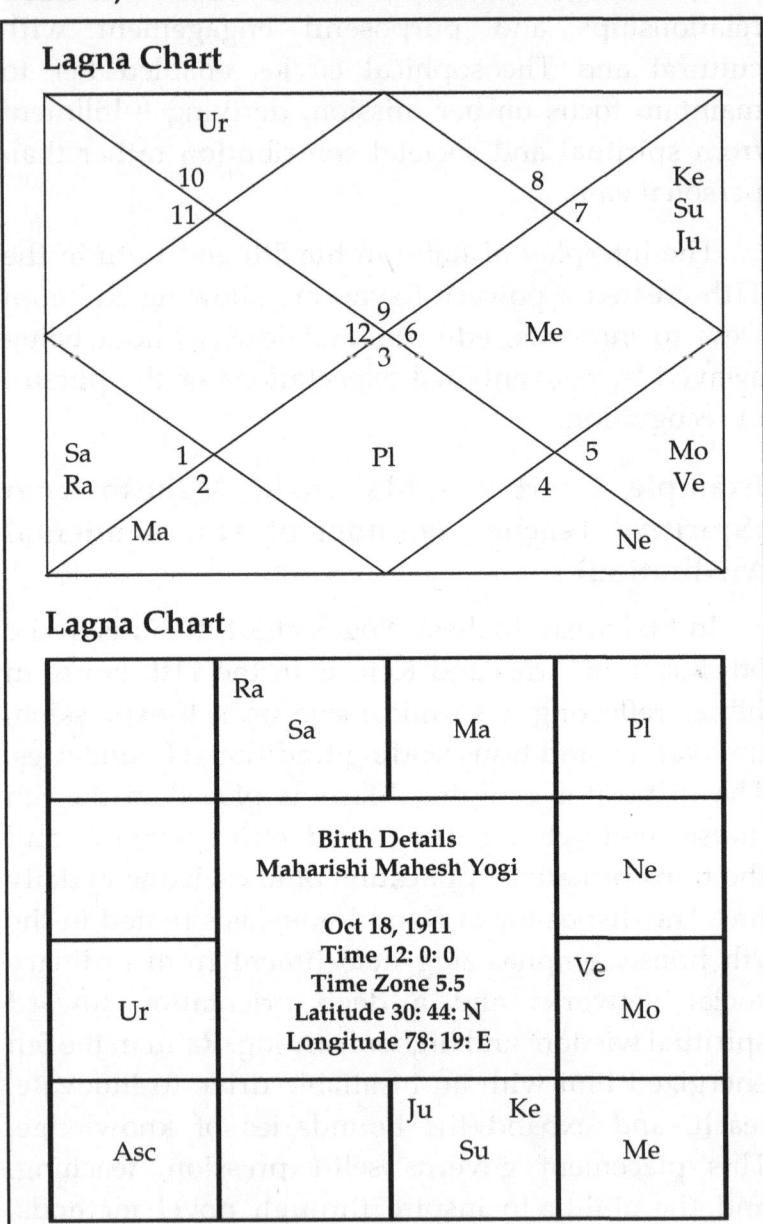

and Rahu here manifested as his remarkable ability to make ancient Vedic wisdom accessible to modern audiences. The creation of Transcendental Meditation exemplifies this energy: he distilled complex spiritual practices into a simple, practical technique that resonated across cultures, from India to the West.

Rahu's influence also brought courage to step beyond conventional frameworks. Maharishi's methods were unorthodox, such as merging ritual simplicity with mass appeal, using modern media to propagate spiritual knowledge, and teaching meditation to both monks and global leaders. Alongside, the debilitated 3rd lord Saturn is conjunct Rahu, which amplified his diligence, discipline, and physical effort, channeling them into spiritual practice and teaching.

Ketu in the 11th house provided a natural detachment from societal approval, collective expectations, and material rewards, but it came regardless, as the soul had mastered this all in past lives. While Rahu drew him into public prominence, Ketu allowed him to maintain spiritual focus and selective engagement. His past-life mastery in social strategy and collective endeavors enabled him to form purposeful communities and institutions, like the global TM movement, without being entangled in conventional social or organizational pressures. The dispositor of Ketu in the 9th house reinforced this karmic inheritance, connecting him to higher spiritual wisdom and global vision, while the 9th Lord (Sun) conjoined Ketu in debilitation emphasizes mastery carried from previous lifetimes, fully realized in this life.

Rahu in the 5th drove creativity, audacity, and global impact, while Ketu in the 11th ensured discernment, detachment, and spiritual integrity. Maharishi Mahesh Yogi's life reflects how a soul equipped with past-life mastery (Ketu) can harness present-life potential (Rahu) to create enduring transformative influence, bridging East and West and preserving the purity of spiritual teaching while achieving unprecedented global reach.

Case Study 10
Ketu in the 5th House, Rahu in the 11th House

Example Chart 1 - Dev Anand (actor, writer, director and producer)

In Dev Anand's chart, Ketu is in the 5th house in Aquarius, and Rahu is in the 11th house in Leo. The dispositors of both Ketu and Rahu are placed in the 12th house. We must note that Mercury (9th house lord) and Venus (Ascendant lord) are also in the 12th house, in turn emphasizing a deep, behind-the-scenes cultivation of talent, spiritual sensitivity, and refinement of artistic skills.

Ketu in the 5th house endowed Dev Anand with an innate mastery over self-expression, artistry, and creativity, suggesting talents and skills carried forward from past lives. The 5th house governs creative abilities, and Ketu's presence here reflects a natural, effortless aptitude in acting, writing,

Example Chart 1: Dev Anand (Actor, Writer, Director and Producer)

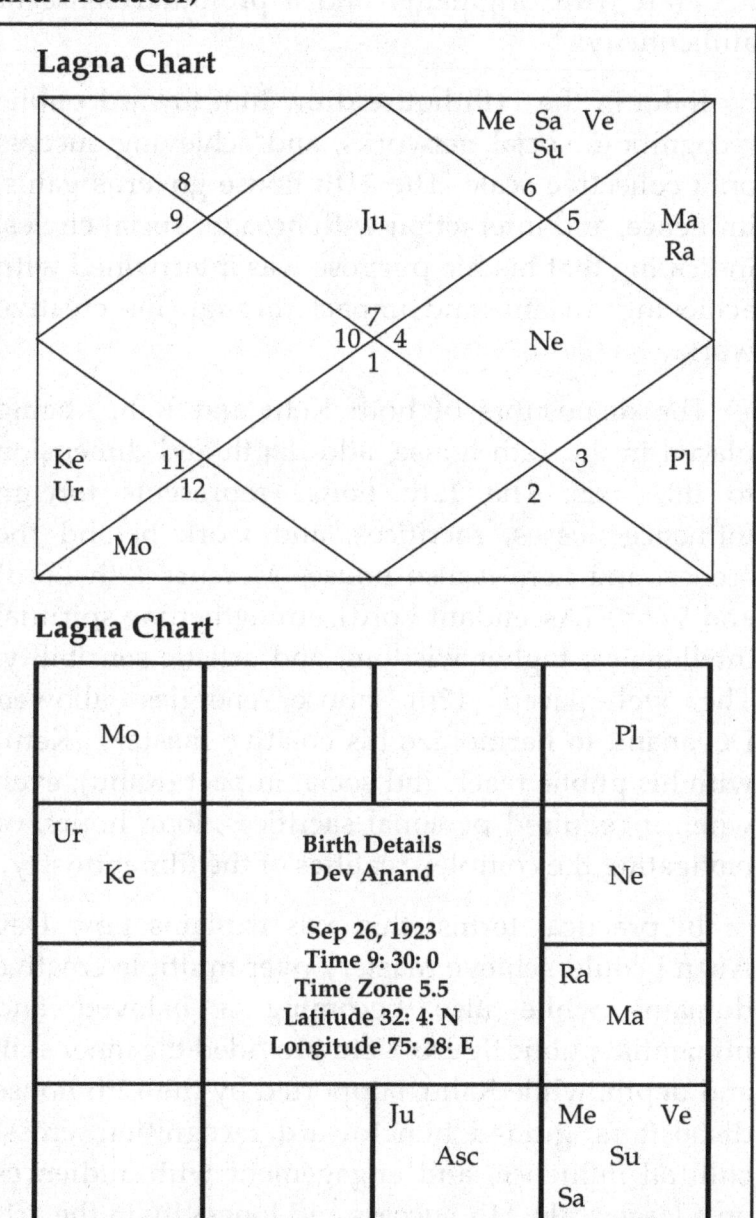

directing, and producing, allowing him to approach his craft with originality and a profound sense of authenticity.

Rahu in the 11th house drew him toward public recognition, social networks, and achieving success on a collective scale. The 11th house governs gains, influence, and interaction with broader social circles, indicating that his life purpose was intertwined with achieving acclaim and impact through his creative work.

The dispositors of both Ketu and Rahu, being placed in the 12th house, add depth and dimension to this axis. The 12th house represents foreign influence, losses, sacrifices, and work behind the scenes, and here it also houses Mercury (9th Lord) and Venus (Ascendant Lord), strengthening spiritual intelligence, higher wisdom, and artistic sensibility. The well-placed 12th house energies allowed Devanand to harmonize his creative mastery (Ketu) with his public reach and social impact (Rahu), even when it required personal sacrifices, long hours, or navigating the complex realities of the film industry.

In practical terms, this axis explains how Dev Anand could achieve mastery over multiple creative domains while also becoming a beloved and influential public figure. Ketu provided the inner skill and depth, while Rahu, supported by the 12th house dispositors, guided him toward recognition, cross-cultural influence, and engagement with audiences on a large scale. His success and longevity in the arts can be attributed to the seamless functioning of this

Rahu–Ketu axis, supported by a strong 12th house that transformed discipline, study, and sacrifice into creative and social achievements.

Example Chart 2 - Acharya Rajneesh (Osho) - Spiritual Teacher, Mystic

In Osho's chart, Ketu is in the 5th house in Virgo and Rahu is in the 11th house in Pisces, reflecting a karmic axis of creative mastery and societal influence. Ketu in the 5th house granted Osho an innate mastery over self-expression, intellect, and the art of teaching, reflecting a karmic inheritance of creative and spiritual abilities carried from past lives. Besides creativity, the 5th house signifies the ability to communicate profound ideas with clarity, which aligns with his skill in delivering discourses, writing books, and presenting complex spiritual philosophies in a transformative way.

Rahu in the 11th house propelled him toward societal influence, collective engagement, and forming communities. The 11th house governs large networks, followers, and social impact, indicating that Osho's life purpose was to create movements, connect with large audiences, and transform social consciousness through his teachings.

Rahu's dispositor, Jupiter, exalted in the 3rd house of communication, magnified his ability to teach, articulate, and expand ideas widely. This placement gave him philosophical depth, rhetorical skill, and strategic vision to reach followers across continents. Ketu's dispositor, Mercury in the 8th house along

Example Chart 2: Acharya Rajneesh (Osho) – Spiritual Teacher, Mystic

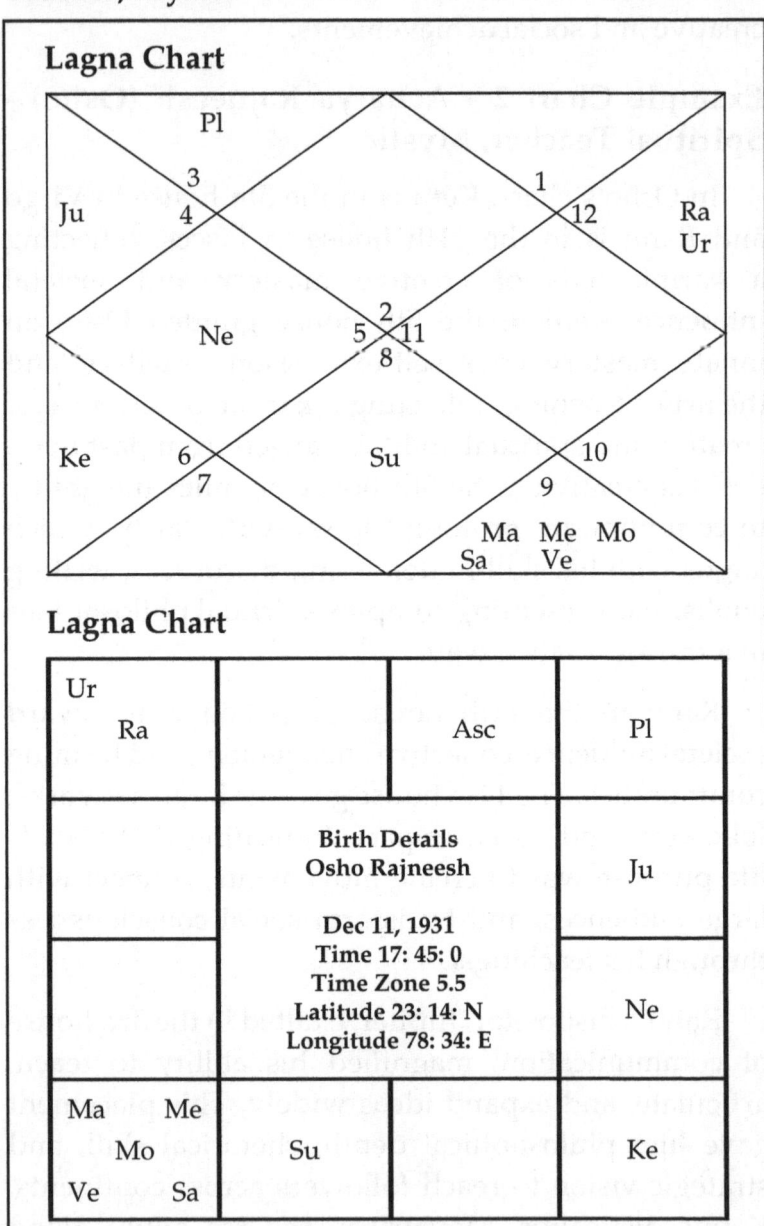

with the 9th Lord (He has a stellium in 8th house; multiple planets) provided an intense capacity for insight, investigation, and spiritual mastery, allowing him to approach occult, mystical, and transformative knowledge with precision and depth.

The interplay of Ketu and Rahu here explains the combination of inner detachment and outer social influence. Ketu in the 5th provided detachment from personal ego and mastery over creative-spiritual faculties, while Rahu in the 11th, amplified by its exalted dispositor - Jupiter, propelled him into global prominence, forming institutions and communities aligned with his vision. The axis also indicates the unconventionality, boundary-breaking, and transformative nature of his teachings: the 8th house influence (through Ketu's dispositor) and the 3rd house Jupiter enabled him to channel profound insights into widespread educational and spiritual outreach.

Case Study 11
Rahu in the 6th House, Ketu in the 12th House

Example Chart 1 - Munshi Premchand (Novelist, Social Reformer)

In Munshi Premchand's chart, Rahu is in the 6th house in Sagittarius and Ketu is in the 12th house in Gemini, reflecting a karmic axis of service, discipline, and detachment from worldly attachments. Rahu's dispositor, Jupiter in its own sign in the 9th house, provided philosophical depth, higher vision, and

Example Chart 1: Munshi Premchand (Novelist, Social Reformer)

Lagna Chart

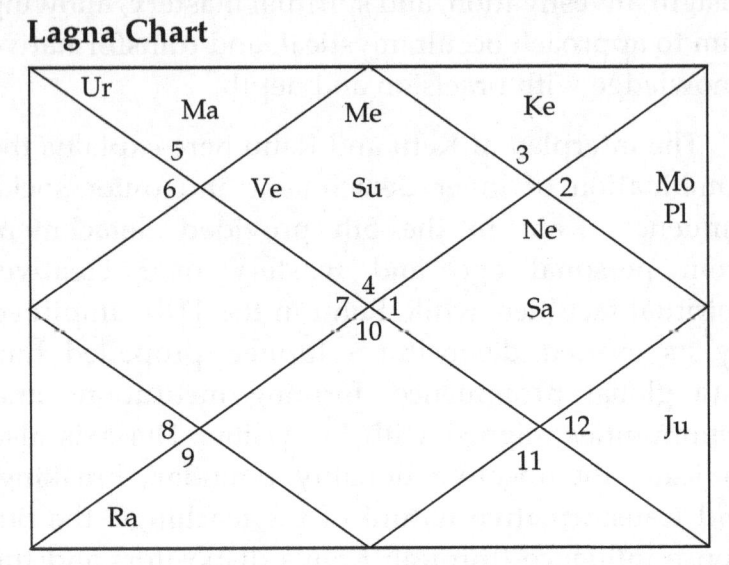

Lagna Chart

	Ne	Pl	
Ju	Sa	Mo	Ke
			Su Me
	Birth Details		Asc
	Munshi Premchand		Ve
	Feb 29, 1904		
	Time 12: 20: 32		Ur
	Time Zone 5.5		Ma
	Latitude 9: 58: N		
	Longitude 78: 10: E		
Ra			

a strong ethical framework, which further allowed Premchand to approach the societal challenges (6th house) with wisdom, compassion, and a purposeful message, blending literary skill with moral insight while the dispositor of Ketu, Mercury in the Ascendant in Cancer, endowed him with emotional intelligence, literary skill, clarity of expression, and the ability to communicate complex social truths in a manner was both accessible and deeply moving.

This rare synthesis of Jupiter's moral vision and Mercury's expressive clarity enabled Premchand to craft narratives that touched the hearts of ordinary readers while at the same time awakening their conscience. We must note here how this in 12th Ketu ensured that his detachment from worldly pursuits did not hinder productivity but instead enhanced the precision and impact of his literary work. Ketu here indicates past-life mastery over matters of isolation, inner reflection, and transcendent work, giving him the capacity to dedicate himself to writing and social commentary without being attached to fame or worldly rewards. He was carrying the gift of letting go and complete immersion from past lives which he nurtured adequately to attain his Rahu's objective of social reform through academia (Sagittarius).

Rahu in the 6th house propelled him toward confronting societal challenges, injustices, and adversities, which was his soul's purpose as well. The 6th house governs competition, service, enemies, and overcoming obstacles, highlighting Premchand's vocation in depicting the struggles of ordinary people, addressing social inequities, and critiquing entrenched hierarchies. Rahu energized him to tackle these challenges creatively, making his narratives powerful instruments for social awareness and transformation.

We must note how Sun is in the ascendant conjunct the dispositor of ketu (Merurcy) - it earned him the title of *Upanyas Samrat* (Emperor of Novels). Works such as *Godaan, Nirmala, Kafan,* and *Idgah* stand as shining examples of how Rahu in the 6th house expressed itself through narratives of poverty, injustice, and human struggle, while Mercury's clarity in the Ascendant ensured that these themes were conveyed in simple yet piercing language. In *Godaan*, the plight of peasants crushed under debt reflects Rahu's call to confront the inequities of the 6th house, whereas *Kafan*, with its stark portrayal of poverty, detachment, and the inevitability of death, mirrors the spiritual aloofness and transcendence of Ketu in the 12th house. By turning literature into a faithful mirror of Indian society, Premchand fulfilled the karmic call of Rahu in Sagittarius which was to reform, to educate, and to raise collective awareness, while drawing upon the spiritual reserves of Ketu, which allowed him to write with sincerity, compassion, and detachment from worldly gain.

Example Chart 2 - Sarojini Naidu (Poet, Freedom Fighter, First Woman Governor of India)

In Sarojini Naidu's chart, Rahu is in the 6th house in Capricorn and Ketu is in the 12th house in Cancer,

Example Chart 2: Sarojini Naidu (Poet, Freedom Fighter, First Woman Governor of India)

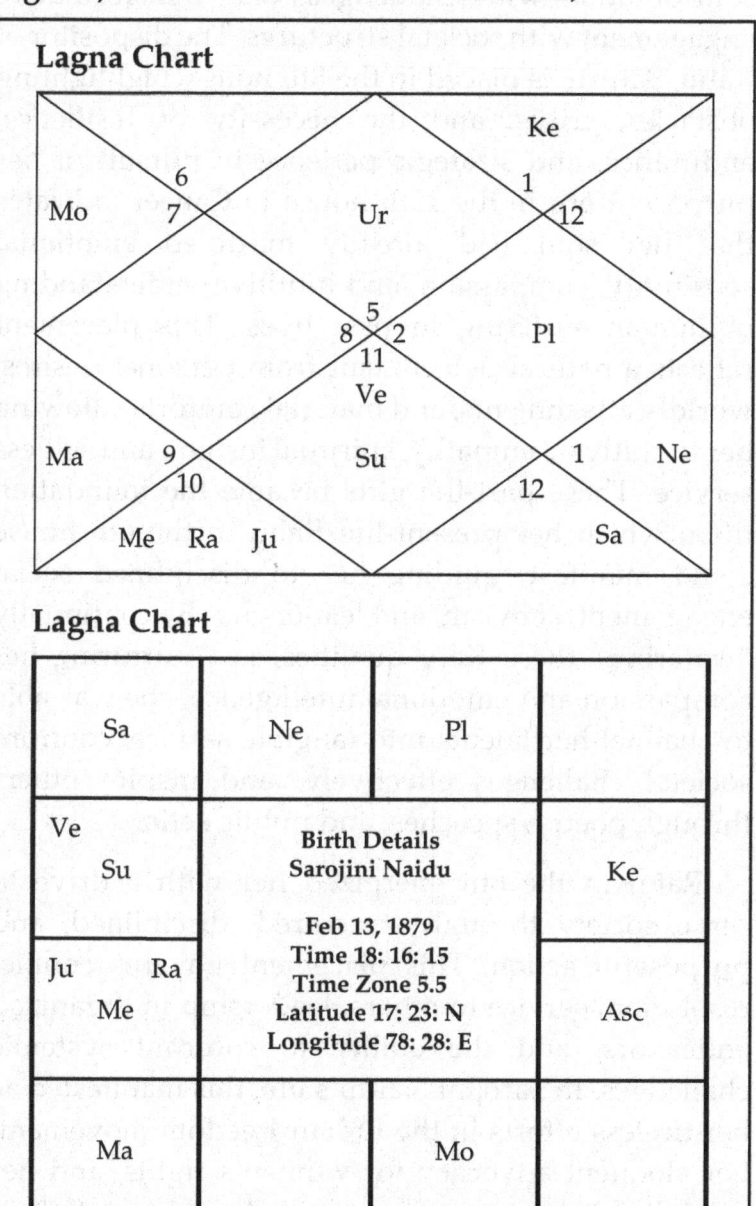

reflecting a karmic focus on disciplined service, confrontation with challenges, and transformative engagement with societal structures. The dispositor of Rahu, Saturn, is placed in the 8th house, highlighting obstacles, crises, and the necessity of resilience, endurance, and strategic patience in pursuit of her purpose. Ketu in the 12th house in Cancer indicates that her soul had already mastered emotional sensitivity, compassion, and intuitive understanding of human suffering in past lives. This placement reflects a natural detachment from personal desires, worldly attachments, and material comforts, allowing her to cultivate empathy, spiritual insight, and selfless service. These past-life gifts became the foundation upon which her present-life Rahu in the 6th house could manifest, guiding her to disciplined social engagement, activism, and leadership. By continually "watering" these Ketu qualities, i.e., nurturing her compassion and emotional intelligence, she was able to channel her talents into tangible service, confront societal challenges effectively, and inspire others through poetry, speeches, and public action.

Rahu in the 6th energized her with a drive to serve society through structured, disciplined, and purposeful action. This placement governs conflict resolution, service to others, leadership in organized endeavors, and the ability to confront systemic challenges. In Sarojini Naidu's life, this manifested as her tireless efforts in the Indian freedom movement, her eloquent advocacy for women's rights, and her disciplined engagement in social reforms. Rahu's influence pushed her to embrace responsibility, public service, and activism, compelling her to navigate political opposition, colonial constraints, and personal sacrifices with unwavering commitment.

The dispositor of Rahu in the 8th house intensified these challenges. Saturn here brought periods of delay, resistance, and hidden obstacles, requiring patience, strategic maneuvering, and endurance. While Rahu directed her toward public service and activism, the 8th house Saturn meant that her path was rarely straightforward; struggles, imprisonment, and personal hardships became catalysts for her growth and deepened her understanding of human suffering and resilience.

The Moon in Libra in the 3rd house, the dispositor of Ketu, reinforced her literary talent, persuasive eloquence, and courageous expression, enabling her to channel her innate sensitivity into poetry, speeches, and public communication. Her mastery of language and the power to inspire through words reflect Ketu's past-life gifts, actively supporting Rahu's present-life mission; her literary brilliance, sensitivity to human suffering, and intuitive understanding of people became tools through which she could enact meaningful societal change.

It was this gift of expression that earned her the title *Bharat Kokila*, the Nightingale of India, for her poetry combined lyrical beauty with patriotic fervor, awakening collective consciousness at a time when the nation yearned for freedom. Her verses, flowing from the emotional sensitivity of Ketu in Cancer, gave voice to the aspirations of millions, while her activism, fueled by Rahu in the 6th house of service and struggle, translated those ideals into action. The hardships she faced such as imprisonment and personal sacrifices, mirror the weight of Saturn in the 8th house, yet each challenge only strengthened her resolve. Rising above these trials, she became the first woman Governor of India, a testament to how the karmic axis of detachment (Ketu) and disciplined service (Rahu) harmonized in her life. By channeling her poetic sensitivity into public leadership, she turned her destiny into a synthesis of art and activism, embodying the very union of Ketu's past-life mastery with Rahu's purposeful striving for social reform.

Case Study 12
Ketu in the 6th House, Rahu in the 12th House

Example Chart 1 - Sri Anandmayi Maa (Saint, Teacher, Mystic)

In Sri Anandamayi Ma's chart, Ketu is placed in the 6th house in Leo and Rahu in the 12th house in Aquarius, revealing a karmic alignment between discipline, service, and transcendence. Ketu in the 6th signifies that in past lifetimes her soul had already mastered the realm of daily struggles, conflicts, and obstacles. She had learnt the art of facing challenges without being bound by them, of transforming the friction of material existence into fuel for inner growth. This mastery endowed her in this life with a natural detachment from personal struggle;

Example Chart 1: Anandmayi Maa (Saint, Teacher, Mystic)

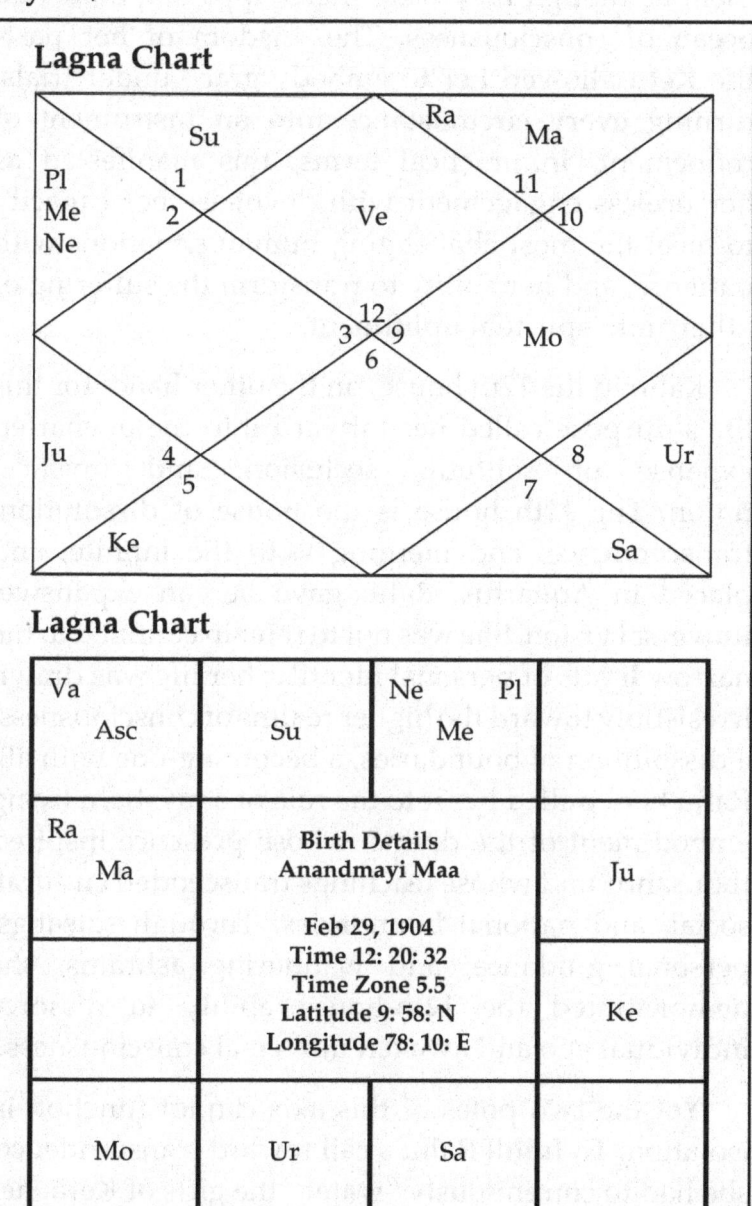

difficulties appeared before her, yet she glided past them as though they were mere ripples upon a vast ocean of consciousness. The wisdom of her past-life Ketu allowed her to embody grace under trials, turning every circumstance into an instrument of refinement. In practical terms, this manifested as her tireless engagement with devotees, her capacity to meet the most challenging human situations with patience, and her ability to transform the suffering of others into spiritual upliftment.

Rahu in the 12th house, on the other hand, for this life's purpose called her forward into the uncharted expanse of solitude, seclusion, and mystical union. The 12th house is the house of dissolution, transcendence, and merging with the infinite, and placed in Aquarius, Rahu gave her an expansive, universal vision. She was not to remain confined to the narrow limits of personal identity; her life was drawn irresistibly toward the higher realms of consciousness, a dissolution of boundaries, a becoming-one with all. Rahu here pulled her into the role of a mystic, a living embodiment of the divine, whose presence inspired thousands and whose teachings transcended cultural, social, and national boundaries. Through satsangs, personal guidance, and wandering ashrams, she demonstrated the 12th-house ability to dissolve individual ego and awaken universal consciousness.

Yet the two poles of this axis cannot function in isolation. To fulfill Rahu's call toward transcendence, she had to continuously "water" the gifts of Ketu: her past-life mastery in service, discipline, and endurance.

It was her natural detachment from struggle (Ketu in the 6th) that enabled her to walk the path of Rahu (12th house transcendence) without faltering. Every time she returned inward to the humility and discipline symbolized by Ketu, she found the strength to expand into Rahu's infinite horizons. Her service to devotees, her gentle but firm guidance, her willingness to meet each person in their struggles with patience and compassion were the fruits of her Ketu that nourished the flowering of Rahu's boundless vision.

Ketu's dispositor, the Sun, exalted in the 2nd house, granted her clarity of speech, moral luminosity, and a radiant presence, so that even her simplest words carried the weight of eternal truth. Rahu's dispositor, Saturn, exalted in the 8th house, gave her immense patience, depth of sadhana, and an ability to guide seekers through their darkest crises. She could meet people in suffering, help them transform their lives, and remain untouched by worldly distractions which is a reflection of Saturn's stabilizing, transformative influence.

Anandamayi Ma's chart reflects a rare and extraordinary configuration that amplifies the potency of her Rahu–Ketu axis - both dispositors, the Sun for Ketu and Saturn for Rahu, are exalted, a rare phenomenon that imbues her axis with exceptional clarity, and transformative power. Furthermore, Venus is exalted in the Ascendant and Jupiter exalted in the 5th house further reinforcing her spiritual authority, creative vision, and capacity for insight. It was a blend of all this that earned her reverence as *Anandamayi Ma*, the "Mother of Bliss". In addition we must note, how these exalted planetary positions are not common in ordinary charts and signify a soul of advanced evolution. The power of her Rahu–Ketu axis was magnified by this constellation of exalted energies, making her presence, guidance, and life purpose resonate with the force and clarity of an avatar, rather than an ordinary human being.

Example Chart 2 - Kapil Dev (Cricketer)

Kapil Dev's Rahu-Ketu axis, with Ketu in the 6th house in Pisces and Rahu in the 12th house in Virgo, demonstrates a seamless integration of resilience, strategic intellect, and latent mastery in high-pressure environments. Ketu in the 6th endowed him with an intrinsic ability to overcome challenges, rivalries, and competitive pressures, reflecting a past-life proficiency in handling adversity. This placement, combined with the 2nd house Jupiter conjunct Moon as Ketu's dispositor, reinforced his emotional intelligence, leadership qualities, and capacity to inspire those around him. He could channel pressure into performance, transforming the arena of competition into a stage for excellence, much as a seasoned warrior of past lives would navigate battlefields with intuition and poise.

Rahu in the 12th house and its dispositor, Mercury in the 3rd house conjunct Sun and Saturn, provided Kapil Dev with strategic foresight, analytical acuity, and disciplined execution, allowing him to navigate the tactical and intellectual demands of cricket with

Example Chart 2: Kapil Dev (Cricketer)

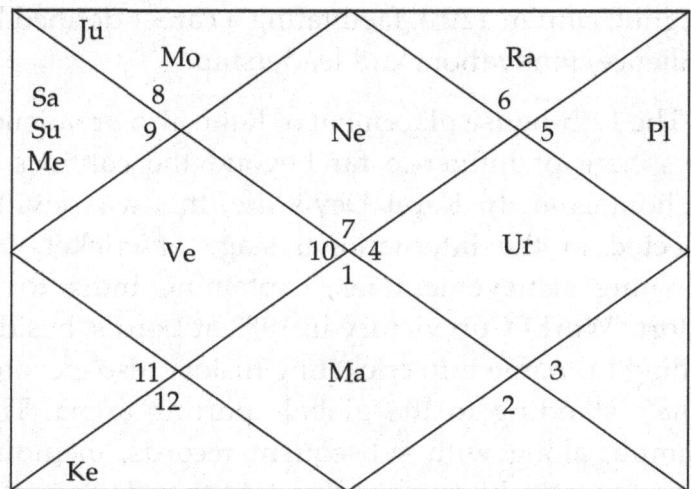

remarkable precision. The axis thus harmonized detachment and disciplined mastery (Ketu in 6th) with expansive ambition, global reach, and visionary insight (Rahu in 12th), facilitating a career defined by resilience, innovation, and leadership.

The 12th-house placement of Rahu also broadened his sphere of influence far beyond the confines of his homeland. In Kapil Dev's life, this was vividly reflected in the international stage of cricket. His crowning achievement i.e., captaining India to its historic World Cup victory in 1983 at Lord's, besides etching his name into cricketing history also elevated India's standing in the global sporting arena. This triumph, along with subsequent records, including becoming the highest wicket-taker in Test cricket at the time, cemented his status as a "Captain of Destiny," which aligns with Rahu's dispositor (Mercury) being conjunct Sun (Captain) in the sign of 'Destiny' (Sagittarius).

It is crucial to recognize that the extraordinary fruits of Rahu in the 12th could only manifest because Kapil Dev remained rooted in the discipline and perseverance of Ketu in the 6th house. The 6th house demanded tireless service, humility, and relentless effort, while Pisces infused his efforts with faith, devotion, and a sense of higher purpose. By continually tending to these Ketu qualities of 6th house such as rigorous training, dedication to his team, and steadfastness in adversity, could he lay the very foundation upon which Rahu's promise of international acclaim unfolded. His ability to overcome injuries, physical strain, and fierce competition reflects the strength of his 6th-house mastery of past lives. Every return to this grounding in discipline and service allowed Rahu in the 12th to expand, carrying his name, his achievements, and his leadership far beyond India's borders.

Thus, Kapil Dev's career exemplifies the seamless choreography of the Rahu-Ketu axis: the past-life mastery of Ketu in the 6th enabled Rahu's 12th-house vision to flower, transforming disciplined effort into global glory, personal resilience into collective inspiration, and individual excellence into a legacy that continues to define cricketing history.

Chapter 6

The Impact of Rahu in Different Houses

Note: *Assessing the overall impact of a planet in any house requires joint and thorough consideration of multiple factors. Any planet placed in a house cannot be judged for its full implications in isolation— aspects, conjunctions, and nakshatra lord (in terms of strength, weakness, and support it provides) considerably modify the results of a planet in any house.*

Planetary Aspects, Houses, Signs, and Their Influence

When examining the impact of Rahu in any house, it is of utmost importance to consider the aspects from both temporal and natural benefic and malefic planets. Benefic influences, such as aspects or conjunction with *trikona* house lords (1, 5, 9) or with natural benefics like Jupiter or Venus, can largely mitigate Rahu's negative results while magnifying positive results. Conversely, malefic influences, such as aspects or conjunction with *dushthana* house lords (6, 8, 12) or with natural malefics like Saturn or Mars, can markedly exacerbate Rahu's disruptive tendencies, leading to more daunting challenges.

If natural malefics like Saturn or Mars become *yogakaraka* in a chart, their association with Rahu will not necessarily cause serious problems, which potentially would be the case if they lord *dushthana* houses.

Irrespective of other factors, owing to the principle that malefic planets give good results in *upachaya* houses—the overall output of which is further amplified or weakened by benefic or malefic aspects, respectively—Rahu performs well in the 3rd, 6th, and 11th houses. Furthermore, Rahu is considered exalted in Taurus and finds the environment of Mercurial signs conducive, thereby performing well in Gemini and Virgo. It is also considered strong in Aquarius, as the natural significations of the two overlap. These principles apply consistently across all houses and are imperative for understanding the overall effects and results of Rahu in any particular house.

1. Rahu in the First House

The first house in Vedic Astrology also known as the Ascendant or Lagna, governs the self, identity, personality, physical body, and how one projects themselves to the world.

When Rahu is in the first house, it brings extremes in personality. The native can possess an exceptionally good and charming personality or he could be extremely wicked as Rahu magnifies the characteristics associated with the house it occupies. Rahu in the ascendant exacerbates the character, and self-focus of the native, often making him think primarily about himself. This amplification can lead to a strong focus on oneself, with a tendency to prioritize personal ambitions and desires over ethical considerations or societal norms. It gives short-temperedness, cunningness, charisma, wit and a heightened sense of self-development. Such a native can resort to any means to elevate his status or sense of self.

Natives with Rahu in the first house often possess high intelligence and a sharp intellect. They are driven by a relentless pursuit of success and status, willing to adopt unconventional or even controversial methods to achieve their goals. This placement is particularly favourable for individuals aspiring to become prominent figures in politics or business, leveraging Rahu's amplifying effect on personal charisma and ambition.

A well-placed and strong Ascendant lord can moderate Rahu's extreme tendencies, promoting a more balanced expression of personality traits where the native's charisma is working to his advantage.

Secondly, planetary aspects on Rahu play a crucial role in shaping its effects. Benefic influences, such as those from Jupiter or Venus, can mitigate Rahu's negative traits and enhance positive attributes like an undeniable allure and leadership potential, particularly when associated with the Sun. On the contrary, malefic influences like that of Saturn or Mars can exacerbate Rahu's disruptive tendencies, leading to issues such as impulsiveness, temperamental behaviour, or health concerns related to the head region. The magnitude of the same would depend upon and be modified based on the lordship of Saturn or Mars.

Marital life for individuals with Rahu in the first house may be problematic, as their primary focus tends to be on personal ambitions rather than nurturing relationships. They may struggle to empathize with others' emotions, potentially leading to misunderstandings or conflicts in partnerships. Furthermore, natives with Rahu in the first house often harbour a strong desire to travel abroad or settle in foreign lands. This inclination stems from Rahu's association with foreign connections and its penchant for seeking novelty and expansion beyond the known or the usual. Physically, this placement can manifest as issues related to the head, such as headaches, migraines, or accidents involving the head region, especially when Rahu is aspected by natural or temporal malefic planets.

In essence, Rahu in the first house signifies a dynamic and intense personality, driven by ambition, intelligence, and a relentless pursuit of personal success. Understanding and managing the influences of Rahu through planetary aspects and the strength of the Ascendant lord is essential for harnessing its positive potential while efficaciously navigating its challenges.

Rahu's placement in the 1st house brings a distinctive energy to the native's personality. According to the BPHS, "Rahu in the 1st house makes the native courageous, sinful, of crooked nature, but with strong determination" (Chapter 45, Verse 30).

The presence of Rahu in the Ascendant can give the native a restless mind and a deceitful nature, as noted in Jataka Parijata. This combination often indicates a drive to achieve, albeit through unconventional means.

2. Rahu in the Second House

The second house in Vedic Astrology governs our family, wealth, speech, finances, and the accumulation of financial assets. When Rahu is positioned in the second house, it dramatically influences these areas, owing to its natural tendency towards extremism or surplus. Rahu's presence in the 2nd house intensifies the native's focus on multiplying his wealth and elevating the family's financial status. This drive for financial gain can lead to an overwhelming desire to control and possess family assets, potentially causing conflicts or even separation from family members.

One of the notable impacts of Rahu in the second house is on the native's speech. The native may exhibit harsh or blunt communication, often speaking without forethought. This can result in misunderstandings or hurt feelings among family and friends while on the positive spectrum, Rahu here gives a highly influential speech or enchanting voice as well. It is crucial for the native to develop a more thoughtful and considerate way of speaking to avoid unnecessary conflicts and maintain harmony within the family.

Financially, Rahu in the second house can bring sudden and substantial windfalls of money. However, this financial gain tends to be volatile and unpredictable. The wealth accumulated through Rahu's influence is not stable; the native might experience periods of significant earnings followed by times of substantial spending. This fluctuation in financial stability can lead to a cycle of boom and bust, making it difficult for the native to maintain consistency in terms of his financial status.

Given this volatility, it is advisable for individuals with Rahu in the second house to avoid making large investments solely in their name or keeping substantial amounts of money in their personal bank accounts. Instead, they should focus on balanced financial planning and avoid impulsive financial decisions. Moreover, it is essential for the native to strive for good relationships with family members. Understanding and cooperation within the family can help mitigate the tensions caused by Rahu's influence in the 2nd house.

Individuals with Rahu in the second house often face challenges in family dynamics due to differences in opinion or a desire to evade familial responsibilities. This placement can lead to a sense of detachment from family ties, rooted in the native's intense focus on personal financial success. To counteract this, the native should work on building strong, supportive relationships with family members and finding a balance between their financial ambitions and familial duties.

Rahu in the second house brings a powerful focus on wealth accumulation and financial success, but it also introduces volatility and challenges in family relationships and communication. By being mindful of their speech, avoiding impulsive financial decisions, and striving for harmonious family interactions, natives can better navigate the complexities introduced by Rahu's presence in this house.

When Rahu occupies the 2nd house, the native faces challenges related to speech defects and eye troubles, and may gain wealth through questionable means, as described in BPHS (Chapter 45, Verse 31). The Phaladeepika further mentions that this placement can lead to financial instability but also provides the native with sharp intellectual abilities. The tension between material gains and moral choices often becomes a theme in such individuals' lives.

3. Rahu in the Third House

The third house in Vedic Astrology governs communication, media, neighbourhood, social projections, willpower, hard work, and friend circle. Rahu's placement in the third house is considered among one of the favourable placements for Rahu. This position intensifies the native's efforts to enhance their business ventures and expand their social network, ultimately aiming to generate profit and achieve success.

Natives with Rahu in the third house are very enterprising, often irresistibly drawn to fields that involve communication and networking. They may find themselves in professions such as transport, media, or even family businesses, provided that the third lord is well-positioned in the chart. Rahu's influence in the 3rd house of *"purushartha"* drives the natives to work hard and leverage their social connections to further their professional endeavours. Further benefic influences can enhance the native's ability to communicate effectively, build strong social networks, and achieve significant commercial success.

However, individuals with Rahu in the third house often have a propensity for gossip and may struggle with keeping secrets. This tendency can tarnish their image and affect their reputation in society. Such natives must be mindful of their words and avoid engaging in gossip or spreading rumours. Maintaining a reputation for discretion and reliability will help them build trust and respect within their social and professional circles.

In terms of willpower and hard work, Rahu in the third house instils a strong drive to succeed. The native is likely to possess a high level of determination and a relentless work ethic. They are willing to put in the necessary effort to achieve their goals, often going above and beyond to ensure success. This tenacity can lead to significant achievements in their chosen fields, especially when they focus on enhancing their communication skills and making use of their social networks effectively.

Rahu's influence on the native's environment and social projections can also be remarkable. The natives may find themselves in dynamic and ever-changing environments, constantly adapting and evolving to stay ahead. Their social projections, or the way they present themselves to the world, are often bold and impactful. They leave a lasting impression on others through their communication and actions.

In conclusion, Rahu in the 3rd House brings a powerful focus on communication, media, social networking, and hard work. The native's efforts to enhance their business and social circle are driven by strong willpower and determination to attain great heights in life. While there are challenges, such as a tendency for gossip and difficulty in keeping secrets. Besides, by being mindful of their communication, avoiding gossip, and leveraging their social connections effectively, natives with Rahu in the 3rd house can achieve substantial success and build a strong, respected reputation in their professional and social circles.

Rahu in the 3rd house brings an ambitious and courageous spirit. BPHS notes that "Rahu in the 3rd house bestows bravery, happiness from siblings, and success in endeavors" (Chapter 45, Verse 32). The Jataka Parijata echoes this sentiment, stating that the native becomes courageous, resourceful, and capable of overcoming challenges. This placement is often associated with a strong desire for recognition and success through personal efforts.

4. Rahu in the Fourth House

The fourth house in Vedic Astrology is the natural house of the Moon, representing home, comfort, luxury, mother, basic education, and the native's basic value system. When Rahu is placed in the fourth house, it intensifies the focus on these areas, particularly emphasizing the pursuit of peace, management of domestic affairs, and the acquisition of luxury and big assets, such as expensive cars and spacious homes.

Rahu's influence in the fourth house increasingly drives the native to aspire for a luxurious and comfortable home environment. The native has a strong desire to multiply their assets, always wanting more than what they currently possess. This ambition is characterised by a constant urge to upgrade their living conditions, whether it be through purchasing a bigger home or acquiring more lavish possessions. However, whether these desires manifest into reality depends significantly on the aspects of other planets on Rahu and the overall condition of the fourth lord.

One key aspect to consider herein is the native's ability to balance their professional and personal life. With Rahu in the fourth house, there is often a tendency to remain preoccupied with domestic affairs, sometimes at the expense of professional growth. The natives may struggle to strike a balance between their career ambitions and the responsibilities at the homefront. This preoccupation with home life can lead to a love for flaunting their status, as they seek to display their achievements in a domestic setting.

The relationship with the mother is another crucial aspect influenced by Rahu in the fourth house.

The native's mother often has high expectations from them, which can be perceived as pressure. This dynamic may lead to a feeling of being overwhelmed by maternal expectations, affecting the native's performance and sense of self-worth. The native might find it challenging to receive love and expectations from their mother in a harmonious way, leading to a strained relationship.

The strength of the Moon in the natal chart plays a significant role in determining the outcomes of Rahu's placement in the fourth house. If the Moon, the natural ruler of the fourth house, is strong and well-placed, Rahu in the fourth house can bring tremendously good results, especially in a material sense. The native may experience significant material gains, leading to an increase in assets and overall comfort. A strong Moon can also mitigate some of the challenges associated with Rahu's influence, such as the tendency to be overwhelmingly preoccupied with home affairs. It could manifest in other ways as well, with regards to other significations of the 4th house such as mother or land.

In essence, Rahu's placement in the fourth house brings an intense focus on home, comfort, luxury, and domestic affairs. The native aspires to have a flamboyant domestic ambience. Balancing work and home responsibilities can be challenging, and the relationship with the mother may be strained due to unrealistically high expectations. The strength of the Moon in unison with the 4th lord in the chart plays a pivotal role in determining the extent of Rahu's positive or negative influence. By striving for balance and understanding in their domestic life, natives can harness Rahu's energy to achieve significant material success and create a harmonious homely environment.

According to BPHS (Chapter 45, Verse 33), Rahu in the 4th house can cause a lack of mental peace, disputes over property, and a wandering nature. Mansagari adds that this placement brings troubles related to land and maternal connections. The native may struggle with emotional security and experience challenges in finding stability at home, which can affect their personal life and overall peace of mind.

5. Rahu in the Fifth House

The fifth house in Vedic Astrology governs intellect, creativity, children, self-expression, fun, and desires. When Rahu is positioned in the fifth house, it significantly impacts these areas of the native's life, leading to a multifaceted influence.

One prevalent misconception regarding Rahu in the 5th house is its alleged negative effect on progeny. Contrary to this belief, when Rahu receives benefic aspects from other planets, it can actually bless the native with intelligent and talented children. The native's primary focus often revolves around their children, investing considerable effort into their grooming and education. However, this intense focus can sometimes lead to opinion differences as the native may dominate their children's upbringing, aiming for their success and well-being.

Apart from children, the fifth house also represents fun and romance in life. With Rahu situated here, the native's orientation towards these aspects is pronounced. They tend to be naturally flirtatious and enjoy indulging in romantic affairs. The moral implications of these tendencies depend largely on the aspects influencing Rahu in the fifth house. When aspected by malefic planets, Rahu can exacerbate these traits, potentially leading the native towards cunning or shrewd behaviour.

The intellectual aspect of the fifth house is crucially influenced by Rahu's placement. Natives with Rahu in the fifth house possess sharp thinking abilities, often using their intellect to strategise and achieve their desires. This intellectual prowess can be utilised either positively in artistic or creative pursuits or negatively to scheme, plot or manipulate others.

In essence, Rahu in the fifth house dynamically influences intellect, creativity, children, self-expression, and desires. Despite misconceptions, this placement can foster positive outcomes for children when supported by natural or temporal benefic planetary aspects. The native's heightened focus on their children's success can sometimes lead to conflicts of opinion. Additionally, the house's association with fun and romance makes the native naturally inclined towards these aspects of life, with outcomes varying based on the planetary influences on Rahu.

Rahu in the 5th house creates challenges related to progeny, a tendency towards gambling, and speculative behavior, as outlined in BPHS (Chapter 45, Verse 34). The Phaladeepika notes that such natives may experience emotional instability but often have a deep interest in occult sciences. This combination can lead to a strong intellectual curiosity but also indicates possible struggles in forming lasting emotional bonds.

6. Rahu in the Sixth House

The sixth house in Vedic Astrology governs conflicts, arguments, health, service to others, and legal matters. Rahu in the sixth house is considered a favorable placement, primarily because it endows the native with exceptional tact and skill in resolving conflicts and disputes. Even as a third party, individuals with Rahu in the sixth house can adeptly mediate and settle disagreements between others. This ability makes them well-suited for professions requiring negotiation and conflict resolution, such as law, corporate management, surgery or diplomacy. For a successful legal career, Rahu here benefits from the supportive influence of Saturn, while for surgical prowess, positive aspects from Mars and Ketu are advantageous. Likewise, to excel in the field of diplomacy, we would be requiring to examine Venus, while for corporate management we will assess Mercury and Venus jointly.

Moreover, when Jupiter aspects Rahu in the sixth house, it forms the auspicious *"Ashtalakshmi Yoga"*, enhancing the native's financial prosperity. Such a congruence of planets can lead to significant material gains, as Rahu's placement in the sixth house shifts the native's effort and focus towards obtaining wealth, activating *"Artha Trikona"* (2nd, 6th, 10th houses), which govern wealth accumulation and material success in totality. Natives with Rahu in the 6th house often take pride in their possessions and enjoy luxury, driven by a strong orientation towards material gains.

In addition, the strength of the sixth lord in the chart plays an indispensable role in determining the outcomes of Rahu's influence in this house. When supported by benefic influences such as Jupiter, a strong Sun, or a prominent 9th house or its lord, the native may even inherit wealth from their father. This further solidifies Rahu's potential to bring financial stability and prosperity through strategic planning, service-oriented careers, and adept management of conflicts and legal matters.

In a nutshell, Rahu's placement in the sixth house signifies an adeptness in managing conflicts and legal issues skillfully. It promotes success in professions involving tact and negotiation skills. The formation of *Ashtalakshmi Yoga* under Jupiter's influence enhances financial prosperity, while the native's materialistic inclinations are supported by the placement in the Artha Trikona. Understanding these dynamics allows individuals to harness Rahu's energy effectively, leveraging it for personal and professional growth in service-oriented fields.

Rahu in the 6th house provides the native with the ability to overcome enemies and gain wealth, as per BPHS (Chapter 45, Verse 35). The Jataka Parijata highlights the native's skill in defeating adversaries, although they may tend to be overly critical. This placement generally indicates a strong drive to excel in competitions or conflicts, with an added focus on health and well-being.

7. Rahu in the Seventh House

The seventh house in astrology signifies partnerships, spouse, business relationships, and public dealings. Rahu's placement in the seventh house often amplifies the native's inclination towards partnerships and relationships to an extreme level. This heightened influence can lead to complexities, especially when Rahu is under further malefic influences. Under such conditions, the native may be prone to engaging in multiple relationships or extramarital affairs. Issues in marital harmony or separations can arise if the seventh lord is also adversely affected, causing instability in partnerships and marriage.

In business dealings, Rahu here can manifest as unfair practices or deceit towards partners, particularly when aspected by natural or temporal malefics in the horoscope. This can lead to breaches of trust and financial losses if not managed carefully. However, when positively influenced, Rahu in the seventh house can elevate the native's career to exceptional heights. The individual may excel as a corporate lawyer, adept at handling complex legal matters or taxation issues with finesse.

A beneficially disposed Rahu in the seventh house enhances the native's ability to maintain strong and passionate relationships with their spouse. On the other hand, if Rahu is further afflicted, it may lead to significant financial setbacks, such as hefty alimony payments post-separation or huge losses in business partnerships.

In essence, Rahu in the 7th house carries the potential for both positive and challenging outcomes in partnerships, business relationships, and marital life, by utilising strengths and mitigating negative tendencies, individuals can harness Rahu's energy to cultivate successful partnerships and maintain integrity in business dealings, thereby achieving stability and growth in their personal and professional lives.

BPHS (Chapter 45, Verse 36) mentions that Rahu in the 7th house can lead to difficulties in marriage, challenges in relationships with foreigners, and delays in partnerships. Mansagari states that this placement can indicate unconventional or troubled marital ties. The native's approach to relationships is often complex, and they may find themselves drawn to non-traditional forms of partnership or experience delays in their romantic life.

8. Rahu in the Eighth House

The eighth house in Vedic Astrology governs hidden and deep aspects of life such as death, transformation, longevity, inheritance, tragedy and unexpected or sudden events like accidents. Rahu in the eighth house, when afflicted by malefic planets, and if the eighth lord is weak or similarly impaired by negative aspects or decapitating conjunctions, can potentially reduce the native's lifespan. This configuration suggests vulnerability to health issues or accidents that could threaten longevity. However, if Rahu in the eighth house receives mitigating aspects from benefic planets or if the eighth lord is strong and well-placed, these concerns about longevity diminish.

Under benefic influence, Rahu in the eighth house stimulates a deep interest in esoteric subjects such as metaphysics, astronomy, and astrology. The native is driven to explore hidden knowledge and delve into secretive realms that are not easily accessible to others. This placement often encourages intensive research and a quest for intense explorations.

Conversely, under negative influences, Rahu in the eighth house can indicate involvement in surreptitious activities or secretive affairs, potentially leading to extramarital relationships for the native or their spouse. Factors like the strength and position of the ascendant lord, Venus along with the seventh lord—benefic or malefic influences on all the three will further portray a clearer picture and, thereby, must be thoroughly analysed concurrently to understand the full implications.

Additionally, there may be challenges with in-laws or deceptive influences from spouse's family members, affecting the native's decision-making. However, when Rahu in the eighth house receives favourable aspects from corresponding house lords like the 11th or 2nd lord, it can bring material abundance and financial gains alongside.

Overall, the placement of Rahu in the eighth house is considered complex and potentially challenging due to its association with transformation and hidden aspects of life which overlap with the significations of the 8th house, thus, demanding mindful navigation and a balanced approach to channelise its positive attributes while mitigating negative effects ensuring the native's growth and stability amidst life's uncertainties.

Rahu in the 8th house brings challenges related to health, accidents, and secrecy. BPHS (Chapter 45, Verse 37) mentions that the native may face fear of accidents and health issues, coupled with a tendency to keep things hidden. Phaladeepika adds that such natives might be drawn to research or hidden knowledge, often developing an interest in the occult or the mysteries of life.

9. Rahu in the Ninth House

In Vedic Astrology, the ninth house governs higher learning, religion, father figures, and mentors. When Rahu is positioned in the ninth house, it influences native's beliefs and spiritual inclinations in distinctive ways.

Rahu in the ninth house often manifests as extremism in the native's approach to spirituality or religion. This can lead to two contrasting paths:

either the native becomes deeply spiritual, embracing religious practices and traditions with fervour, or they reject religion altogether, questioning established beliefs and authority figures such as their father or spiritual mentors. This radical polarisation can result in a strong inclination towards propagating their religious beliefs or being adamantly opposed to them.

A positively functioning Rahu in the 9th house can empower the native to become a religious leader, preacher, or someone deeply committed to spiritual or religious growth and exploration. Such individuals may actively promote matters of their faith or religion, engage in religious studies, and pursue meditative practices with dedication. They may also honour and carry forward the traditions of their lineage. Whereas, a negatively functioning Rahu in the ninth house may lead to scepticism or disregard for religious teachings, resulting in a rebellious stance against established faiths or gurus. The native might challenge authority figures like their father or mentors, potentially disrupting family traditions or spiritual lineages.

When Rahu in the ninth house gets positively associated with either Jupiter or Saturn, it signifies a possibility towards a highly spiritual life, with the native turning into a monk, yogi or other form of spiritual guide, influencing others positively through their wisdom and teachings as it facilitates a deeper understanding of religious principles.

In essence, Rahu's placement in the ninth house underscores a significant journey of spiritual exploration and belief formation for the native. It can either give rise to profound devotion or prompt scepticism towards the whole concept and institution of religion; this placement challenges the individual to navigate their spiritual path with integrity and purpose, ultimately carving their role in the broader spiritual community.

Rahu in the 9th house often results in irreligious tendencies and a disregard for traditional values. BPHS (Chapter 45, Verse 38) notes that the native may be prone to foreign travels and conflicts with spiritual authorities. The Jataka Parijata suggests that this placement can create tensions with spiritual or traditional beliefs, pushing the individual towards a more independent or unconventional path in life.

10. Rahu in the Tenth House

In Vedic Astrology, the tenth house governs career, public reputation, authority, and achievements in life. When Rahu is positioned in the tenth house, it signifies a compelling influence that deeply shapes the native's professional life and public persona.

Rahu in the tenth house is one of the most favourable and advantageous placements. It imbues the native with ambition, intelligence, and a relentless drive to achieve significant success in their chosen field. Individuals with Rahu in the tenth house often ascend to prominent positions such as renowned politicians, CEOs, or leaders of state. They are driven by a strong sense of purpose and ambition, refusing to settle for anything less than remarkable excellence in their career.

The influence of Rahu here amplifies the native's capabilities and determination to expand their professional sphere. They possess an inherent belief that they are destined for greatness, which motivates them to constantly innovate and adopt new strategies to advance their careers. This placement gives rise to a workaholic mentality, where the native is tirelessly striving to reach new heights and make a lasting impact in their professional endeavours.

When Rahu forms a conjunction or beneficial association with the tenth lord in the birth chart, it creates *rajyoga* of the highest order. This alignment enhances the native's prospects for massive success as well as international recognition. They may become trendsetters in their field, pioneering new initiatives or setting new standards of excellence. Such individuals are adept at utilising their intelligence and strategic acumen to accelerate their professional journey.

Overall, Rahu in the tenth house symbolizes a journey marked by ambition, perseverance, and a relentless pursuit of success. It bestows the native with the determination and resilience needed to overcome challenges and achieve remarkable feats in their professional and public life, leaving a lasting legacy of accomplishment and influence.

Rahu in the 10th house brings fame and success in professional life, especially through unconventional methods. According to BPHS (Chapter 45, Verse

39), this placement is linked to associations with influential people and the attainment of high status. Phaladeepika elaborates that natives with Rahu in the 10th house may achieve great success, but it is often attained through non-traditional or even controversial means.

11. Rahu in the Eleventh House

In Vedic Astrology, the eleventh house governs gains, income, friendships, and networks. When Rahu occupies the eleventh house, it exerts a significant influence on the native's approach to wealth, social connections, and aspirations in life.

Rahu's placement in the eleventh house is indicative of a pressing desire and drive to accumulate wealth and boost income throughout life. The native is ambitious and persistent in his pursuit of financial success, often ensuring multiple income streams and financial stability. If a native with Rahu in the eleventh house happens to run his Rahu's Mahadasha, particularly in his prime years of life, he can amass tremendous wealth and experience significant gains, stepping into a high-income bracket. Furthermore, this placement of Rahu also enhances the native's ability to build extensive networks and cultivate influential friendships. They are likely to have a wide circle of friends and acquaintances who play instrumental roles in their professional success and personal growth. The influence of Rahu here can lead to unexpected windfalls of money or opportunities, contributing to overall financial prosperity.

Conversely, Rahu in the eleventh house can also manifest negatively depending on the aspects and conjunctions as stated above, prompting the native to engage in dubious financial practices, including potential involvement in tax evasion or manipulative behaviours to increase wealth. Such natives may form friendships or alliances based primarily on the material benefits they can derive, rather than a genuine sense of companionship or affection.

This placement of Rahu also hints towards the possibility of having foreign connections and income sources from international ventures. If other placements support, the native is highly likely to benefit financially through dealings with foreign countries or investments in overseas markets.

In terms of familial dynamics, as the 11th house signifies elder siblings, Rahu's placement herein suggests that the native could either be the eldest or youngest in the family. There may be financial gains or support received through elder siblings, who themselves are likely to be materialistic and considerably successful.

Overall, Rahu's presence in the eleventh house underscores a dynamic where the native is driven by ambitions for financial success, adept at building influential networks, and receives material support or benefits from foreign countries, network circles, and elder siblings.

Rahu in the 11th house indicates gains from multiple sources and the fulfillment of desires, as per BPHS (Chapter 45, Verse 40). Mansagari adds that the native tends to earn wealth through diverse means and enjoys material comforts. This placement is associated with social success and the ability to fulfill one's ambitions, often through networking or unconventional routes.

12. Rahu in the Twelfth House

In Vedic Astrology, the twelfth house governs isolation, spirituality, the subconscious mind, hidden enemies, and confinement. Rahu's placement in the twelfth house is considered challenging, often leading to involvement in legal issues, court cases, or even imprisonment in extreme cases. The native may face obstacles related to hidden enemies or covert activities, which can hamper their peace of mind and create a penetrating sense of isolation.

This placement also enhances the native's imaginative and intuitive faculties. They possess a strong imagination and may be drawn to mystical or occult pursuits. However, this heightened sensitivity can also lead to sleep disorders *viz.* Insomnia, Parasomnias, or Sleep Paralysis. The native is likely to have vivid dreams both literally and metaphorically, they could have their head in the clouds, dreaming without any practical basis, hesitant to act towards the materialisation of their dreams— depending upon other factors like planetary aspects to this Rahu in unison with the strength and overall condition of the 12th lord. For instance, if Jupiter is strong in the birth chart and Mars aspects Rahu from the sixth house, it can mitigate some of the negative effects, leading to positive outcomes as Mars is one of the planets that can regulate Rahu, dominating and directing its raw and unbridled energy in a constructive way.

When Rahu is placed in certain signs like Aries, Taurus, or Capricorn in the twelfth house, it can lead to considerable financial abundance but may tempt the native towards unethical or illegal means of earning money, such as through activities like drug dealing.

On the spiritual front, if Rahu in the twelfth house is under benefic influences, like Jupiter's aspect, the native will wish to explore the spiritual side of life, becoming deeply involved in spiritual practices, meditation, or even pursue a life as a yogi, seeking enlightenment and transcendence from worldly attachments.

In a nutshell, Rahu's placement in the twelfth house signifies a journey marked by challenges, potential legal entanglements, and a deep exploration of spirituality and the subconscious mind.

Rahu in the 12th house can lead to unnecessary expenditures, foreign travels, and an interest in spiritual practices, according to BPHS (Chapter 45, Verse 41). Phaladeepika further suggests that this placement can cause detachment from worldly pleasures and lead the native toward occult studies. There is often a tendency towards introspection and the exploration of spiritual or mystical pursuits.

Chapter 7

The Impact of Ketu in Different Houses

Note: *Assessing the overall impact of a planet in any house requires joint and thorough consideration of multiple factors. Any planet placed in a house can't be judged for its full implications, in isolation – aspects, conjunctions, ascendant lord (in terms of strength and association), corresponding house lord (in terms of strength, weakness and support it's providing) and nakshatra lord (in terms of strength, weakness and support it's providing) considerably modify the results of a planet in any house.*

Planetary Aspects, Houses, Signs, and Their Influence

When examining the impact of Ketu in any house, it's of utmost importance to consider the aspects from both temporal and natural benefic and malefic planets. Benefic influences, such as aspects or conjunction with *trikona* house lords (1,5,9) or with natural benefics like Jupiter can largely mitigate Ketu's negative results, magnifying positive results. On the contrary, further malefic influences like aspects or conjunction with *dushthana* house lords (6,8,12) or with natural malefic or cruel planets like Saturn or Mars can markedly exacerbate Ketu's disruptive tendencies in a particular house, leading to more daunting challenges.

If natural malefic or cruel planets like Saturn or Mars become *yogakaraka* in a chart, their association with Ketu won't necessarily cause problems of a grave nature which potentially would be the case if they lord *dushtana* houses.

Irrespective of all other factors, owing to the principle that malefic planets give good results in *upachaya* houses, the overall output of which is further amplified or weakened by benefic or malefic aspects, respectively, Ketu does well in the 3rd, 6th, and 11th house. Besides, Ketu is the natural significator of the 5th, 8th and 12th house, thus, producing relatively good results therein. Furthermore, Ketu is considered to be exalted in Scorpio and finds the environment of Jupiterian signs conducive, and thereby performs well in Sagittarius and Pisces. Kindly note that these principles apply consistently across all houses and are imperative for understanding the overall effects and results of Ketu in any particular house.

1. Ketu in the First House

The first house in Vedic Astrology also known as the Ascendant or Lagna, governs the self, identity, personality, physical body, and how one projects themselves to the world. If Ketu is benefically positioned here, in Jupiterian signs *viz.* Sagittarius or Pisces, conjoined mercury, or aspected by benefic planets, it suggests that the native will have an introspective and spiritual bent to his personality, his focus will be towards self-discovery and individuality. They are often driven by a strong desire to delve into existential questions and pursue spiritual enlightenment throughout their lives. When functioning positively, Ketu in the 1st house leads to introspection, prompting the native to explore their true purpose and spiritual dimensions.

These natives tend to be reserved and not overly expressive. They prefer not to speak or express more than necessary unless they have thoroughly researched and are confident about the subject. This tendency makes them cautious communicators, ensuring they have a solid understanding before engaging in discussions. They prefer depth over superficiality in their interactions and communications. An essential aspect of their focus is on their children. The nature of this focus, whether it manifests as nurturing their children's excellence or stems from concern, is contingent upon the overall configuration of the chart.

Conversely, if Ketu is unfavourably positioned in the first house, it can lead to lethargy, aloofness, and confusion in the native. Such natives may be reluctant to socialise and could potentially engage in less desirable activities, including criminal behaviour. However, when Ketu's influence is positive, it can manifest positively, such as in the roles of spies or detectives who excel in maintaining a low profile and uncovering hidden truths.

In essence, the positioning of Ketu in the first house significantly shapes the native's personality and life path, influencing their spiritual journey, introspective tendencies, and approach to personal expression and engagement with the world.

Brihat Parashara Hora Shastra (BPHS) describe Ketu in the 1st house as creating a person who may seem aloof or eccentric but possesses a sharp intellect. "Ketu in the Lagna makes the native spiritually inclined, often detached from material pursuits, and blessed with insight into mystical knowledge." Meanwhile, Jataka Parijata, note that this position often gives a visionary outlook but with a tendency toward solitude.

2. Ketu in the Second House

The second house in Vedic Astrology governs our family, wealth, speech, finances, and the accumulation of financial assets. When Ketu occupies the 2nd house, the natives may experience challenges in communication or may possess a unique way of expressing themselves. They may have karmic lessons related to family dynamics or inherited wealth, often learning the importance of detachment from material possessions.

If the Ketu is beneficially disposed of here and the 2nd house lord is strong as well, it bestows the native with sudden wealth, particularly from the maternal grandparents' side. This positioning enhances the individual's intellectual faculties, making them deeply thoughtful and deliberate in their speech. Such natives measure their words carefully, often thinking before speaking, which can make them appear wise and introspective.

This placement also fosters a profound interest in various philosophies and subjects that delve into the mysteries of life. These individuals are likely to be well-read and have a keen interest in metaphysics, astrology, history, and other esoteric disciplines. Their quest for knowledge often leads them to explore and understand different belief systems and historical contexts, enriching their intellectual and spiritual lives.

Conversely, when Ketu is negatively positioned in the 2nd house, it can bring about several challenges, particularly related to family wealth and relationships. Natives with this placement might face significant issues in receiving family wealth, often encountering disputes or delays that hinder their financial stability. The negative influence of Ketu can strain familial relationships, creating conflicts and misunderstandings that further complicate the accumulation of wealth.

Financially, these individuals might have to struggle more than others to achieve stability and prosperity. The challenges posed by a malefic Ketu can lead to a sense of insecurity regarding wealth accumulation, compelling the native to work harder to secure their financial future. Additionally, a negatively positioned Ketu can diminish their interest in learning and studying, making them less inclined towards intellectual pursuits or academic achievements.

In summary, Ketu in the 2nd house creates a multifaceted impact on the native's life, significantly influenced by its positioning and the strength of the

2nd house lord. When positively placed, it brings sudden wealth, intellectual depth, and a measured communication style. However, when negatively placed, it can lead to financial struggles, strained family relations, and a lack of interest in learning. The overall influence of Ketu in the 2nd house is thus a blend of potential benefits and challenges, heavily dependent on the broader context of the individual's astrological chart.

Phaladeepika suggests that Ketu in the 2nd house can lead to difficulties in acquiring wealth or strained family relations. However, it emphasizes that natives can excel in philosophical or esoteric fields. "The native, though detached from wealth, may gain sudden financial fortune from unexpected sources, including inheritance." Brihat Jataka highlights speech-related difficulties but acknowledges the potential for profound wisdom in the native's words.

3. Ketu in the Third House

The third house in Vedic Astrology governs communication skills, media, neighbourhood, social projections, willpower, hard work, and friend circle. Individuals with this placement may experience a sense of detachment from their immediate environment or struggle with assertiveness. They may excel in spiritual or occult pursuits and have a deep-seated urge to fulfil past life responsibilities related to siblings or neighbours.

When Ketu is positively positioned in the 3rd house, it bestows the native with a number of favourable traits and opportunities. Such individuals often have influential friends who play a significant role in their lives. These connections can provide valuable support, advice, and opportunities, enhancing the native's social standing and professional network. Travel plays a crucial role in the life of someone with Ketu in the 3rd house. The native is likely to travel frequently, especially for short distances, and these journeys are often associated with learning and personal growth. Each trip enriches the native's knowledge and experiences, and travel itself becomes a source of fortune and good luck.

This placement also fosters a strong bond with younger siblings. The native will likely have a supportive and harmonious relationship with them, often playing a mentoring or helping role. This close-knit familial bond extends to the native's broader social interactions as well. In terms of personality, the native is generally talkative and well-read, possessing excellent communication skills. They are knowledgeable about international affairs and current events, making them engaging conversationalists and effective communicators. This intellectual curiosity and ability to articulate thoughts clearly contribute to their overall charisma and influence.

On the other hand, a negatively positioned Ketu in the 3rd house can lead to several challenges. The native might not have younger siblings at all, or if they do, the relationship could be strained or distant. This lack of familial support can create a sense of isolation. Moreover, when Ketu in the 3rd house comes into close association with malefic planets such as Mars or Saturn, it may impart a stubborn and unyielding nature. Such individuals may develop a rigid sense of superiority regarding their lineage or background and can sometimes harbor socially negative traits, making interactions strained and relationships less harmonious.

Additionally, the native may struggle with social interactions in their immediate environment. They might develop a reputation among neighbours as introverts who don't engage much in social activities or conversations. This can lead to misunderstandings and a perception of aloofness or detachment.

The negative influence of Ketu can also impact the native's communication skills and social presence. They might find it difficult to express themselves effectively or to engage in meaningful conversations. This can lead to a feeling of being misunderstood or underappreciated in their community. Ketu in the 3rd house brings a blend of positive and negative influences, shaping various aspects of the native's life. When positively positioned, it grants influential friendships, frequent and fruitful travel, strong bonds with younger siblings, and excellent communication skills. These natives are likely to be well-read and knowledgeable, particularly about international affairs.

However, when Ketu is negatively positioned, the native may face significant challenges, including a lack of younger siblings or strained relationships with them, poor social reputation, and difficulties in communication. These challenges can lead to a sense of isolation and misunderstanding within their community.

Overall, the impact of Ketu in the 3rd house depends greatly on its positioning and the broader context of the individual's astrological chart, balancing between the potential for intellectual and social enrichment and the risk of social and familial challenges.

According to Saravali, Ketu in the 3rd house can create a person with sharp intellect and great courage but potentially distant relationships with siblings. "The native excels in fields requiring secrecy and precision, such as espionage or research, and may derive benefits from foreign lands." Additionally, Brihat Parashara Hora Shastra notes that such natives often gain fame through their writings or communications.

4. Ketu in the Fourth House

In the 4th house, Ketu influences home, mother, and emotional stability. Individuals may have karmic ties related to their roots, homeland, or mother. They may feel a strong sense of detachment from domestic affairs or experience unconventional living situations. Ketu here encourages spiritual growth through detachment from emotional attachments and nurturing environments.

When Ketu is positively positioned in the 4th house, it brings several beneficial influences to the native's life, particularly in relation to their mother, home, and material assets. The native's mother is likely to be a spiritual person with a good reputation in society. This spirituality and esteemed social standing of the mother can have a profound impact on the natives, shaping their values and worldview. The mother's influence is significant, and the native often feels a deep connection with her, seeing her as a central figure in their identity and personal development.

Affection and support from the mother are strong with this placement, providing a nurturing and stable home environment. This maternal bond plays a critical role in the native's emotional well-being and personal growth, fostering a sense of security and belonging.

In terms of material benefits, Ketu in the 4th house often indicates good fortune in acquiring assets. The native is likely to own luxury items, including high-end cars and well-appointed homes. These possessions not only reflect the native's financial success but also contribute to their overall sense of comfort and status. The positive positioning of Ketu here encourages a balanced pursuit of both spiritual and material goals. The native appreciates the finer things in life while maintaining a spiritual perspective, thanks to the mother's influence and the inherent introspective nature of Ketu.

Conversely, a negatively positioned Ketu in the 4th house can bring several challenges and obstacles, particularly concerning the native's home life, emotional stability, and material possessions. The relationship with the mother might be strained or distant, lacking the warmth and support that characterise a positively positioned Ketu. This can lead to feelings of emotional neglect or disconnection, impacting the native's overall sense of security and well-being.

The native could experience a deep longing for motherly love, feeling a profound sense of absence and emptiness in their childhood. This emotional void can create a sense of having a bland and meaningless childhood, where the native perceives a lack of achievement and fulfilment. Such experiences can make the native introverted and perpetually worried about matters related to home, peace, and comfort. Materially, the native might face difficulties in acquiring and maintaining assets. The luxurious lifestyle indicated by a positively positioned Ketu may be out of reach, and the native could experience financial instability or loss of property. The pursuit of comfort and security in the home may be fraught with obstacles, leading to a sense of dissatisfaction and frustration.

The negative influence of Ketu can also foster a sense of detachment or disinterest in material and domestic matters. The native might feel disconnected from their roots and heritage, leading to an ongoing internal struggle between the desire for stability and the inclination towards detachment and introspection. Additionally, there could be struggles with building assets such as homes, frequent vehicle accidents, and even heart-related troubles, further complicating the native's pursuit of a stable and comfortable life.

Ketu in the 4th house has a significant impact on the native's life, particularly in relation to their mother, home, and material possessions. When positively positioned, it brings a spiritual and esteemed mother, strong maternal affection, significant material assets, and a harmonious blend of spiritual and material pursuits. The native enjoys a nurturing home environment and the influence of a mother who is central to their identity and personal development.

However, when Ketu is negatively positioned, it can lead to emotional neglect, strained maternal relationships, social embarrassment, financial instability, and a sense of disconnection from domestic and material matters. The native might struggle with maintaining a sense of security and comfort in their home life, leading to internal conflicts and dissatisfaction. Additionally, there could be a deep longing for motherly love, a sense of a bland and unfulfilled childhood, introversion, constant worry about home matters, struggles with building assets, frequent vehicle accidents, and heart-related issues.

Overall, the effects of Ketu in the 4th house are deeply intertwined with the native's emotional well-being, family dynamics, and material success, highlighting the importance of this placement in shaping the individual's life experiences and personal growth.

Brihat Parashara Hora Shastra states, "Ketu in the 4th makes the native fortunate in acquiring lands and properties but emotionally distant from familial attachments." Additionally, Jataka Parijata mentions that natives with this placement may experience karmic connections with their homeland, often leading to foreign travel or relocation.

5. Ketu in the Fifth House

Ketu's presence in the 5th house affects creativity, intellect, and children. Individuals may possess a profound interest in spirituality, occult sciences, or unconventional forms of self-expression. They may have karmic lessons related to children or speculative ventures, often leading to spiritual transformation and mastery in esoteric fields.

When Ketu is positively positioned in the 5th house, it bestows the native with exceptional communication skills and a strong ability for self-expression. These individuals are often regarded as wise and highly intelligent, standing out for their profound understanding and insightful perspectives. Ketu in this house enhances their ability to articulate complex ideas clearly, making them effective communicators and teachers.

In terms of relationships with children, a positively placed Ketu in the 5th house suggests harmonious and beneficial dynamics. The native is likely to experience pride and joy through their offspring, who may achieve significant success and bring prestige to the family. The presence of Ketu here often indicates that the native's children will be intelligent, successful, and possibly spiritually inclined, reflecting the positive influence of Ketu. This placement encourages the native to foster a nurturing and supportive environment for their children, facilitating their growth and accomplishments.

Furthermore, Ketu in the 5th house can enhance the native's creativity and artistic talents. They may excel in fields that require innovative thinking and originality, gaining recognition and respect for their contributions. This placement also supports a strong intuitive ability, allowing the native to perceive and understand subtle nuances in various situations, which can be particularly beneficial in creative and intellectual pursuits.

On the other hand, when Ketu is negatively positioned in the 5th house, it can bring several challenges and difficulties. One significant issue that may arise is related to childbearing and child-rearing. The native might experience difficulties in conceiving or face the heartbreak of abortions. Even if children are born, there could be complications or strained relationships, affecting the overall harmony and happiness within the family.

Health-wise, a negatively placed Ketu in the 5th house can cause gastric issues, stomach or abdominal problems, and ulcers. These health concerns can impact the native's quality of life, requiring careful attention and management. In terms of self-expression, the natives might struggle to convey their thoughts and ideas effectively. Their communication may lack clarity and coherence, leading to misunderstandings and misinterpretations. This can hinder their ability to connect with others and express their true selves.

Moreover, the native may exhibit negative traits such as wickedness or deceitfulness. While their intuitive abilities remain strong, they might predominantly receive harmful intuitions, influencing their actions and decisions in detrimental ways. This can lead to a skewed perception of reality and difficulties in maintaining positive relationships.

Ketu in the 5th house has a profound impact on the native's life, particularly in terms of communication, intelligence, creativity, relationships with children, and health. When positively positioned, it bestows exceptional communication skills, wisdom, and intelligence, along with harmonious and beneficial relationships with children who achieve significant success. This placement also enhances creativity, artistic talents, and intuitive abilities, making the native effective in intellectual and creative pursuits.

Conversely, when Ketu is negatively positioned, it brings challenges such as difficulties in conceiving, abortions, gastric and abdominal issues, and struggles with effective self-expression. The native may exhibit negative traits and receive predominantly harmful intuitions, affecting their actions and relationships.

Overall, the effects of Ketu in the 5th house are deeply intertwined with the native's intellectual capabilities, creative expression, family dynamics, and health, highlighting the importance of this placement in shaping the individual's life experiences and personal growth.

According to Phaladeepika, "Ketu in the 5th makes the native a seeker of spiritual wisdom, often through unconventional means." It also warns of potential challenges in parenting or romantic relationships. Brihat Parashara Hora Shastra emphasizes that the native's intelligence is profound but often directed toward spiritual or esoteric subjects.

6. Ketu in the Sixth House

When Ketu occupies the 6th house, it influences health, enemies, and service. Individuals with this placement may have a heightened awareness of physical well-being and may excel in healing professions or service-oriented careers. They may face challenges related to health or enemies from past lives, prompting them to overcome obstacles through spiritual practices.

When Ketu is positively positioned in the 6th house, it bestows the native with remarkable strength and resilience to overcome adversaries. Such individuals possess a formidable ability to annihilate their enemies and emerge victorious in conflicts. This placement can make them exceptionally skilled in professions that require precision, determination, and a strategic mindset, such as doctors, lawyers, or surgeons. Their enemies are often defeated effortlessly, as Ketu in this position acts similarly to Mars, imparting a warrior-like spirit.

Natives with Ketu in the 6th house are known for their incredible work ethic. They set clear, result-oriented goals and pursue them with relentless dedication. This drive and determination earn them respect and admiration in their professional environments. Their colleagues and superiors praise their work style and their disciplined approach to tasks. Their ability to focus on objectives and deliver outstanding results makes them invaluable assets in any workplace. They often excel in fields that demand meticulous attention to detail and the ability to remain calm under pressure.

Moreover, these individuals tend to have a robust constitution, enabling them to withstand physical and mental stress. Their resilience and endurance contribute to their success in competitive environments. They thrive in challenging situations and possess the tenacity to overcome obstacles, making them natural leaders and achievers in their chosen fields.

Conversely, when Ketu is negatively positioned in the 6th house, it can bring a host of challenges and difficulties. One significant concern is the native's susceptibility to accidents and injuries. They might find themselves prone to multiple accidents, leading to physical harm and setbacks. Additionally, this placement can make the individual vulnerable to diseases and illnesses, resulting in frequent health issues and a weakened immune system.

The native's maternal uncle may also face troubles, as Ketu's negative influence can extend to family members. There could be strained relationships or unfortunate events affecting the maternal side of the family. Another critical aspect is the native's temperament. A negatively placed Ketu in the 6th house can result in a bad temper, leading to impulsive actions and decisions. This volatile nature can create conflicts and misunderstandings, both in personal and professional relationships. Their tendency to react aggressively can generate more enemies and adversaries, leading to unnecessary strife and challenges.

Furthermore, the native's inability to manage their temper and emotions can result in significant losses. They might make hasty decisions that negatively impact their career, relationships, and overall well-being. This placement requires a conscious effort to cultivate patience, self-control, and a balanced approach to handling conflicts and challenges. Ketu in the 6th house plays a pivotal role in shaping the native's ability to handle adversities, achieve professional success, and maintain physical health. When positively positioned, it endows the individual with the strength to defeat enemies, excel in demanding professions, and earn admiration for their work ethic. These natives are hardworking, goal-oriented, and resilient, making them successful in competitive environments.

On the other hand, a negatively positioned Ketu in the 6th house brings challenges such as susceptibility to accidents, health issues, and troubles related to the maternal family. The native may struggle with a bad temper, leading to conflicts and losses. Managing these challenges requires a conscious effort to cultivate patience and self-control.

Overall, Ketu's placement in the 6th house significantly influences the native's approach to adversities, professional achievements, health, and interpersonal relationships, highlighting the importance of this position in determining the individual's life experiences and growth.

Saravali states, "Ketu in the 6th house destroys enemies and obstacles, granting the native victory in disputes or litigation." Brihat Parashara Hora Shastra also mentions that this placement can enhance the native's ability to handle challenges effectively, often through unconventional or spiritual means.

7. Ketu in the Seventh House

In the 7th house, Ketu influences marriage, partnerships, and business relationships. Individuals may experience a sense of detachment or an unconventional approach towards relationships. They may attract partners who are spiritually inclined or face karmic lessons related to partnerships. Ketu encourages them to seek spiritual fulfilment through harmonious partnerships.

When Ketu is positively positioned in the 7th house, it brings forth a range of beneficial influences, particularly in the realms of marriage and business partnerships. One of the most prominent effects is the likelihood of having a spiritual spouse. While the native might not initially be spiritual, this difference can initially cause disruptions in marital life. However, as time progresses and the native learns to accept and appreciate the spiritual nature of their spouse, marital harmony improves significantly. This journey towards mutual acceptance and understanding can lead to a fulfilling and supportive marital relationship.

In terms of business partnerships, a positively placed Ketu in the 7th house can attract simple, honest, and reliable partners. The native's approach to business is characterized by integrity and straightforwardness, fostering successful collaborations. If the 7th house lord is strong, the native has the potential to achieve great success in business, possibly becoming a prominent entrepreneur. Their skills in technology and computer-related fields are noteworthy, allowing them to excel in these areas with considerable adeptness. Furthermore, they may engage in international collaborations, expanding their business horizons and achieving global recognition.

Conversely, when Ketu is negatively positioned in the 7th house, it brings about a series of challenges, particularly in personal and professional relationships. Marital life is likely to be fraught with conflicts, leading to frequent fights and a higher likelihood of separation. This placement often indicates the possibility of two marriages, as the natives struggle to maintain harmony in their relationships. The tendency for partnerships, whether marital or business-related, to dissolve prematurely is pronounced, resulting in instability and recurrent losses in business ventures.

The native's introverted nature and reluctance to express their thoughts and feelings further exacerbate relationship issues. This lack of communication creates misunderstandings and emotional distance, making it difficult for the natives to connect deeply with their spouse or business partners. Additionally, if the spouse is also non-expressive, the native may find it challenging to understand their spouse's inner thoughts and emotions, leading to further marital discord. Ketu's placement in the 7th house plays a crucial role in shaping the native's experiences in marriage and business partnerships. When positively positioned, it fosters spiritual growth within the marital relationship and attracts reliable business partners, enabling significant achievements, especially in technology-related fields and international collaborations. The native's journey towards accepting and appreciating their spouse's spiritual nature leads to a harmonious and fulfilling marital life.

However, a negatively positioned Ketu in the 7th house brings about considerable challenges. Marital life is marked by conflicts, separations, and the possibility of multiple marriages. Business partnerships are unstable, leading to frequent losses. The native's introverted nature and reluctance to express emotions contribute to relationship difficulties, making it hard to connect deeply with others.

Overall, Ketu's influence in the 7th house underscores the importance of communication, acceptance, and mutual understanding in both personal and professional relationships. This placement significantly impacts the native's journey towards building lasting connections and achieving success in their endeavours.

Ketu in the 7th house, as per Brihat Parashara Hora Shastra, "causes difficulties in maintaining harmonious marital relationships and brings separative tendencies." This placement often signifies unconventional relationships or partners and challenges in sustaining long-term partnerships. Similarly, Phaladeepika notes that "natives with Ketu in the 7th house may experience delays or instability in marriage unless counteracted by benefic aspects." On the positive side, this placement can foster deep karmic connections and partnerships with individuals involved in spiritual or unconventional domains.

8. Ketu in the Eighth House

Ketu in the 8th house affects transformation, hidden knowledge, and longevity. Individuals may have a deep interest in occult sciences, mysticism, or research. They may face challenges related to inheritance, sudden changes, or fears from past lives. Ketu here promotes spiritual growth through understanding the mysteries of life and death.

When Ketu is positively positioned in the 8th house, it brings about a host of beneficial influences that can significantly impact various aspects of the native's life. The 8th house governs areas such as longevity, in-laws, taxes, insurance, and the occult. A well-placed Ketu here endows the native with remarkable skills in research and an aptitude for delving into the depths of complex subjects. This placement can make the native a renowned researcher, excelling in fields such as occult studies, astrology, metaphysics, and even technology or computer science.

The native's career in tech-related fields can flourish, as Ketu's influence enhances their ability to understand intricate systems and work with advanced technologies. Additionally, this placement can bring support from in-laws, fostering a harmonious and beneficial relationship with them. The native may also excel as a taxation lawyer, leveraging their analytical skills and attention to detail to navigate complex tax laws effectively. In terms of marriage, a positively positioned Ketu in the 8th house can contribute to the longevity of the marital relationship, ensuring stability and mutual support over the long term.

On the other hand, when Ketu is negatively positioned in the 8th house, it introduces a series of challenges and obstacles that the native must navigate. This placement can lead to a higher likelihood of accidents and the need for surgeries, indicating potential health concerns. The native may feel that their in-laws are secretive, leading to mistrust and strained relationships. This sense of secrecy and lack of transparency can create a barrier between the native and their in-laws, resulting in a less supportive and more contentious dynamic.

Marital life may also suffer due to the negative influence of Ketu in the 8th house. The stability of the marriage can be compromised, with frequent conflicts and misunderstandings leading to an unstable relationship. In extreme cases, this placement can result in separation, either from the spouse or from the in-laws. The native may struggle to find common ground and maintain a harmonious marital life, leading to feelings of isolation and dissatisfaction. Ketu's placement in the 8th house is a powerful indicator of the native's potential in various complex and intellectually demanding fields. When positively positioned, it fosters exceptional research skills and an aptitude for the occult, technology, and metaphysics. The native can enjoy a supportive relationship with in-laws, a successful career in tech or taxation law, and a stable, long-lasting marriage.

However, a negatively positioned Ketu in the 8th house brings about significant challenges. Health issues, accidents, and surgeries may be more common, and the native may feel mistrust towards their in-laws. Marital stability is jeopardized, with a higher risk of conflicts and separations. The native must work hard to overcome these obstacles, striving for transparency and communication in their relationships to mitigate the negative effects of this placement.

Overall, Ketu's influence in the 8th house underscores the importance of balance, trust, and open communication in both personal and professional spheres. This placement highlights the potential for great success and profound understanding in specialized fields, while also cautioning against the pitfalls of secrecy and mistrust in relationships.

According to BPHS, Ketu in the 8th house can "lead to an extraordinary interest in occult sciences, mysticism, and hidden knowledge." While it enhances the native's capacity for research and spiritual transformation, Phaladeepika warns that "this placement may bring health complications, marital discord, or accidents caused by sudden events." Despite its challenges, it can empower the native to navigate profound transformations and karmic lessons tied to the mysteries of life and death.

According to BPHS, Ketu in the 8th house can "lead to an extraordinary interest in occult sciences, mysticism, and hidden knowledge." While it enhances the native's capacity for research and spiritual transformation, Phaladeepika warns that "this placement may bring health complications, marital discord, or accidents caused by sudden events." Despite its challenges, it can empower the native to navigate profound transformations and karmic lessons tied to the mysteries of life and death.

9. Ketu in the Ninth House

When Ketu occupies the 9th house, it influences religion, spirituality, and father. Individuals may feel detached from conventional religious practices and may seek spiritual truths independently. They may face karmic lessons related to paternal relationships or religious beliefs, prompting a deep exploration of philosophical and spiritual ideologies.

When Ketu is positively positioned in the 9th house, it brings a profound influence on the native's spiritual and intellectual life. This placement often indicates a very spiritual and knowledgeable father whose philosophy and wisdom deeply shape the native's own beliefs and understanding. The native is likely to have been a very knowledgeable person in past lives, carrying forward that wisdom into the present life. This can make them an excellent preacher, adept in consultancy, and highly respected in advisory roles.

The influence of Ketu in the 9th house also encourages long-distance travels, especially those with a spiritual or educational purpose. These journeys enhance the native's knowledge and spiritual growth, contributing to their overall development. The native may also possess strong counselling abilities, making them a good counsellor who can provide valuable guidance to others. Relationships with the father are generally positive, characterised by mutual respect and admiration. The native often follows in their father's footsteps, embracing the philosophical and spiritual teachings imparted by him.

However, when Ketu is negatively positioned in the 9th house, it can create significant challenges and disruptions. The native may become a non-believer, rebelling against the religious and spiritual beliefs of their family. This rebellion can damage the family's social prestige and tarnish the lineage's reputation. Acts of defiance against established beliefs and traditions may lead to societal disapproval and isolation. The native may also engage in actions that harm the father's dignity and image in society.

In some cases, the father himself may be involved in illegal or criminal activities, further complicating the relationship and adding to the native's internal conflict. The negative placement of Ketu in the 9th house can lead to a loss of direction and purpose, causing the native to question their beliefs and struggle with finding a meaningful path.

Ketu's placement in the 9th house significantly influences the native's spiritual and philosophical outlook. When positively positioned, it fosters deep spiritual wisdom, strong influence from a knowledgeable father, and a propensity for long-distance spiritual travels. The native excels in advisory roles, becoming an effective preacher or counsellor, and maintaining a positive relationship with their father.

Conversely, a negatively positioned Ketu in the 9th house brings rebellion against family beliefs, societal disapproval, and potential disgrace to the family name. The native may struggle with religious and spiritual beliefs, leading to actions that harm the father's reputation. This placement underscores the importance of understanding and integrating spiritual beliefs with personal identity, balancing respect for tradition with individual growth.

Overall, Ketu in the 9th house highlights the profound impact of spiritual and philosophical teachings on the native's life. It emphasizes the need for balance and respect in navigating personal beliefs and family traditions, ensuring that the quest for knowledge and spiritual growth is pursued with integrity and wisdom.

The placement of Ketu in the 9th house is described in BPHS as one that "causes detachment from orthodox beliefs and a strong inclination toward spiritual liberation." This position may result in strained relationships with the father or gurus, as Phaladeepika explains: "The native may face difficulties in following family traditions or religious practices." Despite potential conflicts with authority figures or tradition, this placement enhances the native's philosophical depth and capacity for exploring higher truths.

10. Ketu in the Tenth House

Ketu's presence in the 10th house affects the native's career, status, and public image. Individuals may experience a sense of detachment from worldly ambitions or conventional career paths. They may excel in unconventional professions or leadership roles that involve spiritual guidance. Ketu encourages them to find fulfilment by aligning their career with higher spiritual goals.

When Ketu is positively positioned in the 10th house, the natives channel all their energy toward achieving great heights in their profession. Their ambition is driven by a desire to make a significant impact on society, and they may dream of accomplishing something monumental. The individual could potentially become a renowned preacher of religion or a spiritual leader with a global following. Their approach to work is characterized by innovation and novel ideas, which often influence and inspire others. The native's unique work style and attitude towards their profession earn them admiration and respect, and they have a strong desire to reach the pinnacle of success. Whether this ambition materializes depends on the overall horoscope, but the drive and determination are undoubtedly instilled by Ketu's presence. The native is likely to be very outspoken with exceptional oratory skills, enhancing their ability to communicate and persuade effectively. Additionally, the social status of their father could be noteworthy, indicating a family background of respect and recognition.

On the contrary, when Ketu is negatively placed in the 10th house, the native faces significant challenges in their professional journey. Despite striving for success, they may struggle with laziness or lethargy, often resorting to shortcuts that undermine their efforts. This lack of perseverance and diligence can prevent them from achieving their professional goals. The native might also exhibit weak willpower or a negative mindset, which can further hinder their progress. Socially, their image could suffer, potentially becoming weak or tarnished due to their inability to commit fully to their work. This placement can lead to a preference for isolation, making the individual reluctant to engage with others or put in the necessary hard work. These challenges and tendencies may also extend to their father, reflecting similar difficulties in the professional and social spheres.

In summary, Ketu's placement in the 10th house significantly influences the native's professional and social life. When positively aligned, it fosters ambition, innovation, and leadership qualities, leading to potential success and admiration. However, when negatively positioned, it can result in professional struggles, laziness, and social isolation, requiring the native to overcome these obstacles to achieve their desired success.

In the 10th house, Ketu, as mentioned in BPHS, "grants unique professional skills, particularly in unconventional fields, but causes dissatisfaction with societal roles." Similarly, Phaladeepika highlights the potential for "professional instability unless mitigated by benefic influences." While this placement can lead to career disruptions, it fosters success in innovative or technological fields and helps the native break free from societal constraints to pursue authentic aspirations.

11. Ketu in the Eleventh House

In the 11th house, Ketu influences gains, friendships, and social circles. Individuals may feel detached from material desires or may experience unconventional friendships. They may have karmic lessons related to social networks or aspirations, often leading to spiritual growth through detachment from worldly attachments.

When Ketu is positively positioned in the 11th house, the native is often endowed with qualities that make them effective leaders, doctors, politicians, preachers, or consultants. They might also find success in businesses related to watches or clocks. These individuals are likely to excel in networking, and becoming part of highly influential circles, such as those involving prominent politicians or key societal figures. Their entire energy is directed toward building and maintaining powerful networks, gradually weaving a web of influential contacts. This strategic networking can lead to sudden recognition, awards, and unexpected financial windfalls. Ensuring a stable and substantial regular income is a significant focus, and they work diligently to maintain financial stability. Furthermore, their elder sibling may be highly successful, and their relationship with their elder siblings is generally positive and supportive, contributing to their social and emotional well-being.

Conversely, when Ketu is negatively positioned in the 11th house, the native may face several challenges, particularly in their relationships and financial stability. This placement can result in separation or strained relations with elder siblings, causing emotional distress. The native's regular income is often unstable, characterized by periods of substantial earnings followed by times of financial drought, leading to a precarious economic situation. Breaks in earnings and financial instability become a recurring issue. Additionally, the native may find themselves networking with individuals of questionable character, potentially leading to associations with people whose social reputation is poor or who are involved in dubious activities.

This negative influence requires the native to be extremely cautious in choosing their social circle and professional networks to avoid getting entangled in financial or economic offenses. Such connections can further complicate their financial and social standing, emphasizing the need for careful selection of friends and associates.

In conclusion, Ketu's placement in the 11th house significantly impacts the native's social and financial life. When positively aligned, it enhances leadership qualities, effective networking, and financial gains, fostering strong relationships with elder siblings. However, when negatively positioned, it brings challenges in maintaining stable income, potential involvement with undesirable associations, and strained sibling relationships, requiring vigilance and careful management to mitigate these adverse effects.

BPHS observes that Ketu in the 11th house "causes sudden gains through unique channels but brings difficulty in maintaining social networks and long-term alliances." According to Phaladeepika, "the native may experience fluctuations in income and challenges in fulfilling their desires." Despite social challenges, this placement often brings unexpected financial gains, particularly through foreign connections or unconventional means.

12. Ketu in the Twelfth House

Ketu in the 12th house influences spirituality, isolation, and hidden enemies. Individuals may have a strong inclination towards solitude, meditation, or spiritual retreats. They may face challenges related to isolation, past life karma, or subconscious fears. Ketu here promotes spiritual liberation through detachment from materialism and ego.

When Ketu is positively positioned in the 12th house, it naturally aligns with the house's significations, as Ketu itself is one of the natural significators of the 12th house. This placement often yields favourable outcomes, given that the 12th house represents a boundaryless space where Ketu's quest for spiritual identity and detachment can thrive. Individuals with this placement are likely to develop a sense of renunciation, embracing detachment from worldly possessions and relationships. This can lead them to travel far distances, often leaving their homes in pursuit of spiritual enlightenment or higher knowledge. They might engage deeply in spiritual practices, meditation, and other forms of inner exploration, finding solace in solitude and introspection.

Conversely, when Ketu is negatively positioned in the 12th house, the native may experience a lack of marital happiness due to their inherent detachment and a nature inclined towards renunciation. Their approach to life can resemble that of a yogi, preferring solitude and spiritual pursuits over worldly attachments. However, if Ketu receives aspects from benefic planets and the lords of the 12th and 7th houses are strong, the native's marital life may sustain until a certain age before they fully embrace renunciation, moving towards spiritualism, detachment, and ultimate liberation. A negatively functioning Ketu in the 12th house can also bring significant challenges, such as leading the native towards asylums or creating a "Bandhan yoga," which indicates imprisonment or confinement. Mental imbalances and other psychological issues may arise, resulting in frequent visits to hospitals or healthcare facilities.

In essence, Ketu in the 12th house profoundly influences the native's spiritual journey and detachment from material life. When positively positioned, it fosters spiritual growth, renunciation, and a deep sense of inner peace through solitude. On the other hand, a negatively positioned Ketu can lead to challenges in marital happiness, mental health issues, and periods of confinement or hospitalization. The overall impact of Ketu in this house is greatly influenced by the aspects of benefic planets and the strength of the 12th and 7th house lords, which can mitigate or exacerbate the effects of this placement.

The 12th house placement of Ketu, as per BPHS, "promotes spiritual liberation and detachment from material concerns but may lead to health issues and excessive expenditures." Phaladeepika elaborates that "natives with Ketu in this house are inclined toward isolation, foreign settlement, or spiritual pursuits." While this placement challenges the native with financial and physical difficulties, it paves the way for deep introspection, spiritual growth, and eventual liberation from worldly attachments.

Chapter 8

The Impact of Rahu in Different Zodiac Signs

Note: Assessing the overall impact of a planet in any sign requires joint and thorough consideration of multiple factors. Any planet placed in a sign can't be judged for its full implications, in isolation – aspects, conjunctions, ascendant lord (in terms of strength and association), corresponding sign lord (in terms of strength, weakness and support it's providing) and nakshatra lord (in terms of strength, weakness and support it's providing) considerably modify the results of a planet in any house.

Planetary Aspects, Houses, Signs, and Their Influence

When examining the impact of Rahu in any sign, it's of utmost importance to consider the aspects from both temporal and natural benefic and malefic planets. Benefic influences, such as aspects or conjunction with *trikona* house lords (1,5,9) or with natural benefics like Jupiter or Venus, can largely mitigate Rahu's negative results, magnifying positive results. On the contrary, further malefic influences like aspects or conjunction with *dushthana* house lords (6,8,12) or with natural malefic or cruel planets like Saturn or Mars can markedly exacerbate Rahu's disruptive tendencies in a particular sign, leading to more daunting challenges.

If natural malefic or cruel planets like Saturn or Mars become *yogakaraka* in a chart, their association with Rahu won't necessarily cause problems of a grave nature which potentially would be the case if they lord *dushthana* houses.

Irrespective of all other factors, owing to the principle that malefic planets give good results in *upachaya* houses—the overall output of which is further amplified or weakened by benefic or malefic aspects, respectively, Rahu does well in the 3rd, 6th, and 11th house. Furthermore, Rahu is considered to be exalted in Taurus and finds the environment of Mercurial signs conducive, and thereby performs well in Gemini and Virgo. It's considered strong in Aquarius as well as the natural significations of the two overlap. Kindly note that these principles apply consistently across all signs and are imperative for understanding the overall effects and results of Rahu in any particular sign.

1. Rahu in Aries

Rahu's placement in the zodiac sign of Aries intensifies the native's inherent qualities associated with energy, assertiveness, and ambition of Aries ruled by Mars. This placement imbues the individual with an energetic and vigorous approach to life, driving them to pursue their goals with passion and determination. The impulsive nature of Aries is heightened by Rahu as Rahu amplifies all that it comes in contact with, leading the native to act hastily or rashly at times, often without fully considering the consequences. This energy can manifest in quick decisions with regard to new ventures or relationships, driven by a sense of urgency or desire for immediate results.

Innovation and a pioneering spirit characterise Rahu in Aries, encouraging the natives to explore unconventional ideas and approaches. They are inclined to push boundaries and challenge existing norms, often hammering out new paths or making breakthroughs in their chosen fields. Rahu in Aries induces in natives a propensity for risk-taking behaviour, where the native displays daring and adventurous tendencies. They are inclined towards taking calculated risks that others may shy away from, which can result in both successes and failures depending on the level of foresight allowed by the overall planetary interplay in the horoscope.

Independence and autonomy are strongly emphasised, as Aries symbolizes freedom from constraints. Rahu magnifies this desire for self-reliance, prompting the native to resist authority and conventional expectations. They prefer to lead rather than follow, asserting their independence in all areas of life. Leadership qualities are a natural extension of Rahu in Aries, where the native tends to take charge in group settings or organisational roles. Their enthusiastic and driven demeanour inspires others to follow their lead, making them effective motivators and initiators of change.

However, challenges arise from conflicts that may stem from their assertiveness and impatience. Rahu in Aries can lead to clashes with others, especially when opposing viewpoints or interests come into play. The native may need to cultivate patience and tolerance towards differing perspectives to navigate these conflicts in an efficacious manner.

2. Rahu in Taurus

Rahu's placement in the zodiac sign of Taurus, governed by Venus, intensifies the inherent qualities of materialism, stability, and sensual pleasures associated with this sign. The native is driven by strong desires for wealth, luxury, and material possessions, seeing them as symbols of security and value.

This placement fosters a tendency, rooted in insecurity, towards possessiveness and attachment. The native may fear loss deeply, which prompts them to accumulate and hold onto possessions, relationships, or resources tightly. This can result in resistance to change and reluctance to let go of what they have acquired.

Taurus symbolizes sensual pleasures and enjoyment of life's comforts, and Rahu here amplifies these tendencies. The native may indulge excessively in sensual experiences, seeking gratification through food, drink, or physical comforts. There can be a hedonistic streak where pleasure-seeking becomes a dominant theme in their life.

Financial ambition is heightened with Rahu in Taurus. The native is motivated to pursue career paths or business ventures that promise financial stability and rewards. They demonstrate resourcefulness in managing finances and actively seek opportunities for wealth accumulation. Stability and routine are valued by individuals with Rahu in Taurus. They strive to establish and maintain stable environments, both in personal life and career. Change or disruptions can be challenging for them, as they prefer predictable and secure situations where they feel comfortable and in control.

Despite their preference for stability, if the 2nd lord is negatively aspected or under malefic influence, Rahu in Taurus can also present challenges when unexpected changes occur. The natives may struggle to adapt to new circumstances that disrupt their sense of security or established routines. Taurus also governs artistic talents and creativity, which are enhanced by Rahu's influence. The native may excel in areas such as music, fine arts, or crafts, finding fulfilment in creative expression. They may utilise their artistic skills to generate income or pursue hobbies passionately.

3. Rahu in Gemini

Rahu's placement in Gemini is characterised by an emphasis on communication, intellect, curiosity, and adaptability. Governed by Mercury, Gemini embodies qualities of intellectual agility and a profound thirst for knowledge. With Rahu influencing this placement, individuals often showcase heightened curiosity, a keen intellect, and a strong drive to acquire diverse knowledge from various sources. They excel in fields demanding analytical thinking, effective communication, and versatility, effortlessly juggling multiple interests and roles.

These natives are skilled communicators, adept at articulating ideas persuasively across different platforms. Whether in writing, public speaking, teaching, or media, they shine due to their ability to convey complex concepts with clarity. However, Rahu's influence can also manifest as mental restlessness, leading to scattered thoughts and occasional indecisiveness. They must channel this energy productively to avoid feeling overwhelmed.

Gemini's symbol of the Twins underscores the sign's inherent dualistic nature, reflected in the native's penchant for exploring contrasting viewpoints and interests. This dualism can occasionally create internal conflicts or confusion. Rahu in Gemini fosters a deep interest in technology and modern communication tools, drawing individuals towards fields like computer science, telecommunications, or digital media, where they leverage their skills in networking and information exchange.

Despite their adaptability and versatility, individuals with Rahu in Gemini may encounter challenges with commitment and long-term focus. Their inherent curiosity drives them to explore new ideas and opportunities, sometimes at the expense of consistency. Managing these tendencies effectively can help them harness their full potential in both personal and professional pursuits.

4. Rahu in Cancer

Rahu's placement in Cancer infuses the native with a distinctive blend of characteristics centred around emotions, nurturing instincts, security, and domesticity. Rahu in Cancer intensifies emotional sensitivity and intuition, attributes associated with Cancer's ruler, the Moon. This positioning often endows individuals with a profound empathy and insight into others' feelings and motivations. Such heightened emotional awareness can prove advantageous in personal relationships and caregiving roles.

Individuals with Rahu in Cancer have a strong attachment to home, family, and ancestral roots. They prioritise emotional security and stability, finding comfort in familiar environments and traditions. Family ties hold significant importance, and they may derive a deep sense of fulfilment from maintaining these connections.

Nurturing instincts are enhanced with Rahu in Cancer, making the native naturally protective and caring towards loved ones. They excel in roles involving caregiving, homemaking, or providing emotional support. This placement gives rise to a strong sense of responsibility and devotion to family members and close friends.

Cancer's association with psychic abilities and the unseen realms is heightened by Rahu's influence. Individuals may possess a keen interest in paranormal phenomena, spirituality, and metaphysical subjects. This curiosity often leads them to explore mystical aspects of life and develop intuitive gifts.

There is a pronounced desire for financial security and material comforts within the context of home and family life with Rahu in Cancer. These natives strive to create a nurturing environment, investing resources in property, real estate, or domestic endeavours to enhance comfort and stability.

Despite their nurturing qualities, individuals may experience moodiness or emotional vulnerability under Rahu in Cancer. They are sensitive to environmental changes and interpersonal dynamics, requiring a stable and supportive environment to maintain emotional well-being. Challenges related to setting emotional boundaries may arise. The native may struggle with over-attachment to family members or difficulty asserting their own needs amidst caregiving responsibilities. Learning to balance emotional closeness with healthy boundaries becomes crucial for personal growth and harmony.

5. Rahu in Leo

Rahu in Leo enhances the native's inherent qualities associated with creativity, leadership, and the pursuit of recognition. Leo, governed by the Sun, signifies a natural inclination towards authority and creativity. With Rahu in Leo, these traits are intensified, leading to an ambitious drive for fame and admiration. Natives tend to excel in artistic fields such as drama, entertainment, or speculative ventures, leveraging their creative expression and enjoying the limelight.

Their charismatic persona draws others effortlessly, often using their charm in leadership roles or artistic endeavours. However, there's a notable tendency towards self-centeredness and egoism, where personal ambitions may overshadow the needs of others, potentially causing conflicts.

Rahu's influence in Leo also manifests in dramatic life events, triggering sudden changes related to ego, recognition, or creative pursuits. These events can thrust the natives into public attention, challenging their sense of identity and self-worth. Consequently, they may navigate fluctuations in self-image, seeking validation and approval to bolster their confidence.

This placement often sparks a desire for power and authority, compelling them to aspire to prominent positions in society where they can assert their influence. Despite the challenges, Rahu in Leo provides an opportunity for dynamic growth through creative expression and leadership, albeit with the need to balance ego-driven ambitions with humility and consideration for others.

6. Rahu in Virgo

Rahu in Virgo influences individuals with a unique combination of traits centred around meticulousness, analytical prowess, service orientation, and a quest for perfection. Virgo, governed by Mercury, emphasises analytical thinking, attention to detail, and practicality. When Rahu is in Virgo, these qualities are intensified, making the native exceptionally analytical, methodical, and detail-oriented. They excel in tasks requiring precision, organisation, and problem-solving skills, often thriving in roles that demand meticulous attention.

Individuals with Rahu in Virgo often feel a strong inclination towards service-oriented professions. They derive fulfilment from assisting others through practical aid, guidance, or healing practices. This placement instils a sense of duty and responsibility towards improving the lives of those around them, driven by a desire to contribute meaningfully. Virgo's association with perfectionism and high standards is amplified with Rahu in this sign. The natives may strive for excellence in their work and daily routines, setting rigorous expectations for themselves and others. However, this pursuit of perfection can lead to self-criticism and dissatisfaction if their exacting standards are not met.

Health and wellness become significant areas of focus with Rahu in Virgo. The native develops a heightened awareness of physical well-being and may adopt health-conscious habits such as diet, nutrition, and fitness regimes. They are often drawn to holistic healing methods and may explore alternative therapies to maintain optimal health. Practical intelligence and problem-solving abilities are enhanced with Rahu in Virgo. The native exhibits adeptness in analysing situations, identifying solutions, and implementing efficient strategies. They excel in professions that demand technical expertise, research, or systematic approaches, demonstrating a knack for navigating complex challenges.

Despite their analytical strengths, individuals with Rahu in Virgo may encounter challenges with flexibility and adaptability. They may resist change and become overly fixated on routines and procedures, which can hinder their ability to innovate or embrace new opportunities for growth. Virgo's association with esoteric knowledge and hidden wisdom also intrigues those with Rahu in this sign – the native may develop a fascination with occult sciences, astrology, metaphysics, or alternative healing modalities.

7. Rahu in Libra

Rahu in Libra influences individuals with a complex blend of characteristics revolving around relationships, harmony, justice, and a quest for balance. Governed by Venus, Libra symbolizes partnerships, aesthetic appreciation, and a pursuit of fairness. When Rahu occupies this sign, it intensifies these qualities. Firstly, individuals with Rahu in Libra tend to have a pronounced focus on relationships and interpersonal dynamics. They prioritise social connections and partnerships, seeking harmony and mutual understanding in their interactions. This placement enhances their diplomatic skills, enabling them to navigate conflicts and maintain peace effectively. They value fairness, justice, and mutual respect, often striving to foster harmonious relationships both personally and professionally.

From the lens of creativity, Rahu in Libra amplifies artistic talents and aesthetic sensibilities. The native may possess a heightened appreciation for beauty and artistic expression, excelling in fields such as music, visual arts, design, or fashion. They are drawn to environments and experiences that enhance their aesthetic surroundings, showing a preference for luxury, fine things, and elegant lifestyles.

Seeking balance and equilibrium is a central theme for those with Rahu in Libra. They aim to harmonise various aspects of life, including relationships, career pursuits, and personal growth. Despite this inclination towards balance, they may struggle with indecision and wavering choices, finding it challenging to make definitive decisions amidst conflicting options. Legal and social justice issues also hold significant interest for individuals with Rahu in Libra. They may be drawn to professions or activities that involve advocacy, mediation, or legal matters, driven by a keen awareness of ethical principles and a commitment to upholding moral standards. Their sense of justice aligns with their desire to create fair and equitable outcomes in society.

Overall, Rahu's placement in Libra underscores a life path characterised by a deep engagement with relationships, a pursuit of aesthetic and creative fulfilment, a quest for balance and harmony, challenges with decision-making, and a strong interest in legal and social justice issues.

8. Rahu in Scorpio

Rahu's placement in Scorpio gives rise to traits focused on intensity, transformation, secrecy, and the exploration of hidden truths. Scorpio, governed by Mars, embodies deep emotions, passion, and a relentless quest for profound experiences. When Rahu occupies Scorpio, these intrinsic qualities are heightened, shaping the native's personality and life path.

Firstly, individuals with Rahu in Scorpio experience emotions with unparalleled intensity. They navigate life driven by deep desires and passions, constantly seeking transformative experiences that profoundly impact their inner selves. This placement amplifies their emotional complexity, enabling them to navigate life's highs and lows with heightened sensitivity and resilience.

Furthermore, Scorpio's association with the occult, mysteries, and hidden knowledge finds a natural resonance with Rahu's influence. Those with this placement are often drawn to explore esoteric subjects, psychic phenomena, and metaphysical realms. They possess an innate curiosity and intuitive abilities that propel them towards uncovering deeper truths beyond the ordinary, delving into realms others may find mysterious or enigmatic.

Rahu in Scorpio also enhances the native's desire for power, control, and influence. They are naturally attracted to situations where they can assert authority or manipulate circumstances to achieve their goals. This inclination can lead to a strong need for dominance, occasionally manifesting as power struggles in both personal relationships and professional endeavours.

In matters of sexuality and intimacy, Scorpio's governance over deep emotional bonds is intensified by Rahu's presence. Natives with this placement exude a magnetic allure, drawing others into relationships marked by profound psychological depth and transformative experiences. Their sexual energy is potent and intertwined with their quest for intimate connections that are both passionate and emotionally resonant.

The investigative and research-oriented nature inherent to Scorpio is sharpened by Rahu's influence, endowing these individuals with a keen intellect and an innate talent for uncovering hidden truths. They excel in professions requiring deep analysis, such as detective work, research, or psychology, where their penetrating insights prove invaluable in unravelling complex issues.

Despite their profound connections, individuals with Rahu in Scorpio may grapple with trust issues and a fear of betrayal. They can be secretive or guarded about their emotions and intentions, often testing the loyalty of others before fully opening up emotionally. This cautious approach stems from a deep-seated need to protect themselves amidst the intensity of their emotional entanglements.

Finally, Scorpio's symbolism of transformation, regeneration, and rebirth is amplified by Rahu's presence. Natives undergo significant personal growth through intense life experiences, crises, or upheavals that catalyse inner transformations. These events ultimately lead to profound spiritual evolution and empowerment, guiding them towards a deeper understanding of themselves and their place in the world.

9. Rahu in Sagittarius

When Rahu is placed in Sagittarius, it bestows characteristics centred around exploration, knowledge-seeking, expansion, and philosophical pursuits. Sagittarius, ruled by Jupiter, embodies themes of expansion, higher learning, and philosophical exploration, which are amplified by Rahu's influence. Firstly, individuals with Rahu in Sagittarius possess a deep-seated quest for knowledge and exploration. They are inherently curious, adventurous, and eager to expand their horizons by exploring new ideas, cultures, and belief systems. This placement encourages a profound interest in spiritual or philosophical truths that broaden their understanding of the world and their place within it.

Furthermore, Rahu in Sagittarius instils a sense of restlessness and wanderlust in the native. They are drawn to both physical and mental travel, seeking experiences that challenge their beliefs and expand their perspective. This adventurous spirit fuels their desire to break free from limitations and embrace new opportunities for growth and discovery.

Philosophical and spiritual growth are also prominent themes for those with Rahu in Sagittarius. They are inclined to delve into spiritual teachings, philosophical inquiries, or religious studies, seeking higher knowledge and wisdom that enrich their spiritual consciousness. This placement encourages a lifelong journey of exploring various belief systems and integrating profound insights into their worldview.

Optimism, enthusiasm, and a positive outlook on life characterize individuals with Rahu in Sagittarius. They approach challenges with confidence, viewing obstacles as opportunities for growth and learning. This resilient spirit and sense of purpose propel them forward in pursuing their ideals and aspirations with unwavering determination.

Ethical and moral principles hold significant importance for natives with Rahu in Sagittarius. They uphold strong convictions about justice, fairness, and truth, actively engaging in activities that promote social justice or humanitarian causes aligned with their beliefs. Their actions are guided by a deep sense of ethics, striving to make a positive impact on society.

Sagittarius symbolizes freedom and independence, qualities that are amplified by Rahu's influence. Natives with this placement value personal autonomy and freedom of thought, resisting constraints or limitations that hinder their growth or limit their exploration of new possibilities. They embrace opportunities that allow them to express their individuality and pursue their passions without inhibition.

Despite their expansive nature, individuals with Rahu in Sagittarius may encounter challenges with dogmatism or overzealous beliefs. They may become overly idealistic in their pursuit of truth, sometimes disregarding practical considerations or opposing viewpoints in their quest to uphold their convictions. Balancing their expansive worldview with practicality and openness to diverse perspectives is crucial for their personal and intellectual growth.

In essence, Rahu in Sagittarius shapes individuals who are seekers of truth and wisdom, driven by a profound curiosity about the world and a relentless pursuit of personal and spiritual growth.

10. Rahu in Capricorn

When Rahu is placed in Capricorn, it bestows traits centred around ambition, discipline, responsibility, and the pursuit of worldly success. Capricorn, governed by Saturn, signifies hard work, practicality, and perseverance, and these qualities are intensified by Rahu's influence.

Individuals with Rahu in Capricorn are characterised by their strong ambition and relentless drive for success in their careers and public life. They set high aspirations and are willing to exert considerable effort to achieve them. This placement augments their determination, leadership abilities, and adeptness in navigating complex organisational structures.

Capricorn's association with discipline and perseverance is further fortified by Rahu. Natives with this placement are known for their ability to withstand challenges, overcome obstacles, and remain steadfast in pursuit of long-term objectives. They excel in professions that demand systematic planning, hard work, and strategic foresight.

Practicality and realism define the approach of those with Rahu in Capricorn. They are grounded in practical considerations and prefer tangible outcomes over speculative ventures. Decision-making is based on calculated risks, and they exhibit proficiency in resource management, ensuring efficiency and sustainability in their endeavours. Authority and leadership come naturally to individuals with Rahu in Capricorn. They are inclined to assume roles where they can exert control and influence, leveraging their pragmatic approach and strong organisational skills. Their ability to command respect and manage responsibilities effectively contributes to their success in managerial positions.

Financial security and stability are paramount concerns for those with Rahu in Capricorn. They possess a keen acumen for financial planning, investment strategies, and wealth accumulation, prioritising long-term financial goals to secure their future. This placement underscores their commitment to fiscal prudence and achieving economic independence. Capricorn's reverence for tradition, structure, and adherence to established norms is reinforced by Rahu. Natives often exhibit a strong sense of duty and responsibility towards family, community, or societal expectations. They strive to uphold traditional values while navigating the complexities of modern life, seeking to maintain stability and respect for cultural heritage.

Despite their outward success, individuals with Rahu in Capricorn may encounter challenges with emotional expression. They tend to prioritise professional responsibilities over personal relationships, and they may find it difficult to open up emotionally. Balancing their career ambitions with emotional fulfilment becomes a central theme, requiring introspection and conscious effort to achieve harmony in both domains.

11. Rahu in Aquarius

Rahu's placement in Aquarius is one of the best placements as it co-rules Aquarius with Saturn. It bestows the native with traits that revolve around innovation, independence, humanitarianism, and unconventional thinking. Aquarius symbolizes intellectual prowess, humanitarian ideals, and a forward-thinking approach to life.

Individuals with Rahu in Aquarius are characterised by their innovative and progressive thinking. They possess a sharp intellect and an innate curiosity that drives them to explore new ideas, technologies, and unconventional concepts. This placement fosters a sense of originality and a pioneering spirit, often leading them to challenge and break free from traditional norms in pursuit of cutting-edge innovations. Aquarius symbolizes independence and individuality, qualities that are intensified by Rahu's influence. Those with this placement value personal freedom and autonomy, often resisting conformity and societal expectations. They exhibit a strong sense of self-expression and a willingness to challenge the status quo, advocating for personal liberties and unconventional approaches to life's challenges.

Rahu in Aquarius amplifies the native's commitment to humanitarian causes and social justice. They possess a deep-seated concern for the welfare of society, striving to promote equality, freedom, and progressive reforms. This placement frequently motivates them to engage in activism, advocacy work, or community service aimed at effecting positive societal change and uplifting marginalized groups. Aquarius governs intellectual pursuits and scientific exploration, traits that are heightened by Rahu's presence. Individuals with this placement often excel in fields such as science, technology, astrology, or metaphysics. They are adept at analytical thinking, problem-solving, and exploring abstract concepts that contribute to their intellectual growth and innovative contributions to society.

Those with Rahu in Aquarius are drawn to unconventional dynamics and intellectual connections. They value partnerships that foster independence and allow them to pursue shared interests freely. This placement encourages non-traditional relationship structures that prioritise mutual respect and intellectual compatibility over conventional romantic norms. Rahu in Aquarius manifests as a rebellious spirit against authority and restrictive norms. The native may challenge established institutions, ideologies, or conventions that they perceive as outdated or limiting. This placement fosters a desire to revolutionise existing systems and promote progressive change in society, often through unconventional means.

Aquarius is associated with objectivity and a detached perspective, qualities that are emphasised by Rahu in this sign. Natives approach life's challenges with rationality and a focus on finding solutions that benefit the greater good rather than personal gain. They strive to maintain emotional detachment while pursuing their intellectual and humanitarian goals, prioritising impartiality and fairness in their decision-making processes.

12. Rahu in Pisces

Rahu's placement in Pisces manifests as a profound influence shaping individuals with a blend of characteristics deeply rooted in spirituality, imagination, sensitivity, and a propensity for escapism. Pisces, ruled traditionally by Jupiter symbolizes the spiritual realms, isolated spaces, sleep, feet, mysticism, and transcendental experiences. When

Rahu, known for amplification and craving, occupies Pisces, these qualities are magnified, defining both the inner essence and outward expression of the native.

Those with Rahu in Pisces are naturally inclined towards spiritual and mystical pursuits. They possess an acute sensitivity to metaphysical realms, often engaging in meditation, spiritual practices, or philosophical studies that expand their connection with higher consciousness and universal truths. Their rich imagination and creative potential find profound expression in art, music, poetry, and other forms of creative endeavour, serving as channels for their deep emotional and spiritual insights.

Empathy and compassion are hallmarks of individuals with Rahu in Pisces. They possess an innate ability to resonate with the pain and suffering of others, leading them to actively engage in acts of kindness, charity, or humanitarian efforts aimed at alleviating human suffering. Their compassion extends beyond personal boundaries, driven by a deep emotional connection to humanity and a sincere desire to contribute positively to society.

The heightened sensitivity to their surroundings is a significant trait of those with Rahu in Pisces. They absorb energies and emotions from their environment, experiencing profound emotional fluctuations influenced by the moods and energies of others. This heightened sensitivity necessitates periods of solitude or retreat to recharge their emotional and spiritual energies, maintaining inner equilibrium amidst external influences.

Despite their spiritual depth, individuals with Rahu in Pisces may grapple with tendencies towards escapism or indulgence in fantasy realms. They may seek solace from harsh realities through daydreaming, creative pursuits, or temporary escapes that provide respite from emotional overwhelm. Balancing their spiritual aspirations with grounded, practical realities becomes an ongoing challenge in their quest for emotional and spiritual fulfilment.

Pisces' fluid boundaries and porous sense of self are further accentuated by Rahu's influence, making individuals susceptible to emotional blending and challenges in maintaining clear boundaries in relationships. This vulnerability can leave them open to manipulation or deception if they are not vigilant in safeguarding their emotional and spiritual integrity.

The journey of healing and redemption is central to those with Rahu in Pisces. They undergo profound spiritual growth through experiences of suffering, sacrifice, or selfless service, leading to inner purification, enlightenment, and a deeper connection with their higher self and spiritual truths. These transformative journeys guide them towards spiritual fulfilment, transcendence, and a deeper understanding of their place in the cosmos.

Chapter 9

The Impact of Ketu in Different Zodiac Signs

Note: *Assessing the overall impact of a planet in any sign requires joint and thorough consideration of multiple factors. Any planet placed in a sign can't be judged for its full implications, in isolation – aspects, conjunctions, ascendant lord (in terms of strength and association), corresponding sign lord (in terms of strength, weakness and support it's providing and nakshatra lord (in terms of strength, weakness and support it's providing) considerably modify the results of a planet in any house.*

Planetary Aspects, Houses, Signs and Their Influence

When examining the impact of Ketu in any sign, it's of utmost importance to consider the aspects from both temporal and natural benefic and malefic planets. Benefic influences, such as aspects or conjunction with *trikona* house lords (1,5,9) or with natural benefics like Jupiter or Venus, can largely mitigate Ketu's negative results, magnifying positive results. On the contrary, further malefic influences like aspects or conjunction with *dushthana* house lords (6,8,12) or with natural malefic or cruel planets like Saturn or Mars can markedly exacerbate Ketu's disruptive tendencies in a particular sign, leading to more daunting challenges.

If natural malefic or cruel planets like Saturn or Mars become *yogakaraka* in a chart, their association with Ketu won't necessarily cause problems of a grave nature which potentially would be the case if they lord *dushthana* houses.

Irrespective of all other factors, owing to the principle that malefic planets give good results in *upachaya* houses—the overall output of which is further amplified or weakened by benefic or malefic aspects, respectively, Ketu does well in the 3rd, 6th, and 11th house. Besides, Ketu is the natural significator of the 5th, 8th and 12th house, thus, producing relatively good results therein. Furthermore, Ketu is considered to be exalted in Scorpio and finds the environment of Jupiterian signs conducive, and thereby performs well in Sagittarius and Pisces. Kindly note that these principles apply consistently across all signs and are imperative for understanding the overall effects and results of Ketu in any particular sign.

1. Ketu in Aries

When Ketu is positioned in Aries, it endows the individual with a pioneering spirit and a robust sense of independence. This placement can lead to a fearless attitude and a profound desire to carve out a unique path in life. The combination of Aries, ruled by Mars, with the spiritual and otherworldly influence of Ketu can push the native toward spiritual pursuits with great vigour, often resulting in sudden spiritual awakenings and transformative experiences.

The behavioural traits associated with Ketu in Aries may include impulsiveness and aggression. This placement can sometimes lead to a quick temper and a tendency to act before thinking. While challenges related to anger and impatience may arise, the native also possesses a unique courage and the ability to take risks that others might avoid. With regard to health, Ketu in Aries might impact the native's physical well-being, leading to issues related to the head or face, given that Aries rules the head and Ketu signifies cuts, there might also be a tendency towards accidents or injuries due to the impulsive nature influenced by Ketu.

In terms of career and ambition, this placement can create a strong drive for success in the chosen field, often pushing the native to take unconventional routes to achieve their goals. There is a deep desire to lead and innovate, driven by the restless energy of Ketu in Aries. This restless mind constantly seeks new challenges and experiences, leading to a dynamic life but also causing instability if not properly channelled. Relationships might be marked by intensity and passion, with challenges in maintaining long-term harmony due to the aggressive and independent streak influenced by Aries, Ketu is the significator of breaks as well, which could lead to disruptions or discontinuity in relationships.

Ketu in Aries also brings significant karmic implications, often related to lessons about ego, courage, and leadership. The native might face situations that test their patience and humility, pushing them toward spiritual growth and self-realization. There might be a tendency towards renunciation or a strong disinterest in material pursuits, especially if other spiritual indicators are strong in the chart.

In essence, Ketu in Aries combines the fiery, assertive energy of Aries with the mystical, detached nature of Ketu. This placement is marked by a strong drive for independence, a fearless approach to life, and significant potential for spiritual growth. However, it also brings challenges related to impulsiveness, aggression, and restlessness.

2. Ketu in Taurus

Ketu, being a planet of detachment and spiritual pursuit, when placed in Taurus influences the native to seek a balance between material and spiritual realms. Taurus, ruled by Venus, is associated with stability, wealth, and sensual pleasures. This often leads to an unconventional approach to wealth and comfort, with a tendency to find deeper meanings beyond material possessions.

When Ketu is positioned in Taurus, it can cause the native to appear aloof or indifferent towards material gains, despite having an innate understanding of wealth and resources. There might be a natural inclination towards minimalism and simplicity, shunning excessive indulgence. This placement can foster a profound appreciation for nature and beauty without attachment.

The influence of Ketu in Taurus can also impact the native's physical health, particularly in areas related to the throat, neck, and voice, as Taurus rules these areas. There might be susceptibility to ailments involving the thyroid gland or vocal cords. However, this placement can also endow the native with a distinct, melodious voice if other chart factors are favourable.

In terms of career and ambition, Ketu in Taurus can lead to an unconventional career path, often in fields that blend material and spiritual pursuits. The native might excel in professions related to arts, music, healing, or environmental conservation. There might be a strong desire to achieve financial stability while maintaining ethical and spiritual values. This placement often encourages a career that allows for personal growth and societal contribution.

Mentally, a native with Ketu in Taurus can experience an inner conflict between the desire for material security and a quest for spiritual liberation. This can lead to periods of introspection and self-discovery. The native might experience moments of disinterest in worldly affairs, preferring solitude and contemplation. There is potential for significant spiritual growth, especially if the native can balance their material desires with spiritual aspirations.

In relationships, Ketu in Taurus can bring a sense of detachment and independence. The native might value personal space and freedom, sometimes leading to challenges in forming deep emotional bonds. However, this placement can also foster a relationship dynamic based on mutual respect and understanding, where both partners appreciate each other's individuality.

Ketu in Taurus brings karmic lessons related to the proper use of wealth and resources. The native might face situations that challenge their attachment to material possessions, pushing them towards a more balanced and enlightened perspective on wealth. There is potential for renunciation or a shift towards a simpler, more meaningful lifestyle, especially during pivotal transits and major or sub-periods.

In a nutshell, Ketu in Taurus combines the materialistic and stable energy of Taurus with the detached, spiritual nature of Ketu. This placement encourages a balance between enjoying material comforts and pursuing spiritual growth. The native may experience an unconventional approach to wealth, a preference for simplicity, and a deep appreciation for nature.

3. Ketu in Gemini

When Ketu occupied Mercury-ruled Gemini, it blends intellectual curiosity and spiritual detachment. Gemini is a sign associated with communication, intellect, and adaptability. When Ketu, a planet symbolizing detachment and spiritual pursuit, is placed in Gemini, it influences the native to seek knowledge and truth beyond the mundane. This combination often heightens intuition and fosters an unconventional approach to learning and communication.

Individuals with Ketu in Gemini tend to exhibit an unpredictable and restless nature, driven by a strong desire to explore various fields of knowledge. This can lead to a jack-of-all-trades mentality, where the individual has a unique perspective on communication, sometimes appearing eccentric or detached. This placement may also cultivate an interest in occult sciences, mysticism, and metaphysical subjects.

From a health perspective, Ketu in Gemini can impact physical well-being, particularly concerning the respiratory system, arms, and hands, as Gemini governs these areas. There may be susceptibility to ailments involving the lungs or nervous system. However, if other chart factors are favourable, this placement can also bestow quick reflexes and dexterity.

In terms of career and ambition, Ketu in Gemini often leads to unconventional career paths in fields requiring intellectual agility and adaptability. Natives might excel in professions related to writing, teaching, technology, or research. There is a strong desire to innovate and explore new ideas, frequently resulting in breakthroughs. This placement encourages careers that allow for intellectual freedom and creative expression.

Mentally, a native with Ketu in Gemini is likely to be in a constant search for deeper meanings and truths, experiencing periods of introspection and self-discovery that lead to profound insights. Mental restlessness might be prevalent, with a preference for solitude and contemplation to recharge. Balancing intellectual pursuits with spiritual aspirations can lead to significant spiritual growth.

In relationships, Ketu in Gemini can bring a sense of detachment and independence. The native might prioritise intellectual compatibility and stimulating conversations, which can sometimes challenge the formation of deep emotional bonds. However, this placement can also create a relationship dynamic based on mutual respect and understanding, where both partners appreciate each other's individuality and intellect.

Ketu in Gemini often brings karmic lessons related to the use of intellect and communication. Natives might face situations challenging their perception and understanding, pushing them towards a more enlightened perspective on knowledge and truth. There is potential for renunciation or a shift towards a simpler, more meaningful lifestyle, particularly during key transits and periods.

Overall, Ketu in Gemini combines the intellectual and communicative energy of Gemini with Ketu's detached, spiritual nature. This placement encourages balancing the exploration of knowledge with spiritual growth. The native may experience an unconventional approach to learning, a preference for simplicity, and a deep appreciation for intellectual pursuits.

4. Ketu in Cancer

Ketu in Cancer is a significant placement in Vedic astrology, bringing together emotional sensitivity and spiritual detachment. Cancer, ruled by the Moon, governs emotions, nurturing, and domestic life, while Ketu represents detachment and spiritual pursuits. This combination influences individuals to seek a deeper understanding of emotional and familial connections beyond their surface-level manifestations, often leading to a profound sense of introspection and a quest for emotional and spiritual balance.

Natives with Ketu in Cancer tend to have a complex emotional composition. They may appear detached or indifferent on the surface but harbour deep, intense feelings internally. This internal emotional struggle can enhance their intuition and provide an uncanny ability to understand the emotional undercurrents around them. However, this placement can also cause mood swings and emotional instability if not balanced properly.

Health-wise, Ketu in Cancer can affect the chest, lungs, and digestive system, as Cancer rules these areas. There may be a tendency towards ailments involving the stomach, breast, or respiratory system. On the positive side, this placement can endow the native with strong nurturing instincts and a natural ability to heal others emotionally.

In terms of career and ambition, Ketu in Cancer often leads to an unconventional approach to work and professional life. Natives might excel in fields related to healing, counselling, psychology, or any profession that requires empathy and understanding of human emotions. They often seek work environments that provide emotional satisfaction and align with their spiritual values, encouraging a career path that allows for emotional expression and nurturing others.

Mentally, individuals with Ketu in Cancer are often in a constant search for emotional security and inner peace. Periods of introspection and self-discovery frequently lead to profound insights into their own emotional needs and those of others. These natives may experience moments of emotional detachment, preferring solitude and contemplation to recharge. There is significant potential for spiritual growth, especially if they can balance their emotional needs with their spiritual aspirations.

In relationships, Ketu in Cancer can bring a sense of emotional independence and detachment. Natives might value emotional space and freedom, which can sometimes lead to challenges in forming deep, lasting emotional bonds. However, this placement can also foster a relationship dynamic based on mutual emotional support and understanding, where both partners appreciate each other's need for emotional independence.

Ketu in Cancer often brings karmic lessons related to emotions and familial connections. Natives might face situations that challenge their emotional attachments, pushing them towards a more balanced and enlightened perspective on relationships and family life. There is potential for renunciation or a shift towards a simpler, more emotionally fulfilling lifestyle, especially during crucial transits and periods.

In essence, Ketu in Cancer combines the emotional and nurturing energy of Cancer with the detached, spiritual nature of Ketu. This placement encourages a balance between seeking emotional security and pursuing spiritual growth. Natives may experience an unconventional approach to emotions and family life, a preference for simplicity, and a deep appreciation for emotional and spiritual connections.

5. Ketu in Leo

When Ketu occupies Leo, we get a blend of creative expression and spiritual detachment. Leo, ruled by the Sun, is associated with leadership, creativity, and self-expression, while Ketu symbolizes detachment, spirituality, and past-life skills or influences.

When Ketu is positioned in Leo, it imparts a unique blend of charisma and humility. Leo is a sign that thrives on recognition, authority, and self-expression, whereas Ketu's energy is more introverted, emphasising spiritual growth and the release from worldly attachments. This juxtaposition creates a dynamic where the native possesses natural leadership qualities and creative talents but is often uninterested in the limelight or external validation. They may prefer working behind the scenes or pursuing their passions quietly, exhibiting a distinctive personal style and a strong sense of individuality. A non-conformist streak may lead them to express themselves in unconventional or ahead-of-their-time ways, fostering a deep-seated need to understand their true self and embarking on a journey of self-discovery and spiritual exploration. Despite their innate talents and potential for leadership, these individuals may shun traditional paths to success, seeking instead to define success on their own terms.

Health-wise, Ketu in Leo can affect the heart and spine, as Leo rules these areas. There might be a susceptibility to issues involving the cardiovascular system or back problems. However, the native might also possess a robust constitution and a resilient nature if other chart factors are favourable. Individuals with this placement need to maintain a healthy lifestyle and manage stress effectively to prevent health issues.

In terms of career and ambition, Ketu in Leo often leads to an unconventional approach to professional life. Natives might excel in creative fields such as art, music, drama, or any profession that allows for self-expression. They may also be drawn to spiritual or humanitarian work, where they can make a meaningful impact without seeking personal glory. This placement encourages a career path that aligns with their inner values and desire for personal fulfilment rather than external recognition. Mentally, individuals with Ketu in Leo may experience a constant search for inner truth and a higher purpose. They are often introspective and reflective, seeking to understand their place in the world and the larger spiritual context. This introspection can lead to significant personal growth and enlightenment, especially if they can balance their creative desires with their spiritual aspirations.

In relationships, Ketu in Leo can bring a sense of independence and detachment. Natives might value their personal freedom and may have difficulty forming deep, lasting emotional bonds. However, this placement can also create a relationship dynamic based on mutual respect and understanding, where both partners appreciate each other's individuality and need for personal space. There may be challenges in traditional relationship structures, prompting the native to seek more unconventional or spiritually-oriented partnerships. Ketu in Leo often brings karmic lessons related to ego, creativity, and personal power. Natives might face situations that challenge their sense of self and push them towards a more balanced and enlightened perspective on self-expression and leadership. There is potential for renunciation of ego-driven pursuits and a shift towards a life centred on spiritual and creative fulfilment, especially during key transits and periods.

Overall, Ketu in Leo combines the creative and authoritative energy of Leo with the detached, spiritual nature of Ketu. This placement encourages a balance between pursuing personal expression and seeking spiritual growth. Natives may experience an unconventional approach to creativity and leadership, a preference for humility and simplicity, and a deep appreciation for spiritual and personal growth.

6. Ketu in Virgo

When Ketu occupies Virgo, it creates a blend of analytical acumen and spiritual detachment. Virgo, ruled by Mercury, is associated with intellect, precision, and service, while Ketu represents detachment, spirituality, and past-life influences. It results in a distinctive mix of analytical prowess and a quest for spiritual insight. Virgo's emphasis on detail, logic, and practicality contrasts with Ketu's focus on the mystical and the unseen. This dynamic can lead to individuals who are exceptionally meticulous and methodical, yet who also seek deeper, often spiritual, meanings behind everyday occurrences. They might find themselves drawn to exploring the hidden aspects of life, such as the occult, metaphysics, or esoteric philosophies, blending these interests with their natural analytical skills.

Individuals with Ketu in Virgo often possess a strong sense of service and a desire to help others, albeit in unconventional ways. They may approach problem-solving and caregiving with a unique perspective, often integrating intuitive insights with practical methods. This placement fosters a profound sense of duty and responsibility, but it also encourages the native to transcend mundane concerns and focus on higher, spiritual goals. Despite their analytical nature, they might occasionally find themselves at odds with rigid structures, preferring to follow their inner guidance over external rules and conventions.

Health-wise, Ketu in Virgo can affect the digestive and nervous systems, as Virgo rules these areas.

There might be a tendency towards digestive issues, anxiety, or stress-related ailments. However, this placement can also bestow a keen understanding of health and wellness, prompting individuals to seek natural or alternative healing methods. Maintaining a balanced lifestyle and managing stress effectively is crucial for those with this placement to avoid health complications.

In terms of career and ambition, Ketu in Virgo often leads to an unconventional approach to work and professional life. Natives might excel in fields that require precision and analytical thinking, such as research, medicine, writing, or technology. They may also be drawn to spiritual or healing professions, where they can combine their analytical skills with their spiritual inclinations. This placement encourages a career path that allows for both intellectual stimulation and spiritual growth, often leading to innovative contributions in their chosen field.

Mentally, individuals with Ketu in Virgo may experience a constant search for perfection and a deeper understanding of life's complexities. They are often introspective and reflective, seeking to reconcile their need for order and precision with the more chaotic, spiritual aspects of existence. This introspection can lead to significant personal growth and enlightenment, especially if they can balance their intellectual pursuits with their spiritual aspirations.

In relationships, Ketu in Virgo can bring a sense of detachment and independence. Natives might value intellectual compatibility and mutual respect, sometimes leading to challenges in forming deep, emotional bonds. However, this placement can also foster relationships based on shared values and goals, where both partners appreciate each other's need for personal space and intellectual freedom. There may be a focus on practical and supportive relationships rather than overly emotional or dramatic ones.

Ketu in Virgo often brings karmic lessons related to service, health, and intellectual pursuits. Natives might face situations that challenge their need for perfection and push them towards a more balanced and holistic perspective on life. There is potential for renunciation of overly analytical or critical tendencies and a shift towards a more compassionate and understanding approach to themselves and others, especially during key transits and periods.

Overall, Ketu in Virgo combines the analytical and practical energy of Virgo with the detached, spiritual nature of Ketu. This placement encourages a balance between intellectual rigour and spiritual exploration. Natives may experience an unconventional approach to service and healing, a preference for simplicity and practicality, and a deep appreciation for both intellectual and spiritual growth.

7. Ketu in Libra

When Ketu is in Libra, it creates a blend of social dynamics and spiritual detachment. Libra, ruled by Venus, is associated with balance, relationships, and harmony, while Ketu represents detachment, spirituality, and past-life influences – Libra's emphasis on relationships, aesthetics, and balance contrasts with Ketu's focus on the mystical and the unseen. This dynamic can lead to individuals who are adept at navigating social situations and building harmonious relationships, yet who also seek deeper, often spiritual, meanings behind these interactions. They might find themselves drawn to exploring the hidden aspects of relationships and social structures, blending these interests with their natural charm and diplomacy.

Individuals with Ketu in Libra often harbour a strong sense of fairness and a desire to maintain harmony in their surroundings, albeit in unconventional ways. They may approach relationships and social interactions with a unique perspective, often integrating intuitive insights with a desire for balance. This placement fosters a profound sense of justice and equity, but it also encourages the native to transcend mundane social concerns and focus on higher, spiritual goals. Despite their social nature, they might occasionally find themselves at odds with superficial social norms, preferring to follow their inner guidance over external expectations.

Health-wise, Ketu in Libra can affect the kidneys, lower back, and skin, as Libra rules these areas. There might be a tendency towards issues involving these parts of the body, as well as stress-related ailments due to their sensitivity to social disharmony. However, this placement can also bestow a keen understanding of health and wellness, prompting individuals to seek natural or alternative healing methods. Maintaining a balanced lifestyle and managing stress effectively is crucial for those with this placement to avoid health complications.

In terms of career and ambition, Natives with Ketu might excel in fields that require negotiation, mediation, or artistic expression, such as law, diplomacy, art, or design. They may also be drawn to spiritual or humanitarian work, where they can combine their social skills with their spiritual inclinations. This placement encourages a career path that allows for both social engagement and spiritual growth, often leading to innovative contributions in their chosen field.

Mentally, individuals with Ketu in Libra may experience a constant search for balance and a deeper understanding of relationships and social dynamics. They are often introspective and reflective, seeking to reconcile their need for harmony with the more chaotic, spiritual aspects of existence. This introspection can lead to significant personal growth and enlightenment, especially if they can balance their social pursuits with their spiritual aspirations.

In relationships, Ketu in Libra can bring a sense of detachment and independence. Natives might value intellectual and emotional compatibility, sometimes leading to challenges in forming deep, lasting emotional bonds. However, this placement can also foster relationships based on mutual respect and understanding, where both partners appreciate each other's need for personal space and balance. There may be a focus on practical and supportive relationships rather than overly emotional or dramatic ones.

Ketu in Libra often brings karmic lessons related to relationships, social harmony, and aesthetic appreciation. Natives might face situations that challenge their social attachments and push them towards a more balanced and enlightened perspective on relationships and social interactions. There is potential for renunciation of superficial social ties and a shift towards a life centred on spiritual and aesthetic fulfilment, especially during key transits and periods.

8. Ketu in Scorpio

Ketu in Scorpio intertwines the intense and transformative qualities of Scorpio with the spiritual and detached nature of Ketu. Scorpio, ruled by Mars and associated with mystery, transformation, and deep emotional experiences, finds a unique expression through Ketu, which represents spirituality, detachment, and karmic influences.

When Ketu is positioned in Scorpio, it creates a compelling blend of intensity and spiritual insight. Scorpio's depth and association with transformation align well with Ketu's inclination toward uncovering hidden truths and spiritual evolution. This placement often makes the native deeply introspective and driven to understand the mysteries of life and the underlying causes of events and behaviours. They might be drawn to esoteric studies, occult sciences, and transformative practices such as meditation and yoga.

Natives with Ketu in Scorpio often exhibit a complex emotional nature. They might appear secretive or enigmatic, with a strong ability to perceive the hidden motives and emotions of others. This placement fosters a heightened intuition and psychic sensitivity, making the native adept at understanding and navigating the deeper layers of emotional and psychological realms. However, this intensity can also lead to emotional turbulence, and the native may experience periods of profound transformation and upheaval.

Health-wise, Ketu in Scorpio can impact the reproductive organs, excretory system, and immune system, as Scorpio rules these areas. There might be a tendency towards ailments involving the reproductive organs, chronic illnesses, or issues related to detoxification and elimination processes. Despite these challenges, this placement can also bestow the native with a strong ability to heal and regenerate, especially when they channel their energies into transformative healing practices.

In terms of career and ambition, Ketu in Scorpio often leads to an unconventional approach to professional life. Natives might excel in fields that require investigation, research, and transformation, such as psychology, medicine, forensics, and occult sciences. They may also be drawn to careers involving crisis management, healing, and therapy. This placement encourages a career path that allows for deep exploration and transformation, aligning with their innate desire to uncover hidden truths and effect profound change.

Mentally, individuals with Ketu in Scorpio are marked by a constant search for deeper meaning and understanding. They are often introspective and reflective, seeking to uncover the roots of their own and others' motivations and behaviours. This introspection can lead to significant personal growth and enlightenment, particularly if they balance their intense emotional and psychological explorations with spiritual practices that promote detachment and inner peace.

In relationships, Ketu in Scorpio can bring a sense of intensity and depth, coupled with a need for emotional independence. Natives might experience powerful emotional connections and transformative relationships, but they may also struggle with issues of trust and control. This placement can foster relationships based on deep emotional and psychological understanding, where both partners support each other's growth and transformation. However, there may be challenges related to possessiveness and emotional volatility.

Ketu in Scorpio often brings karmic lessons related to power, transformation, and emotional depth. Natives might face situations that challenge their control and push them towards a more balanced and enlightened perspective on power and transformation. There is potential for renunciation of ego-driven desires and a shift towards a life centred on spiritual growth and emotional healing, especially during key transits and periods.

Overall, Ketu in Scorpio combines the intense and transformative energy of Scorpio with the detached, spiritual nature of Ketu. This placement encourages a balance between exploring deep emotional and psychological realms and pursuing spiritual growth. Natives may experience an unconventional approach to emotional and psychological understanding, a preference for transformation and healing, and a deep appreciation for the mysteries of life.

9. Ketu in Sagittarius

When Ketu is in Sagittarius, we have the expansive and philosophical nature of Sagittarius merged with the spiritual and detached essence of Ketu. Sagittarius, ruled by Jupiter, is associated with higher learning, spirituality, and exploration, while Ketu signifies detachment, spirituality, and karmic influences.

When Ketu is placed in Sagittarius, it imbues the native with a profound quest for truth and wisdom. Sagittarius's love for adventure, exploration, and philosophical inquiry aligns well with Ketu's inclination towards spiritual growth and detachment from material concerns. This placement often leads to a native who is deeply introspective, seeking to understand life's higher purpose and spiritual truths. They might be drawn to philosophical studies, religious practices, and mystical experiences.

Natives with Ketu in Sagittarius typically exhibit a strong desire for knowledge and a deep-seated need to explore various belief systems and ideologies. They may have an inherent scepticism towards established doctrines and seek their own understanding of spirituality and truth. This placement fosters a unique perspective on life, often leading the native to question societal norms and traditional beliefs.

Ketu in Sagittarius can impact physical health, particularly issues related to the hips, thighs, and liver, as Sagittarius rules these areas. There might be a susceptibility to ailments involving the lower body or liver function. However, this placement can also bestow the native with a robust constitution and a strong ability to recover from illnesses, especially when they engage in practices that promote holistic health and well-being.

In terms of career and ambition, Natives with Ketu in Sagittarius might excel in fields that involve teaching, writing, research, travel, or spirituality. They may also be drawn to careers in philosophy, theology, or social activism, where they can pursue their quest for truth and make a meaningful impact on society. This placement encourages a career path that aligns with their inner values and desire for intellectual and spiritual fulfilment.

Mentally, individuals with Ketu in Sagittarius are marked by a constant search for higher knowledge and understanding. They are often introspective and reflective, seeking to comprehend the deeper meanings behind life's events and experiences. This introspection can lead to significant personal growth and enlightenment, particularly if they balance their intellectual pursuits with spiritual practices that foster inner peace and detachment from worldly distractions.

In relationships, Ketu in Sagittarius can bring a sense of independence and a desire for intellectual companionship. Natives might value personal freedom and may have difficulty forming deep emotional bonds if they feel restricted. However, this placement can also foster relationships based on mutual respect and shared philosophical or spiritual interests, where both partners support each other's growth and exploration of life's mysteries.

Ketu in Sagittarius often brings karmic lessons related to beliefs, higher education, and the pursuit of truth. Natives might face situations that challenge their understanding of spirituality and push them towards a more balanced and enlightened perspective on life and learning. There is potential for renunciation of dogmatic beliefs and a shift towards a more inclusive and expansive view of spirituality and knowledge, especially during key transits and periods.

Overall, Ketu in Sagittarius combines the philosophical and expansive energy of Sagittarius with the detached, spiritual nature of Ketu. This placement encourages a balance between seeking higher knowledge and pursuing spiritual growth. Natives may experience an unconventional approach to beliefs and learning, a preference for independence and exploration, and a deep appreciation for spiritual and intellectual pursuits.

10. Ketu in Capricorn

When Ketu is in Capricorn, we have Capricorn's disciplined, practical nature merged with Ketu's spiritual detachment and karmic influences. Capricorn, ruled by Saturn, is associated with ambition, responsibility, and material success, while Ketu symbolizes detachment, spirituality, and past-life influences.

When Ketu is positioned in Capricorn, it creates a dichotomy where the native may exhibit a strong sense of duty and responsibility but with an underlying sense of detachment from worldly achievements. Capricorn's focus on structure and discipline aligns interestingly with Ketu's tendency to transcend material concerns, often leading the native to be diligent and hardworking yet feel a sense of dissatisfaction or disinterest in conventional success and societal recognition.

Natives with Ketu in Capricorn often display a non-conformist attitude towards traditional paths of success and societal norms. They may be driven by a sense of duty and ambition but often question the ultimate value of their pursuits. This placement fosters a deep introspection about the nature of success and the purpose of their efforts, leading them to seek meaning beyond material accomplishments. Despite their capabilities and potential for leadership, they might prefer roles that allow them to work quietly or in the background, away from the spotlight.

In terms of Health, Ketu in Capricorn can affect the native's physical health, particularly issues related to the knees, bones, and joints, as Capricorn rules these areas. There might be a susceptibility to ailments involving the skeletal system or chronic conditions related to Saturn's influence. However, this placement can also endow the native with a resilient constitution and the ability to endure physical hardships, especially when they maintain a disciplined lifestyle and focus on holistic health practices.

In terms of career and ambition, Natives with Ketu in Capricorn often excel in fields that require meticulous planning, organisation, and long-term commitment, such as research, administration, or any role that involves strategy and management. They may also be drawn to careers that allow for spiritual or ethical contributions, such as social work or environmental conservation. This placement encourages a career path that aligns with their inner values and desire for meaningful impact rather than mere material success.

Mentally, individuals with Ketu in Capricorn are marked by a constant search for purpose and a deeper understanding of their responsibilities. They are often introspective and reflective, seeking to balance their material ambitions with spiritual goals. This introspection can lead to significant personal growth and enlightenment, particularly if they balance their practical efforts with spiritual practices that foster inner peace and detachment from worldly distractions.

In relationships, Ketu in Capricorn can bring a sense of emotional independence and a focus on practical aspects of relationships. Natives might value stability and reliability but may have difficulty forming deep emotional bonds if they feel restricted or overly responsible. However, this placement can also foster relationships based on mutual respect and shared goals, where both partners support each other's growth and responsibilities.

Ketu in Capricorn is likely to bring karmic lessons related to ambition, responsibility, and the true meaning of success. Natives might face situations that challenge their understanding of duty and push them towards a more balanced and enlightened perspective on achievement and societal contributions. There is potential for renunciation of ego-driven pursuits and a shift towards a life centred on spiritual and ethical fulfilment, especially during key transits and periods.

Overall, Ketu in Capricorn combines the disciplined and ambitious energy of Capricorn with the detached, spiritual nature of Ketu. This placement encourages a balance between pursuing material success and seeking spiritual growth. Natives may experience an unconventional approach to ambition and responsibility, a preference for simplicity and ethical living, and a deep appreciation for spiritual and practical pursuits.

11. Ketu in Aquarius

When Ketu is in Aquarius, we have the humanitarian, innovative nature of Aquarius mixed with Ketu's spiritual detachment and karmic influences. Aquarius, ruled by Saturn and co-ruled by Rahu, is associated with innovation, community, and progressive thinking, while Ketu symbolizes detachment, spirituality, and past-life influences.

When Ketu is positioned in Aquarius, native may feel a strong sense of social responsibility and a desire for progress, coupled with an underlying sense of detachment from societal conventions. Aquarius's focus on collective welfare and futuristic ideas aligns intriguingly with Ketu's tendency to transcend material concerns. This combination often leads to a native who is forward-thinking and visionary, yet feels a sense of dissatisfaction or disinterest in traditional social structures and norms.

Natives with Ketu in Aquarius often display a non-conformist attitude towards societal expectations and group dynamics. They may be driven by a sense of innovation and a desire to improve society but often question the ultimate value of conforming to established norms. This placement fosters deep introspection about the nature of social roles and the purpose of their contributions to the collective, leading them to seek meaning beyond conventional social engagements. Despite their capabilities and potential for leadership in social or technological fields, they might prefer roles that allow them to work independently or in unconventional settings.

With regards to health, Ketu in Aquarius can affect the native's physical health, particularly issues related to the circulatory system, ankles, and lower legs, as Aquarius rules these areas. There might be a susceptibility to ailments involving circulation or sudden health issues due to the unpredictable nature of Aquarius. However, this placement can also endow the native with a resilient constitution and an ability to adapt to physical challenges, especially when they focus on holistic health practices and stress management.

In terms of career and ambition, Ketu in Aquarius often leads to an unconventional approach to professional life. Natives might excel in fields that require innovative thinking, research, technology, or social reform. They may also be drawn to careers that allow for humanitarian or ecological contributions, such as working for non-profits, NGOs, or in environmental science. This placement encourages a career path that aligns with their inner values and desires for societal impact rather than personal recognition.

Mentally, individuals with Ketu in Aquarius are marked by a constant search for deeper understanding and higher knowledge. They are often introspective and reflective, seeking to balance their intellectual pursuits with spiritual goals. This introspection can lead to significant personal growth and enlightenment, particularly if they balance their innovative efforts with spiritual practices that foster inner peace and detachment from worldly distractions.

In relationships, Ketu in Aquarius can bring a sense of emotional independence and a focus on intellectual connections. Natives might value freedom and mental stimulation, sometimes leading to challenges in forming deep emotional bonds if they feel restricted or misunderstood. However, this placement can also foster relationships based on mutual respect and shared ideals, where both partners support each other's growth and intellectual pursuits.

Ketu in Aquarius often brings karmic lessons related to innovation, social engagement, and the true meaning of progress. Natives might face situations that challenge their understanding of societal roles and push them towards a more balanced and enlightened perspective on social contributions and personal aspirations. There is potential for renunciation of ego-driven pursuits and a shift towards a life centred on spiritual and intellectual fulfilment, especially during pivotal transits and periods.

Overall, Ketu in Aquarius combines the innovative and humanitarian energy of Aquarius with the detached, spiritual nature of Ketu. This placement encourages a balance between pursuing social progress and seeking spiritual growth. Natives may experience an unconventional approach to social roles and community involvement, a preference for simplicity and ethical living, and a deep appreciation for intellectual and spiritual pursuits.

12. Ketu in Pisces

When Ketu is in Pisces, we have a combination of the mystical, compassionate nature of Pisces and Ketu's spiritual detachment and karmic influences. Pisces, ruled by Jupiter, is associated with spirituality, intuition, and emotional depth, while Ketu represents detachment, past-life influences, and spiritual pursuits.

When Ketu is positioned in Pisces, the native experiences a strong pull towards spiritual and mystical realms. Pisces, being a sign deeply connected with the subconscious and the metaphysical, aligns well with Ketu's inherent nature of seeking beyond the material. This combination often results in a native who is highly intuitive, spiritually inclined, and drawn to exploring the deeper meanings of life. There is an innate understanding of the ephemeral nature of existence, leading to a pursuit of spiritual knowledge and inner peace.

Natives with Ketu in Pisces often possess a profound sense of compassion and empathy. They may feel a deep connection to the suffering of others and are drawn to help in any way they can, often through spiritual or healing practices. This placement can foster a sense of being out of place in the material world, as the native is more attuned to the spiritual or emotional realms. They might seek solitude and prefer to spend time in meditation, prayer, or other spiritual practices to find solace and clarity.

Health-wise, Ketu in Pisces can affect the native's physical health, particularly issues related to the feet and immune system, as Pisces rules these areas. There might be a susceptibility to ailments involving the lymphatic system or psychosomatic illnesses due to their sensitive nature. However, this placement can also endow the native with a strong ability to heal through spiritual practices and a holistic approach to health. Maintaining a balanced lifestyle and avoiding escapism through substances is crucial for their well-being.

In terms of career and ambition, Natives with Ketu in Pisces are likely to excel in fields related to spirituality, healing, the arts, or any profession that involves caring for others. They may also be drawn to careers that allow them to express their creativity and intuition, such as music, poetry, or counselling. This placement encourages a career path that aligns with their inner values and desire for spiritual fulfilment rather than material success.

Mentally, individuals with Ketu in Pisces are often introspective and reflective, constantly seeking deeper understanding and higher knowledge. They may experience periods of intense spiritual insight and profound realizations about the nature of existence. This introspection can lead to significant personal growth and enlightenment, especially if they balance their spiritual pursuits with practical responsibilities. There is a potential for them to develop psychic abilities or have experiences that transcend the ordinary.

In relationships, Ketu in Pisces can bring a sense of emotional depth and spiritual connection. Natives might value a partner who understands their need for spiritual growth and emotional intimacy. However, they might also face challenges in forming stable relationships due to their tendency towards emotional detachment or idealisation of partners. This placement can foster relationships based on mutual spiritual goals and emotional support, where both partners help each other grow spiritually.

Ketu in Pisces is probable to bring karmic lessons related to spirituality, compassion, and the dissolution of the ego. Natives might face situations that challenge their understanding of reality and push them towards a more balanced and enlightened perspective on life. There is potential for renunciation of material pursuits and a shift towards a life centred on spiritual and emotional fulfilment, especially during key transits and periods.

Overall, Ketu in Pisces combines the mystical and compassionate energy of Pisces with the detached, spiritual nature of Ketu. This placement encourages a balance between pursuing spiritual knowledge and living a compassionate, empathetic life. Natives may experience an unconventional approach to spirituality and life, a preference for solitude and meditation, and a deep appreciation for the mystical aspects of existence. Ketu in Pisces brings karmic lessons that guide the native towards a more enlightened perspective on spirituality, compassion, and the true nature of reality.

Chapter 10
Rahu and Ketu Conjunctions With Different Planets

Note: Assessing the overall impact of a conjunction forming in any house requires joint and thorough consideration of multiple factors. Any conjunction in a house can't be judged for its full implications, in isolation – aspects, conjunctions, ascendant lord (in terms of strength and association), corresponding house lord (in terms of strength, weakness and support it's providing and nakshatra lord (in terms of strength, weakness and support it's providing) considerably modify the results of a conjunction. Readers are required to bear the same in mind while understanding the impact of the following conjunctions of different planets with Rahu and Ketu.

Planetary Aspects and Their Influence

When examining the impact of a conjunction in any house, it's of utmost importance to consider the aspects from both temporal and natural benefic and malefic planets. Benefic influences, such as aspects or conjunction with *trikona* house lords (1,5,9) or with natural benefics like Jupiter or Venus, can largely mitigate any conjunction's negative results, magnifying positive results. On the contrary, further malefic influences like aspects or conjunction with *dushthana* house lords (6,8,12) or with natural malefic or cruel planets like Saturn or Mars can markedly exacerbate any conjunction's disruptive outcomes, leading to more daunting challenges. If natural malefic or cruel planets like Saturn or Mars become *yogakaraka* in a chart, their involvement in a conjunction won't necessarily cause problems of a grave nature which potentially would be the case if they lord *dushtana* houses. Kindly note that this principle applies consistently across all the following conjunctions and is imperative for understanding the overall effects and results of any planet's conjunction with the nodes.

The Power of the Dispositors of Rahu and Ketu: When Shadows Borrow Bodies

Rahu and Ketu, in their very essence, as we learnt, are bodiless entities. Unlike the visible grahas, they possess neither substance nor light of their own; their influence, therefore, must operate through a vessel which is the planet that governs the sign they occupy. These governing planets are known as their "dispositors", and they serve as the corporeal medium through which the shadowed will of Rahu and Ketu manifests into tangible experience.

The condition, dignity, and placement of this dispositor consequently determine the very tenor of the Rahu–Ketu axis in a horoscope. A strong and well-placed dispositor, which is to mean one that enjoys directional strength, benefic association (lords of 9th, 5th or ascendant lord) or occupancy in its own or exaltation sign, becomes an able carrier of the serpent's karmic agenda. Such a Rahu can bestow worldly ascent, ingenuity, and recognition, while Ketu may confer detachment born not of deprivation but of wisdom. Conversely, when the dispositor stands debilitated, combust, retrograde without strength, or heavily afflicted, the same nodes become turbulent. Rahu's ambitions then assume distorted forms such as obsession, deceit, or illusion, and Ketu's renunciation turns into isolation, confusion, a headless search/ longing or loss.

It is through the dispositor that Rahu and Ketu engage with the material plane; hence, their results are never autonomous. Consider Rahu in Taurus, whose dispositor Venus is exalted in Pisces; the native's material desires may fructify into artistic eminence, wealth, or magnetic charm. Yet, the same Rahu, when Venus lies debilitated in Virgo and conjoined with malefics, produces moral confusion and emotional barrenness despite external attainment. Similarly, Ketu in Scorpio with Mars exalted in Capricorn can transform instinct into disciplined power and yogic control, whereas a weak Mars may render the same configuration reckless and self-destructive.

Thus, the dispositors of Rahu and Ketu act as the embodied executors of their karmic mandate. They translate subtle, unseen impulses into lived realities. The ancient seers implied that even the most exalted Rahu or the most spiritually poised Ketu must express themselves through their planetary lord's temperament and overall configuration. Hence, while interpreting the axis of destiny, the wise astrologer must always look beyond the serpent's shadow. One must study the luminous or darkened condition of the planet that lends the nodes a 'body'.

1. Understanding Rahu's Conjunction With All Planets

1.1 Rahu and Sun Conjunction

Rahu and Sun's conjunction is traditionally called to form a *'Grahan Dosha'*. This conjunction can lead to significant achievements and recognition, particularly in fields related to politics, government, and public administration. The native may experience a period of immense success and prestige, often marked by high positions, and charismatic leadership – drawing numerous favours and support from influential figures.

Despite the potential for great success, the conjunction of Rahu and the Sun is plagued by underlying instability. Rahu, mythologically, seeks vengeance on the Sun and the Moon for revealing its disguise as Svarbhanu during the churning of the ocean for *Amrit*. This grudge gives rise to a dynamic where Rahu initially bestows power and freedom, creating an insatiable hunger for more success, power, and fame. However, this relentless pursuit often entraps the native in Rahu's deceptive web.

The native may develop an uncontrollable desire for power, success, and fame, which can lead to overambitious behaviour and potential downfall. The Rahu-Sun conjunction can adversely affect the father's dignity, happiness, or status and the native might experience conflicts or challenges related to paternal relationships and the father's well-being. Rahu's influence can create a sense of invincibility, leading to mistakes and misjudgments. The native may experience a fall from grace, losing the fame, position, and prestige once attained.

In summary, the conjunction of Rahu and the Sun can bring immense success and recognition, particularly in political and governmental fields. However, it also carries risks of instability, pitfall and deception, driven by Rahu's inherent enmity towards luminaries.

1.2 Rahu and Moon Conjunction

Rahu, known for its insatiable hunger, feeds on the essence of the Moon, consuming its *Amrit tattva* (nectar)—soma. This influence can lead the mind astray, causing restlessness and indecision — whether to do this or that, unable to settle into any pursuit with focus. It may augment intelligence and creativity, blessing the native with a fertile brain and a caring nature, as Rahu signifies expansion while the Moon represents nurture and empathy. However, it also gives a critical approach to the native, he has a faultfinding mindset, constantly seeking flaws in everything and dissipating one's attention across multiple endeavours.

For example, when this combination takes place in the 8th house, it can make one intelligent and knowledgeable, yet prone to seeking knowledge obsessively, which may lead to a depressive state due to Rahu's unsettling influence on the Moon. It instils a hunger for knowledge, beauty, and care, but if these desires remain unfulfilled, they can lead to feelings of dissatisfaction and depression.

This conjunction is beneficial for accumulating wealth, beauty, comfort, and luxury. However, it also tends to intensify desires, leading to a never-ending pursuit of materialistic pleasures. This perpetual chase can create inner conflict and discontentment within the mind.

1.3 Rahu and Mars Conjunction

When Rahu and Mars are conjoined in a horoscope, it creates what is known as *Angarak yoga*. Mars, a naturally fiery and aggressive planet, has its raw and impulsive energy further intensified by the presence of Rahu. This combination imbues the individual with an intense passion and drive towards their goals, often without much thought to consequences. It's like setting things on fire metaphorically, driven by overwhelming passion and ambition.

To illustrate, if this conjunction occurs in the 7th house of a chart, the native may exhibit possessive tendencies towards their spouse or partner, seeking to control them, unaware of the negative impact this possessiveness can have on relationships. The innate fighting spirit and impulsiveness of Mars can sometimes turn against the native, causing self-inflicted harm.

However, if this conjunction occurs in auspicious houses and is functioning beneficially for the native, it can lead to significant success, especially in areas related to land, construction, or real estate. The native may become a wealthy real estate developer or builder, acquiring multiple properties or constructing magnificent buildings.

Individuals with a Rahu and Mars conjunction must avoid excessive aggression and impulsiveness, they should refrain from boasting about their abilities or engaging in confrontations unnecessarily. Moreover, misusing their strength or masculinity can lead to legal disputes or other troubles.

1.4 Rahu and Mercury Conjunction

The conjunction of Rahu and Mercury bestows the individual with street-smartness and exceptional communication skills. Such individuals excel in fields requiring persuasive abilities such as sales, marketing, or public speaking.

Although such a native's wit can sometimes border on sarcasm, intending humour but unintentionally hurting others, his command over language is exceptional, leaving an indelible mark on others effortlessly. This combination bestows the natives with communication skills, making them adept in technical fields like AI, engineering, or finance (such as CA), where one can leverage their verbal proficiency or tech finesse to earn heftily. Individuals with this conjunction may excel in legal professions due to their persuasive ability to present arguments effectively.

1.5 Rahu and Jupiter Conjunction

When Rahu and Jupiter combine in a horoscope, they form what is traditionally known as a *Guru Chandal Yoga*. Individuals with this conjunction possess a blend of Rahu's illusionary nature and Jupiter's positive qualities like intelligence, wisdom, and expansiveness. They are highly intelligent, observant, and possess sharp wit, which makes them an expert at navigating complexities. Decision-making for them involves thorough analysis and caution, as they delve deep into all aspects before proceeding. Their knowledge spans vast domains, making them proficient in fields such as medicine, finance, engineering, or any specialised area.

If this conjunction occurs in auspicious houses like angles or trines, particularly when Jupiter is a *yoga karaka* in the chart, the native gains recognition for their extensive expertise and all-encompassing knowledge, they are admired for their wisdom and intellectual prowess within their community or even more broadly, depending upon other factors.

Financially, Jupiter's association with wealth combined with Rahu's amplifying effect indicates the potential for significant financial accumulation. This is particularly true if 2nd house and 2nd house lord are strongly disposed of.

However, individuals with the Rahu-Jupiter conjunction must remain vigilant about maintaining fairness and justice in their actions. Rahu's influence may tempt them towards selfishness or bias, potentially compromising their moral integrity. They must uphold ethical principles and avoid lending support for wrongdoing or injustice, when faced with ethical dilemmas, they should pause, reflect, and ensure their decisions align with the highest standards of fairness and integrity.

1.6 Rahu and Venus Conjunction

When Rahu and Venus conjoin in a horoscope, the combination created is one that of allure and extravagance. This conjunction blends the energies of Venus, associated with beauty, luxury, and art, with Rahu's amplifying and illusionary influence.

Natives with Rahu-Venus conjunction are naturally inclined toward pomp and show, drawn to luxuries, passion, perfumes, and all things that broaden aesthetic appeal. This combination encourages the natives to showcase their assets and talents boldly, living by the principle "What' seen, is sold". Displaying beauty, wealth, luxury items, and artistic talents, such as singing, dancing, or sketching, can bring substantial gains.

However, such individuals need to guard against excessive desires and lust. Rahu's influence can create a craving for immoral pleasures, which, if indulged recklessly, can lead to destructive behaviours. Exercising caution in relationships with women is particularly important; they should be treated with respect, and any attempts to use them for personal gains should be avoided. Disrespecting or mistreating women can lead to significant downfall and losses under Rahu's influence.

Financially, this conjunction indicates the potential for significant wealth and luxury. The native may enjoy financial success and material abundance, but they must manage their desires responsibly. With wealth comes the temptation to fulfil various desires, and it's crucial to assess the moral implications before pursuing them. By maintaining a balanced approach to their ambitions and relationships, natives with this conjunction can navigate its challenges and harness its benefits effectively.

1.7 Rahu and Saturn Conjunction

When Rahu and Saturn come together in a horoscope, it forms what's traditionally called a *Pisach Yoga* or *Shrapit Dosha*. This conjunction brings a blend of challenges and potentials depending on the houses involved and the strength of Saturn.

If the Rahu-Saturn conjunction occurs in Saturnian houses like the 10th (career), 11th (gains), or even the 7th (partnerships), and Saturn is considerably strong in a horoscope, it bestows the native with fame, wealth, and tremendous success in their professional endeavours. Such individuals are unstoppable in their pursuit of success and can achieve great heights in their professions. The influence of Saturn ensures stability and discipline, while Rahu adds ambition and a drive for recognition. This combination in the 10th house, which represents the highest point in the sky, signifies the limitless potential for career success and international recognition. Moreover, with Saturn being in strength, a Rahu-Saturn conjunction forms powerful Dhana Yogas promising substantial financial gains and material success.

On the other hand, if Saturn is weak or afflicted, this conjunction may not yield positive results and can instead lead to challenges and setbacks in professional life.

To illustrate, if this conjunction occurs in the 11th house of a horoscope, and the native happens to run Rahu's *mahadasha*, this conjunction can dramatically alter the course of the native's life, bringing unexpected opportunities and rewards. Yet, despite achieving remarkable success, individuals with this conjunction are often driven to continually aspire for more, which can lead to a sense of dissatisfaction and eventual downfall if not managed with caution and forethought.

One significant aspect of the Rahu-Saturn conjunction is its potential to induce spiritual growth. When the native reaches the pinnacle of success but feels isolated or dissatisfied, it prompts introspection and a turn towards spiritual pursuits. This realization of being alone at the top can lead to penetrating spiritual insights and a deeper understanding of life's purpose.

Individuals with Rahu-Saturn conjunction must strive to remain humble and grounded, regardless of their achievements. It is essential to avoid becoming overly ambitious or neglecting moral values in the relentless pursuit of success. Actively engaging in charitable activities and supporting those less fortunate can help balance the karmic implications of this conjunction and boost its positive outcomes. Additionally, it is crucial to refrain from speaking harshly or belittling others. Maintaining respect for everyone, including family, co-workers and servants, will help prevent feelings of loneliness or isolation at the peak of success. This mindful approach promotes a more fulfilling and harmonious life, ensuring that their accomplishments are accompanied by inner peace and meaningful connections.

2. Understanding Ketu's Conjunction With All Planets

2.1 Ketu and Sun Conjunction

When Ketu conjoins Sun in a horoscope, traditionally it forms *Grahan Yoga*. In this configuration, Ketu feels he has become a king, gaining a sense of power. Natives with this alignment often aspire to reach great heights in politics, driven by a nudging desire to become highly influential personalities. They meticulously plan their path ahead by studying the lives of highly influential figures, learning from their experiences and incorporating their strategies.

In the early stages of their journey, these individuals often humble themselves, literally sitting at the feet of their mentors to absorb knowledge. They start from humble beginnings, never openly declaring anyone as their role model. Instead, they express admiration, stating that their mentor is a great person and they are merely assisting or serving them. However, in reality, the native is secretly learning to emulate their mentor's success.

If a native with a Sun-Ketu conjunction is deeply attracted to power and positions of authority, their attachment can make it challenging to acquire such status. They begin from low levels, working their way up from the ground, and eventually reach the top through sheer perseverance. Their extensive research and understanding of all facets of power enable them to maintain high positions for elongated periods.

However, the misuse of power or position can lead to significant trouble and a massive downfall. Natives with this conjunction may admire political figures or individuals with a strong Sun influence, but they will keep this admiration hidden. They won't overtly display their desire for power, but it remains a driving force within them. Their knowledge of the tricks of the trade, gained from their ground-up journey, equips them with the ability to navigate and sustain their positions effectively.

2.2 Ketu and Moon Conjunction

When Ketu is conjunct with the Moon, the resultant is complex and deeply emotional. The Moon represents the mother and one's emotional composition, and this conjunction can make a native exceedingly emotional, particularly regarding matters related to their mother.

These individuals often experience ongoing internal turmoil—a constant state of emotional conflict.

Natives with Ketu-Moon conjunctions have a deep love for their mother but may hide these feelings, acting detached or indifferent. Their karma is intricately connected to their mother, and this bond significantly influences their life experiences. Ketu-Moon conjunction can also lead to sleep disorders due to overthinking and an inability to rest their mind. They are prone to being influenced by others' words and actions, often overanalysing why someone said something or behaved in a certain way toward them.

These individuals have a strong affinity for comfort and luxury, preferring to stay indoors and enjoy a peaceful environment. However, they may not openly express this desire and instead strive quietly and stealthily to acquire the same. Their emotional complexity and internal struggles make it challenging for them to find peace, but their determination to achieve a comfortable and luxurious life remains a constant driving force.

2.3 Ketu and Mars Conjunction

When Ketu is conjunct Mars it forms what's traditionally called as *Angarak Yoga*. This conjunction makes an individual prone to anger and impulsiveness. Despite an outward appearance of composure and quietness, such an individual may harbour deep-seated cruelty, as both Ketu and Mars act in an equally intense manner beneath the surface. Ketu's latent aggression harmonises with Mars's Scorpion energy, creating a volatile inner landscape.

A person with this combination may internalise their anger, which can lead to damaging repercussions. Unlike a native with Mars-Rahu conjunction, who tends to express and channel their anger immediately, a person with Mars and Ketu will suppress their fury, holding onto it until it possibly manifests later in more destructive ways, until they find a suitable time or circumstance to channelise their resentment.

Additionally, if Ketu is with Mars or in Mars's sign of Scorpio, the native may have a strong inclination towards research, astrology, and delving into profound depths. Such individuals often retaliate when provoked, though their methods of response are unpredictable and can vary greatly.

2.4 Ketu and Mercury Conjunction

When Ketu is conjoined Mercury, it creates a unique blend of communication and introspection. Mercury, governing communication, and Ketu, associated with hands and subtlety, together cultivate an aptitude towards writing. Natives with this placement often excel as writers, drawing inspiration from individuals who have achieved remarkable work while remaining behind the scenes. These individuals may thrive as blog writers, often choosing to write under a pseudonym or different identity.

Communication is a significant aspect of their lives due to Mercury's influence, but it is primarily expressed through writing. While they might sometimes appear slow or confused, it's only because they are thorough and deliberate, delving deeply into subjects before starting any task. This meticulous approach makes them adept at identifying flaws, which is precisely why they can excel as auditors.

Despite their proficiency in communication, these natives are typically quiet and reserved. Ketu's influence encourages them to keep their thoughts and insights to themselves, in contrast to Rahu, which projects outwardly. Their ability to quickly pinpoint shortcomings, coupled with their reflective nature, allows them to contribute significantly in fields requiring detailed analysis and a nuanced understanding of complexities.

2.5 Ketu and Jupiter Conjunction

When Ketu is conjunct Jupiter, the native develops an insatiable thirst for knowledge, always striving to broaden their intellectual horizons. This perpetual desire for wisdom drives them to seek learning from the very roots of any subject. Due to Ketu's nature of doubt, these individuals often harbour scepticism towards their gurus. They frequently question the completeness and correctness of their teachers' teachings, as they are in pursuit of true knowledge that satisfies the depths of their hearts.

Natives with Jupiter conjunct Ketu typically do not adhere to just one guru or may lack a true guru altogether, as their quest for knowledge is never-ending. This conjunction also forms *Ganesh Yoga*,

Yogini Yoga or Dhwaja Yoga, signifying that the individual attains a high level of wisdom, delving deeply into any area they explore as both Ketu and Jupiter have a spiritual nature which overlaps to form this yoga, which makes them exceptionally wise and they often become excellent guides, counsellors or consultants, offering valuable advice based on their vast reservoir of knowledge.

Furthermore, natives with this conjunction are rarely impressed by any form of wisdom, they can't be easily influenced by superficial knowledge. Their nature of persistently inquiring and attaining a deep understanding of all matters they delve into, makes them highly vigilant. Their ability to guide others effectively stems from their comprehensive and deeply rooted insights, making them respected figures in their fields of expertise.

2.6 Ketu and Venus Conjunction

When Ketu is conjunct Venus, the native is drawn towards spirituality and depth in their spouse, creating an intricate dynamic in their pursuit of true love. These natives often keep their romantic feelings hidden, which can sometimes lead to complications, as Ketu also represents intoxication and hidden complexities.

Ketu, embodying inert energy, makes matters related to it difficult to surface, adding layers of complexity to the native's personality and relationships. In a Ketu-Venus conjunction, Ketu urges the native to seek acceptance and completion of incomplete aspects within themselves and their relationships. However, Ketu's critical nature often leads the native to highlight their spouse's flaws, which can strain or even ruin the marriage.

For instance, when such a native visits an art exhibition, they are likely to focus on the imperfections of the artwork rather than appreciating its beauty. This critical tendency extends to their relationships, where they may find it difficult to appreciate their partner until their feelings and acceptance seep deeply into their heart. This dynamic makes the native's personality particularly challenging, as they struggle to balance Ketu's introspective nature with Venus's desire for beauty and harmony.

2.7 Ketu and Saturn Conjunction

When Ketu is conjunct with Saturn, it creates a challenging combination, as both Saturn and Ketu are naturally malefic and critical in nature. Saturn, the taskmaster and significator of the profession, combined with Ketu's introspective qualities, results in a native who is perpetually dissatisfied and critical, especially in their professional life.

Such natives are rarely content with their current job or workplace. They have a tendency to find faults in various aspects of their profession, leading to frequent job changes and a constant sense of discontentment. They are always on a quest, driven by a deep desire to understand how powerful individuals achieve their status. This desire leads them to scrupulously research and imitate the steps necessary to attain similar success. However, they keep these ambitions and plans to themselves, often expressing only general dissatisfaction with their work environment, boss, or profession.

Their approach to work and life is characterised by a critical, reproving nature that is not easily satisfied. This leads to a complex personality that constantly seeks improvement and success but struggles with contentment and clarity in their professional and personal aspirations. These individuals are better suited for social work or unconventional careers. Although they are inclined towards social work and may possess a deep desire to build an NGO, they are reluctant to openly express or pursue these inclinations. They often wish to contribute to society in meaningful ways but prefer to keep their plans and motives hidden.

Chapter 11

Solutions for Rahu and Ketu

Rahu is associated with desires, ambition, and the material world, while Ketu symbolizes detachment, spirituality, and liberation. Balancing their energies can be challenging, yet essential for achieving harmony and success. This chapter outlines effective remedies and precautions for mitigating the negative effects of Rahu and Ketu and harnessing their positive potential.

By following these remedies and precautions with sincerity, individuals can navigate the challenges posed by the Rahu conjunctions while harnessing their potential for success and spiritual growth.

Balancing the energies of Rahu and Ketu through these remedies can significantly improve one's life. By understanding their nature and making conscious changes in habits and practices, individuals can transform the influences of these shadow planets from negative to positive, achieving harmony and success.

1. General Remedies for Rahu

Rahu is linked to the head, smoke, air, uncertainty, and desires. By adopting these simple, cost-free remedies, individuals can channel the positive energy of Rahu and transform its influence from negative to positive.

1.1 Pranayama (Anulom Vilom)

Rahu represents the air element, making pranayama a powerful remedy. Regular practice of anulom vilom (alternate nostril breathing) can help control and regulate prana (vital air), mitigating Rahu's negative effects.

1.2 Surya Darshan

Observing the rising sun (Surya Darshan) in the morning can be particularly beneficial during Rahu's antardasha (sub-period) or mahadasha (major period). This practice helps counteract troubles related to oversleeping, a common issue during these periods.

1.3 Early Sleeping Habits

Maintaining a consistent sleep schedule and going to bed early can change your habits and subsequently alter the planet's influence on your life.

1.4 Cleaning the Temple Entrance (Dehari)

Regularly cleaning the entrance of a temple or your home's temple can be an effective remedy during Rahu's antardasha. Cleaning the "dev dehari" of a Shiva temple is particularly beneficial.

1.5 Worship of Shri Ram Ji

Reciting couplets from Shri Ram Charit Manas or the Ram Raksha Stotra daily can bring significant benefits and help mitigate Rahu's adverse effects.

1.6 Worship of Shakti

Reciting the Durga Chalisa and seeking the blessings of Maa Durga can alleviate Rahu's negative impacts, especially during challenging periods.

1.7 Worship of Maa Saraswati

For students, worshipping Maa Saraswati, the goddess of knowledge and wisdom, can be very beneficial.

2. General Remedies for Ketu

Ketu, associated with detachment and relinquishment, governs spiritual subtraction. By embracing these practices, individuals can balance Ketu's enigmatic forces, paving the way for inner peace and mastery over its energies.

2.1 Devotion to Lord Ganesha

Uttering sacred incantations in honour of Lord Ganesha can provide guidance and balance.

2.2 Planting and Caring for Doorva Plant

Planting a doorva plant (Scutch Grass) and watering it daily can pacify the adverse effects of Ketu.

2.3 Investing in Black and White Hues

Symbols of contrast and equilibrium, black and white can be distributed to those in need, fostering balance with Ketu's energy.

2.4 Meditation and Serenity

Cultivating serenity through meditation, especially focusing on the sacred symbol "Om," can unlock inner harmony and clarity.

2.5 Connecting with Nature

Walking barefoot on the grass invites the Earth's grounding embrace, helping to pacify Ketu's restive currents.

2.6 Harmonising Sibling Relationships

Fostering harmonious relationships with siblings can subtly but profoundly mitigate Ketu's challenges.

3. Rahu and Ketu Remedies With All Planets

3.1 Rahu Remedies with All Planets

(i) Sun and Rahu Remedies

The conjunction of Sun and Rahu can lead to challenges in authority, self-expression, and clarity. However, with the right remedies, one can balance these energies:

- **Worship Surya Narayan Bhagwan**: Regularly offering water to the Sun promotes stability and clarity.
- **Respect Elders and Authority Figures**: Maintaining respect for elders and seniors helps neutralize Rahu's disruptive tendencies.

- **Avoid Misuse of Power**: Stay humble in positions of power to prevent Rahu from bringing ego and arrogance.
- **Maintain a Humble Attitude**: Avoid vanity and practice humility to keep Rahu's disruptive energies in check.

(ii) Moon and Rahu Remedies

The Moon-Rahu conjunction affects mental peace, emotions, and maternal relationships. These remedies can help restore balance:

- **Worship Maa Parvati, Durga, or Saraswati**: Regular worship can soothe the mind and help overcome emotional turmoil.
- **Regulate the Mind**: Practice meditation to stay calm and avoid impulsive emotional reactions.
- **Guard Against Greed**: Be mindful of desires, as Rahu can increase material greed, impacting mental peace.

(iii) Mercury and Rahu Remedies

Mercury and Rahu together can create issues in communication, intelligence, and decision-making. Remedies include:

- **Worship Lord Ganesha or Goddess Saraswati**: Prayers to these deities improve clarity and wisdom, countering Rahu's chaotic influence on Mercury.
- **Practice Mindful Communication**: Avoid harsh speech or sarcasm, and focus on clear, mindful conversations.

(iv) Mars and Rahu Remedies

The Mars-Rahu conjunction can lead to aggression, impulsiveness, and conflicts. The following remedies can help channel the energy positively:

- **Worship Hanuman Ji**: Regular prayers to Lord Hanuman help pacify the aggressive energies of Mars and Rahu.
- **Practice Patience**: Cultivate patience and avoid hasty decisions or impulsive actions.

(v) Jupiter and Rahu Remedies

The conjunction of Jupiter and Rahu, often referred to as Guru Chandal Yoga, can cause confusion in morals and spirituality. The following remedies provide balance:

- **Worship Lord Shiva**: Prayers to Lord Shiva help guide towards righteous decisions and provide spiritual clarity.
- **Adopt Moral Integrity**: Stay true to justice and fairness, avoiding unethical behaviors or shortcuts.

(vi) Venus and Rahu Remedies

Venus and Rahu together can create material desires and disrupt relationships. These remedies can help maintain harmony:

- **Worship Maa Durga or Adi Parashakti**: Prayers to these goddesses channelize the energy of Venus positively.

- **Practice Moderation in Desires**: Maintain a balance in material and sensual pursuits to avoid excesses.
- **Respect Women**: Treat women with integrity and respect, as it pacifies Venus and Rahu's combined influence.

(vii) Saturn and Rahu Remedies

The Saturn-Rahu conjunction can lead to difficulties with discipline, responsibility, and delayed progress. Remedies include:

- **Worship Lord Shiva**: Regular prayers to Lord Shiva, especially on Saturdays, help pacify Saturn and Rahu's challenging energies.
- **Perform Charitable Acts**: Helping the needy and extending acts of selfless service balances Saturn and Rahu's energies.
- **Maintain Discipline**: Cultivating a strict routine and staying committed to responsibilities helps in balancing this conjunction.

3.2 Ketu Remedies with All Planets

(i) Sun and Ketu Remedies

The Sun-Ketu conjunction can affect confidence, authority, and self-expression. These remedies can help balance the energy:

- **Worship Surya Narayan Bhagwan**: Regular prayers to the Sun maintain clarity and enhance self-expression.

- **Seek Guidance from Father Figures**: Stay connected and respectful towards father figures to mitigate Ketu's detachment.
- **Practice Meditation**: Meditation helps overcome the feeling of isolation and confusion caused by Ketu.

(ii) Moon and Ketu Remedies

The Moon-Ketu conjunction can cause emotional instability and mental unrest. The following remedies can bring peace:

- **Worship Maa Durga or Goddess Parvati**: Regular prayers help stabilize emotions and provide mental clarity.

(iii) Mercury and Ketu Remedies

The Mercury-Ketu conjunction can create communication issues, confusion, or lack of focus. These remedies offer relief:

- **Worship Lord Ganesha**: Prayers to Lord Ganesha bring intellectual clarity and help balance the influence of Ketu.
- **Practice Mindful Communication**: Be careful in speech, avoiding miscommunication or harshness.

(iv) Mars and Ketu Remedies

Mars-Ketu conjunction leads to impulsive actions and hidden anger. Remedies include:

- **Worship Hanuman Ji**: Regular prayers to Lord Hanuman help balance Mars and reduce Ketu's unpredictable influence.
- **Engage in Physical Activity**: Channel energy through exercise, martial arts, or any physical activity.

(v) Jupiter and Ketu Remedies

Jupiter-Ketu conjunction may cause confusion in spiritual beliefs or difficulty in grasping wisdom. Remedies include:

- **Worship Lord Vishnu**: Prayers to Lord Vishnu provide spiritual guidance and mitigate confusion.
- **Seek a Guru's Guidance**: A spiritual mentor helps align Ketu's detachment with Jupiter's wisdom.

(vi) Venus and Ketu Remedies

Venus and Ketu can affect relationships and create detachment from material desires. The following remedies can balance these energies:

- **Worship Maa Lakshmi**: Prayers to Goddess Lakshmi or Shukra Dev help in balancing desires and relationships.
- **Practice Moderation**: Avoid overindulgence in luxuries and pleasures.

(vii) Saturn and Ketu Remedies

Saturn-Ketu conjunction can bring isolation, discipline challenges, and detachment from responsibilities. Remedies include:

- **Worship Lord Shiva**: Regular prayers, especially on Saturdays, help balance Saturn's discipline and Ketu's detachment.
- **Maintain a Routine**: Staying disciplined in life routines reduces Ketu's negative influence.